KV-420-033

INDUSTRIAL DISPUTES

INTERNATIONAL LIBRARY OF SOCIOLOGY

AND SOCIAL RECONSTRUCTION

Founded by Karl Mannheim

Editor: W. J. H. Sprott

A catalogue of books available in the INTERNATIONAL LIBRARY OF SOCIOLOGY AND SOCIAL RECONSTRUCTION and new books in preparation for the Library will be found at the end of this volume

INDUSTRIAL DISPUTES

ESSAYS IN THE SOCIOLOGY
OF INDUSTRIAL RELATIONS

by

J. E. T. Eldridge

LONDON
ROUTLEDGE & KEGAN PAUL
NEW YORK: HUMANITIES PRESS

First published 1968
by Routledge & Kegan Paul Limited
Broadway House, 68–74 Carter Lane
London, E.C.4

Printed in Great Britain
by C. Tinling & Co. Ltd., Liverpool

© *J. E. T. Eldridge* 1968

No part of this book may be reproduced
in any form without permission from
the publisher, except for the quotation
of brief passages in criticism

SBN 7100 3503 9

Contents

Tables

Tables

LIST OF ABBREVIATIONS
USED IN THE TEXT

A.E.U.	Amalgamated Engineering Union
A.S.E.	Amalgamated Society of Engineers
A.S.W.	Amalgamated Society of Woodworkers
A.U.B.T.W.	Amalgamated Union of Building Trade Workers
A.S.S.E.T.	Association of Supervisory Staffs, Executives and Technicians
B.I.S.A.K.T.A.	British Iron, Steel and Kindred Trades Association
B.J.I.R.	*British Journal of Industrial Relations*
B.J.S.	*British Journal of Sociology*
B.M.C.	British Motor Corporation
B.M.S.	Boilermakers Society
C.A.W.U.	Clerical and Administrative Union
C.E.U.	Constructional Engineering Union
C.S.E.U.	Confederation of Shipbuilding and Engineering Unions
D.A.T.A.	Draughtsmen's and Allied Technicians' Association
E.T.U.	Electrical Trades Union
I.D.T.	Industrial Disputes Tribunal
N.U.B.	National Union of Blastfurnacemen
N.U.G.M.W.	National Union of General and Municipal Workers
N.U.S.M.W.	National Union of Sheet Metal Workers
P.E.P.	Political and Economic Planning
P.B.R.	Payment by Results
P.T.U.	Plumbing Trades Union
S.R.	*Sociological Review*
T.G.W.U.	Transport and General Workers Union
T.U.C.	Trade Union Congress
U.P.A.	United Pattern Makers Association

Acknowledgements

The impetus to write this book came initially from involvement in an industrial relations research project sponsored by the Department of Scientific and Industrial Research and undertaken by the Business Research Unit at the University of Durham (1961-64). The focus then was upon the elucidation of points of friction existing between management, unions and men in three major North-East industries: engineering, shipbuilding and steel. While these particular essays are written from a sociological perspective, I hope that they bear the marks of the stimulating inter-disciplinary discussions that took place in the course of the Durham research. I refer here particularly to economists Gordon Cameron, Alan Odber and Geoffrey Roberts and psychologist Charles Baker. Two of the essays in this volume (Chapters 2 and 4) are in fact joint ventures and I record here my thanks to Gordon Cameron and Geoffrey Roberts for permission to publish them.

A number of academic colleagues have read and commented helpfully on these essays while they were still in manuscript form. They are Professors N. Elias, R. Fletcher and W. J. H. Sprott. To them I should like to add the name of publisher Norman Franklin, not least for his injunction to keep the text as jargon-free as possible. Other colleagues have commented on particular essays in one or other of their several drafts and I am glad to have this opportunity of thanking them. They are Alan Odber (Chapters 2 and 6), Professor John Rex (Chapter 3), Professor H. A. Turner (Chapter 4) and Professor T. Lupton (Chapter 6).

It remains for me to thank the following publishers for permission to re-publish essays (in slightly altered form) from two learned journals: Basil Blackwell for permission to re-publish 'Redundancy Conflict in an Isolated Steel Community' from *The Journal of Management Studies*, Vol. 3, No. 3, October 1966.

Routledge & Kegan Paul for permission to re-publish 'Unofficial Strikes: some objections considered', from the *British Journal of Sociology*, Vol. XV, No. 1, March 1964.

Introduction

INDUSTRIAL relations in Britain since the Second World War, and more particularly in the 1960s, have come to be socially defined as a 'problem'. This is reflected even in the titles of some well-known books produced during the last few years: *Industrial Relations: Contemporary Problems and Perspectives;*[1] *What's Wrong with the Unions?;*[2] *Industrial Relations: What's Wrong with the System?*[3] In the last named of these studies Allan Flanders has recently written:

> Whether trade union structure is under debate, or the organisation of employers' associations, or the prospect of an incomes policy, or the frequency of unofficial strikes, or the relaxing of restrictive practices, or the failure of joint consultation to realise the earlier hopes that were placed in it, no one is any longer disputing that pressing and largely unresolved problems abound.[4]

The Labour Government has in essence endorsed this viewpoint by setting up a Royal Commission on Trade Unions and Employers' Associations, under Lord Justice Donovan, in 1965, 'to consider relations between managements and employees and the role of trade unions and employers' associations in promoting the interests of their members and in accelerating the social and economic advance of the nation, with particular reference to the law affecting the activities of these bodies'.

It will be evident that the chapters of this book focus on a number of issues and themes prominent in the public debates surrounding British industrial relations. These include: the causes of strikes, demarcation disputes, the handling of redundancy questions, the effects of technical change on management-worker

---

[1] B. C. Roberts (ed.) *Industrial Relations: Contemporary Problems and Perspectives* (Methuen, 1962).

[2] G. Wigham, *What's Wrong with the Unions?* (Penguin, 1960).

[3] A. Flanders, *Industrial Relations: What's Wrong with the System?* (Faber and Faber, 1965).

[4] ibid., pp. 7-8.

relations, the role of plant bargaining and the effectiveness of established procedures in regulating industrial relations in specified contexts. Obviously I hope that what I have written will make a useful contribution to the current discussion, but one thing should be made clear at the outset. I have sub-titled these studies 'essays in the sociology of industrial relations' and I take the view that one essential component of a sociological attitude is, as Aron has put it, 'the ability to look at the problems of one's own society, and yet be detached, in order to understand it'.[1] I have not, therefore, been concerned to make industrial relations policy recommendations in any direct sense. One may contrast the position I have taken with that, say, of Clark Kerr as revealed in his collection of essays, *Labor and Management in Industrial Society*.[2] In them he frankly and ably advocates a policy of liberal pluralism. This implies, among other things, that in industrial societies private associations should have a great deal of autonomy; and the role of the state is to provide minimum protection for the rights of individuals within the private associations. He not only recognises the existence of competing sectional interests but urges 'the necessity for balance in seeking solutions to problems' and advises, 'practical and constant adjustments around the Golden Mean'.[3] In other words he is seeking to legitimate a particular form of capitalism, in which a dynamic equilibrium is maintained between competing groups, thanks to the benevolent existence of the forces of countervailing power. In doing so, he goes beyond the bounds of social science. Clearly one may not wish to start talking about the virtues of the Golden Mean until structural changes are brought about in capitalist societies which equalise more effectively the distribution of wealth and income.[4] In any case it is simply beyond the competence of an empirical science to demonstrate the ethical correctness of a policy whether it be characterised as a middle-of-the-road compromise or an extremist solution.

There are, however, certain specific ways in which a sociologist

[1] Aron, *Eighteen Lectures on Industrial Society* (Weidenfeld and Nicolson, 1967).

[2] Clark Kerr, *Labor and Management in Industrial Society* (Harper, 1964).

[3] ibid., p. xxvi.

[4] See for example, V. L. Allen, 'The Paradox of Militancy', in R. Blackburn and A. Cockburn (eds.) *The Incompatibles: Trade Union Militancy and the Consensus* (Penguin, 1967).

writing about industrial conflict in a detached manner, may legitimately hope to contribute to the public discussion. Among them, the following may be enumerated:

1. One may attempt to clarify or refine the concepts which are employed in industrial relations discussions. To take first an obvious example, one cannot sensibly speak of a strike as though it were a single category of social action. There are varieties of strikes and indeed, the very same social conditions which give rise to certain kinds of strikes may also lead to the diminution of other kinds of strikes. Clearly the student of industrial relations has to distinguish effectively between different kinds of strikes if he is, in subsequent analysis, to compare like with like. There are times however, when one wishes to suggest that existing classifications of types of strike are not as precise as they might be. This is one of the points which Cameron and I bring out in the chapter on unofficial strikes. We make the point that to speak of unofficial strikes in a unitary way is to ignore the fact that we are dealing with a concept which varies in scope, content and tactical significance as between unions and within the same union for that matter. What follows from this of course, is that any public policy which is framed to deal with *the* problem of *the* unofficial strike is grounded on a mistaken assumption. Or to assume that the number of unofficial strikes involving members of a particular union may be taken as an index of the degree of union control over its membership, is inadequate, since there are times when such activity is tacitly encouraged, and many times when it is subsequently legitimated.

2. One may also wish to show, however, that some conventional classificatory devices do not do justice to the social reality they purport to describe, when the categories are treated as mutually exclusive. In Chapter 1, for example, on explanations of strikes, I have shown how political and economic, reformist and revolutionary goals may co-exist in particular strikes, although different goals may dominate at different stages in the proceedings. Similarly in Chapter 5, on industrial relations in the north east steel industry, I have suggested that one might classify disputes not simply in terms of one stated (and allegedly dominant) cause, but rather in terms of a mixture of the known elements. If one takes the Ministry of Labour's categories for classifying disputes,

one may consider how particular elements cluster together in certain industries or situations. One can draw attention to the frequency and range of such clusters. Thus, in applying this form of analysis to bargaining issues raised at plant level in a steel plant over a six month period, I noted that 'wage questions' were often mixed with 'manning' or 'other work arrangements' elements, providing the dominant theme for plant bargaining during this period.

3. One may consider the assumptions underlying particular viewpoints on industrial relations. For example, it is commonly maintained that the settlement of disputes through the use of procedures and the mechanisms of conciliation, mediation and arbitration is preferable to overt conflict in the form of strikes. One tacit assumption here, however, is that the interest groups in dispute accept the legitimacy of the industrial order in which the procedures are operative. And even if this is the case, there is the assumption that the use of procedures leads to preferable outcomes to the parties in dispute as opposed to the use of the strike weapon (or, rather, the parties themselves must believe this to be so). How and why particular interest groups ignore, accept or modify the procedural arrangements which are designed to regulate their activities, is a theme which is taken up in several chapters, notably perhaps in the studies of the demarcation dispute in the shipbuilding industry and industrial relations in the north east steel industry.

4. It may sometimes be possible to indicate the kind of conditions which are necessary before certain policies can be effectively implemented. An example of what I have in mind occurs in Chapter 4 on the official dispute in the constructional engineering industry where one of the questions discussed is, why was the arbitration machinery ineffective in resolving the conflict. Following an earlier analysis by Lockwood, Roberts and I suggest that it is important to distinguish between an arbitration procedure which discharges its function in a judicial way, assuming that 'right' principles can be enunciated and 'correct' solutions arrived at, and a procedure which functions in a political way, seeking a working compromise between interest groups. Equally, it is important to distinguish between the type of conflict itself. Is it predominantly a conflict of interest or a conflict of right? Our

case study bears out the suggestion that only at the conflict of rights level is there likely to be sufficient normative consensus between the parties to make arbitration possible and that the political approach to arbitration is likely to be more effective than the judicial. Clearly, distinctions such as these are of relevance for policy makers.

5. In analysing social processes, one of the central tasks of the sociologist is to discover how those involved in those processes define the situation. In trying thus to interpret observed behaviour, the investigator must attempt to understand what norms the participants decide to follow or not follow, what rules to obey or disobey, and in pursuit of what goals or purposes. Needless to say, the investigator may make wrong assessments and draw wrong inferences. But in looking at conflict situations as an observer he is perhaps less likely to categorise the differences which arise in terms of truth versus error, or rationality versus irrationality. He may point instead to the co-existence of competing logics. Starting from different premises, different groups will have differing conceptions about what constitutes a desirable outcome in terms of the goals to be attained or the priorities to be established. To draw attention to the co-existence of competing logics is not, however, to deny the possibility of irrational behaviour. The logic may not always be clearly articulated in terms of a well thought through means-end schema. There may be times when one would want to say that an individual or group, in the light of the evidence available to them, could have selected certain tactics or developed certain strategies which would have been more effective in achieving their ends. (This is meant to imply, of course, that rational action is not dependent on a perfect knowledge of the costs and consequences of the action. More typically it may be defined as an adequate assessment of costs and consequences in terms of probabilities.)

It is through the use of the case study particularly that the attempt can be made to explain social behaviour in terms of the ways in which the participants in a dispute define the situation. And, since conflict presupposes some kind of interaction between the disputants, it is possible to indicate how the interaction process may lead to changing definitions of the situation. Thus, for example, decisions as to whether to continue with a strike or whether to go to the bargaining table, are likely to be affected by the perceived effectiveness of the method. One may try and calculate in advance how cohesive the striking group is likely to be and how far the employer is likely to be able to withstand the pressure, but re-evaluations have to be made in the light of the on-going experience of the participants. It is precisely this kind of issue that is discussed in Chapter 4.

In commenting on the assumptions, implications or ambiguities of industrial relations viewpoints or policies, one is attempting to clarify the substance of certain 'issues' or 'problems'. What I have said in this context is, in effect, a specific application of the appropriate relations between social policy and social theory as suggested in the writings of, among others, Max Weber and Myrdal.[1] It remains now to say something of the ways in which these essays seek to enhance our theoretical understanding of industrial conflict.

Much attention has been given in these essays to the presentation and analysis of case studies of industrial disputes. But, apart from the empirical information thus provided (and, in the British context it is surprisingly limited) is there any theoretical virtue in such an approach? I think the answer is quite certainly yes, but the theoretical virtues which may be manifest will depend upon the kind of case study we are talking about. It is, in particular, helpful to distinguish between the representative case, the deviant case, and the strategic case.

In the study on redundancy conflict in an isolated steel community, one first attempted to show, by a review of other redundancy studies and surveys, that a generalised belief system concerning the principles recognised as relevant in guiding redundancy policies and procedures, existed in the country at large. One was able to show that the particular case analysed in this chapter conformed to this generalised belief system, in terms of the official policy pursued by the Company. It is in this sense, as Kaplan suggests, that we may speak of a paradigm, 'a particular case considered as representative for a generalisation, whose content is thereby being made manifest'.[2]

[1] See for example, Max Weber, *The Methodology of the Social Sciences* (Glencoe Free Press, 1949) and G. Myrdal, *Value in Social Theory* (Routledge and Kegan Paul, 1958).
[2] Abraham Kaplan, *The Conduct of Inquiry* (Chandler, 1964), p. 118.

It can also be recognised, however, that a case study may serve to throw legitimate doubt on the validity of a sociological proposition. If it does it may be described as a deviant case. For example, as a result of analysing the causes of the dispute in the constructional engineering industry, Roberts and I questioned Baldamus' contention that 'occupational costs are strictly determinate whereas effort is not.[1]' The point of Baldamus' proposition is that, since occupational costs are determinate, this leads to a harmony of interests in the employment situation between worker and manager. Industrial conflict, it is maintained, is centred on the 'effort bargain'. Our case study suggests that this is an oversimplified distinction. Central to the dispute was a conflict between management and labour over the skilled status of the erector: the erectors and their union claimed that it was a skilled category and the management denied this. This inevitably brings an element of indeterminacy into the discussion of occupational costs. This effectively leads to a counter-proposition that it is precisely because differences of opinion may exist on matters relating both to 'effort' and 'occupational costs', in the same dispute, that the difficulties of resolving labour-management conflicts are intensified.

In using the term strategic case, I have in mind the fact that one may choose to describe and analyse a particular dispute situation to give another dimension of meaning to what is already statistically known. Such cases are used, for example, in the study of industrial relations in the north east steel industry. There, both in the discussion of strike patterns and in the analysis of the plant bargaining issues, attention was drawn, not only to the numerically frequent wage disputes but also to less frequent disputes, which, however, served to throw light on the frontiers of control as between one group and another. These included demarcation questions arising between the craft and production side of the industry, recognition issues relating to the unionisation of clerical and supervisory staff and issues of managerial prerogative arising from changing situations created by technical innovations and the introduction of new plant.

If the case study focuses on particular conflict episodes, historical analysis enables one to consider changing patterns of industrial conflict: both their form and content. The chapters

[1] W. Baldamus, *Efficiency and Effort* (Tavistock Publications, 1961), p. 10.

on the north east steel industry and the study of the demarcation dispute in the shipbuilding industry, are two examples of this approach.

The implications of the steel industry study for a sociological theory which seeks to explain the frequency and/or intensity of industrial conflict by primary reference to the technological context of the employment situation, is that, in the light of comparative studies, the theory does not fit the facts. The alternative proposal is put forward that a less tidy but more accurate explanation of the patterning of industrial relations in the industry, is to be found in the interaction of cultural, economic and organisational factors.

A further critique of the theories which relate the nature of industrial conflict to the type of technology in an over-deterministic way, is to be found in the opening chapter. The logical ambiguities of these theories mirror those involved in more general 'economic interpretations' of history, which Weber so lucidly exposed:

> Wherever the strictly economic explanation encounters difficulties, various devices are available for maintaining its general validity as the decisive causal factor. Sometimes every historical event which is *not* explicable by the invocation of economic motives is regarded *for that very reason* as a scientifically insignificant 'accident'. At others, the definition of 'economic' is stretched beyond recognition so that all human interests which are related in any way whatsoever to the use of material means are included in the definition. If it is historically undeniable that different responses occur in two situations which are economically identical – due to political, religious, climatic and countless other non-economic determinants – then in order to maintain the primacy of the economic all these factors are reduced to historically 'accidental' 'conditions' upon which the economic factor operates as a 'cause' . . .[1]

Whether this is a just parallel, the reader may judge by reading not only the critique, but the texts cited in this connection.

In discussions of sociological theories, there is sometimes a rather sharp distinction drawn between those who see power as a scarce resource and, in consequence, emphasise the conflicts of interest which divide society, and those who stress that for society

[1] Objectivity in Social Science and Social Policy, in Max Weber, op. cit. p. 70.

to work at all, there must be some underlying consensus embodied in a value system which asserts the common advantages to be obtained in particular forms of social relationships and organisation. This distinction between the 'conflict theorists', such as Marx and Wright Mills on the one hand, and the 'functionalists' such as Durkheim and Parsons on the other hand, no doubt springs in part from differing images of society. The suggestion is now being made, however, by writers such as Dahrendorf[1] and Lenski,[2] that to posit these approaches as mutually exclusive is misleading. Dahrendorf, for example argues:

> There are sociological problems for the explanation of which the integration theory of society provides adequate assumptions; there are other problems which can be explained only in terms of the coercion theory of society; there are, finally, problems for which both theories appear adequate. For sociological analysis, society is Janus-headed, and its two faces are equivalent aspects of the same reality.[3]

Now in the study of the demarcation dispute in the ship-building industry, I have suggested that in certain circumstances the conflict of interest motif may dominate inter-group relations, while in other circumstances the mutual advantage considerations help to explain social behaviour. One of the crucial questions in this context is why procedures emerged at all to regulate demarcation conflicts. In certain respects the answer given represents a synthesis between the functionalist and conflict of interest perspectives. Given the original conflict over a scarce resource, namely job opportunities, the disputants first discovered the degree of real power they possessed, by drawn out attritional strikes. The parties having thus ascertained in this painful way where they stood vis-à-vis each other, a search for a less costly means of settlement then became realistic. In effect, the balance of power was built into the normative system of conflict regulation. This system can certainly be shown to exercise a constraining effect on the disputants and to influence the mode of conflict settlement by emphasising ideas of reciprocal co-ordination

[1] R. Dahrendorf, *Class and Class Conflict in an Industrial Society* (Routledge and Kegan Paul, 1959).

[2] Lenski, *Power and Privilege. A Theory of Social Stratification* (McGraw Hill, 1966).

[3] Dahrendorf, op. cit. p. 159.

between groups, but it has to be recognised that the balance of power between groups is not a once and for all affair. Technical changes in the industry can affect the bargaining strength of particular unions and economic downturns can affect the willingness of the craft groups to reappraise the situation by reverting to strike action. Normative regulation in this context is thus best viewed as a safety net rather than a strait jacket. There is, in this respect, something of a dialectic between conflict of interest concerns and the commitment to procedural forms of conflict regulation.

One way of attempting to enhance our theoretical understanding of industrial conflict is to examine the methodology which underpins the theory. This in fact is the strategy pursued in the first chapter, which critically reviews the explanations offered for strike activity. There is no need to recapitulate the substantive conclusions reached there, one can simply indicate the kinds of question which such a review leads one to ask. What is the reliability of the statistical data upon which studies of strikes are based? What is the research design employed to explain a strike episode, or the incidence of strike activity? What indices are employed to measure strike activity? Are the concepts utilised in the research design unambiguous? What empirical generalisations about strike activity are put forward and what is the nature of the evidence upon which they are based? What conclusions, if any, may be drawn from the empirical study of industrial conflict in developing sociological theory? If in the process of considering these questions, I have shown that there is no universally applicable explanation of industrial unrest and that even more specific propositions are sometimes of dubious status, I will, I hope, by the same token, have drawn attention to the complexity of the phenomena under investigation.

Although the phrase 'sociology of industrial relations' may have something of a modern ring about it, it represents in fact one dimension, albeit an important one, of sociologists' long-standing interest in the causes, forms and consequences of the division of labour in industrial society. In Appendix A, The Sociology of Work: Trends and Counter-trends, I have suggested that studies of the impact of machine-based technologies and bureaucratic organisations on the labour force (manual and clerical) in the writings of Marx, Engels, Durkheim and Weber, have formed the basis of a tradition of sociological pessimism. The alienation theme is writ large: the mode of production and the means of administration are depicted in a way which suggests that the individual has lost control over the conditions of his working life. And work as an activity is so broken down into a minute division of labour that it has lost its meaning for the individual worker. Moreover, he is so closely circumscribed by an imposed system of impersonal rules that he may properly be described as 'unfree'.

This sociological tradition is not to be lightly discounted. Nevertheless, more recent sociological writing (for example, that of Blauner, Burns and Stalker, Crozier, Dalton, Friedmann and Gouldner) has drawn attention not only to the diversity of work experiences and situations, but to the fact that differential opportunities for control of work patterns, creativity, rule formation and manipulation may be discerned. The differences in the degree of control which one group of employees may exhibit vis-à-vis another, or in relation to their employer may be the product of many factors. But certainly the struggle to maintain or alter the frontiers of control is central to the study of industrial relations. It is to some of the facets of this struggle that I now turn in the chapters which follow.

CHAPTER ONE

Explanations of Strikes

A Critical Review

To consider all strikes as homogeneous occurrences stands in the way of enlightenment.[1]

A 'strike' is a social phenomenon of enormous complexity which, in its totality, is never susceptible to complete description, let alone complete explanation.'[2]

IN this chapter we will look at some of the ways in which strikes and strike patterns have been explained. Given the truth of the two observations which head this page, one is not surprised to find different classifications of the subject matter and a diversity of explanations of the phenomena. In order to bring some coherence to this review, I have chosen to organise it by discussing in sections the research interests which have characterised investigations. One will notice in the course of this that what is discerned at one level of investigation may well have relevance for another level. For example, the conclusions of national comparisons may have to be modified by what is discovered about inter-industrial differences.

This review of some of the major contributions to the study of strikes and their causation is, then, arranged in the following way:

A. A preliminary comment on some of the intrinsic difficulties involved in studying strikes.

[1] Arthur M. Ross and Paul T. Hartman, *Changing Patterns of Industrial Conflict* (Wiley, 1960), p. 24.
[2] Alvin W. Gouldner, *Wildcat Strike* (Routledge and Kegan Paul, 1955). p. 65.

B. A note on the concept of an industrial relations system as an aid to analysis.
C. National comparisons of strike activity.
D. Inter-industry comparisons of strike activity.
E. Intra-industry comparisons of strike activity.
F. The case study approach: three examples.

A. *Preliminary comment*

Whatever the logical strengths and weaknesses of particular explanations of strike activity, one needs to realise that, even at the level of description the record may be 'contaminated'. Kuhn reports, for example, in his American study *Bargaining in Grievance Settlement*,[1] that few firms kept any statistics on walk-outs. And he questioned the objectivity of such statistics as were kept. In one case he compared the management and union records of work stoppages over a seven year period. He found that although the trend was similar, the union record was consistently and markedly below the management's. He further suggests that there is not always agreement within the ranks of management as to what constitutes a stoppage and that, in any case, it is sometimes thought preferable not to report a stoppage when it does occur. Kuhn quotes a foreman who did not report a walk-out in his department because, while it created a difficulty for him, it did not in fact interfere with production. 'As long as I get enough production I'll take the nuisance.' One can also recognise that too many stoppages within a department may be thought to reflect upon a manager's or supervisor's ability to control his work force. This may well provide an incentive not to report a work stoppage where this can be avoided.

Many studies of strikes are based upon official government statistics. As with many social statistics these are collected for administrative convenience and usage. The research worker at his more cynical is inclined to feel that they create almost as many problems as they solve. One finds a certain arbitrariness existing over basic questions of definition. What constitutes a strike? Some countries include lock-outs in the definition, whereas others, more sensibly, separate them. We find also differences between

[1] J. W. Kuhn, *Bargaining in Grievance Settlement* (Columbia, 1961). See Chapter VII, The Influence of Technology.

countries in the minimum amount of time lost and/or workers involved before a strike is officially counted. Ross and Hartman had to face these and other difficulties in their work on international comparisons of strike activity. They maintain however, that the statistics are usable:

> When all is said and done, the dissimilarities in methods and definition are not very great. Furthermore, the conclusions reached in this study do not require a high degree of precision in the basic data. The recorded differences in experience among the countries are so great as to outweigh the relatively minor inaccuracies and ambiguities in the statistics.[1]

They found that the Yearbook of Statistics published by the International Labour Office for the years since 1927, was a most convenient source of data, since it co-ordinated government material from many countries. Data from Communist governments was not, however, available.

The problems of international comparisons were greater for Kerr and Siegel, since they were concerned with inter-industry propensities to strike.[2] Leaving aside the Communist countries, they examined data from eighteen countries and found that, for their purposes only eleven could be included in their analysis. They found, for example, man-days lost through strikes in France were published in aggregate but not broken down by industry; in Denmark, there was an occupational breakdown of man-days lost, but no industry classification, and that in Canada, Finland and South Africa, no adequate employment data was given to match against man-days lost. They were certainly more cautious in evaluating the status of their findings than Ross and Hartman:

> It should be kept in mind that (the data) reflect the experience of only eleven countries over a limited period of time and that the industrial breakdowns are not so numerous or so comparable from one country to another, or even from one time period to another in the same country as would be ideally desirable for the purposes of this analysis.[3]

[1] Ross and Hartman, op. cit., pp. 184–5.
[2] Clark Kerr and Abraham Siegel, 'The Interindustry Propensity to Strike—An International Comparison,' in Arthur Kornhauser, Robert Dubin and Arthur Ross (eds.) *Industrial Conflict* (McGraw Hill, 1954), pp. 189–212.
[3] Ross and Hartman, op cit., p. 189.

Whether a country chooses to 'adjust' its official statistics because, say, it regards a high strike record as bad for its trading image, is a matter for speculation, but certainly the mechanisms by which strike data are collected are likely to vary in efficiency as between countries. In a relatively under-developed country, for example, the channels of communication through which government statistics are obtained and processed, are likely to be less well established than in the older industrial countries. By the same token there is more likely to be a shortage of qualified administrative personnel, which may affect the reliability of the statistics finally produced. On the other hand, some well established administrations may produce statistics which have a misleading precision about them. Thus in the United Kingdom, the practice has long existed of classifying industrial disputes according to their main cause or object. But, as Knowles rightly points out:

> Any such classification must be somewhat subjective, since not only do most strikes break out on a multipicity of issues, the relative importance of which may change in the course of the strike, but the main issue on which the strike is fought may turn out to be more or less relevant to the real cause of discontent.[1]

What this really amounts to is that we have a strait-jacketed account of the reasons people give for striking (strait-jacketed because only one reason appears in the classification). This is not without interest and may provide some valuable clues for the research worker. Indeed, comment is made below on the use Knowles himself makes of these statistics.[2] All that one is concerned to point out for the moment is the weakness of the classificatory system as a descriptive device. Since it is the kind of description which encourages explanatory inferences, which in practice would lay an incorrect emphasis on single factor explanations and the role of precipitant causes of strikes, the imperfections of the system of classification need to be made clear.

The preceding comments draw attention to some of the basic difficulties involved when making comparative or trend studies

[1] K. G. J. C. Knowles, ' "Strike-Proneness" and its Determinants,' in Walter Galenson and Seymour Martin Lipset (eds.) *Labor and Trade Unionism* (Wiley, 1960), pp. 301–18. The quotation is from p. 202.
[2] See section D of this chapter.

of strike patterns. For different reasons, case studies of particular strikes present research problems at the level of description. For example, the method of participant observation may be used: the research worker interested in industrial conflict may join a particular firm as an employee in the hope that he will get 'inside information' and 'the feel of the situation'. But it has to be recognised that his work obligations may cut across his research objective of accurate situational observation, since he may be tied too closely to a particular place. Further his work role, with its concomitant status implications for the enterprise hierarchy, may structure the way he is perceived by the various participants in any dispute which arises. In this way, information from the 'opposite' side may be withheld from him. Conversely, he may not always find it a simple matter to describe events without treating one group in a dispute more sympathetically than another. The possibility of having more than one participant observer, one as manager, another as worker in the case of management-labour conflicts, would seem to commend itself.

If the research worker comes into the situation without trying to conceal his research interest (whether as an open participant observer or interviewer) he may try to cash in on his stranger value. The ambivalence with which strangers are treated, however, is sufficiently well known for us to note that, again, advantages and disadvantages will be found to attach to the position so far as attaining accurate descriptions of conflict episodes are concerned. It is the field worker's task to minimise the disadvantages and it appears that scientific objectivity is not always best served by adopting a role of lofty detachment. Gouldner, for example, studying industrial conflict in a gypsum mine, found that the miners, when being interviewed, were not prepared to accept 'the dependent and passive role involved in a one-way exchange':

> The ideal role of the interviewer could be approximated on the surface (i.e. with surface workers) but it fell flat in the mine. We tentatively conclude from this experience that the dangers of interviewer 'over-identification' and 'over-rapport' can be much exaggerated, and that it is sometimes indispensable to develop friendly ties with certain kinds of respondents in order to obtain their co-operation. . . . Deep rapport has its perils, but to treat the norm of impersonality as sacred, even if it impairs the informants'

co-operation, would seem to be an inexcusable form of scientific ritualism.[1]

Dalton came to similar conclusions in his perceptive study *Men Who Manage*.[2] As a participant observer he found that the expectations of his work colleagues were such that 'any straining toward a detached manner, or pursuit of points with uncommon persistence would – and did until I learned better – defeat the purpose'.[3] And since he was interested in industrial conflict, he did not put all his faith in the cool detachment of the interview situation:

> Usually expecting guarded talk, I sought when possible to catch men in or near critical situations, and to learn in advance when important meetings were coming up and what bearing they would have on the unofficial aspects of various issues. Experience . . . prompted me to get comments or gestures of some kind from certain people before their feelings cooled or they became wary.[4]

The point that I am making here is that there is no simple or mechanical technique available for obtaining descriptions in the case study situation. This is because adequate description for sociological purposes involves the attempt to delineate the meanings people attribute to their behaviour and to the situations in which they find themselves. While certain technical skills are a prerequisite of successful field work, in the last resort it is the sensitivity of the research worker in adopting an appropriate stance in his observer role that conditions the extent to which he is able to maximise his research opportunities.

We have been looking in these preliminary comments at some of the inherent difficulties which exist in trying to describe strikes and strike patterns. We noted earlier some of the problems associated with the use of strike statistics. Finally, let us consider the use of qualitative documentary material. First one may observe that description may be warped through the selection of documentary materials. This may occur either because some relevant material is withheld from or not discovered by the re-

[1] Alvin W. Gouldner, *Patterns of Industrial Bureaucracy* (Routledge and Kegan Paul, 1955), pp. 259–60.

[2] Melville Dalton, *Men Who Manage* (Wiley, 1959).

[3] ibid., p. 280.

[4] ibid., pp. 280–1.

searcher; or because the researcher has so much material to handle that he selects some for the purpose of presentation. Each of these experiences is common enough in social research. The research worker can, of course, qualify his statements where he is aware of gaps in the documentary evidence. Likewise, where he has selected material for presentation he can explain what is assumed in his criteria of relevance and representativeness. The second point however is this. As soon as comments are made about the documentary material we are in the realm of inference and (tentative) explanation rather than description. The dilemma is that if one accepts the documentary evidence at its face value (its manifest content) one's inferences may be naïve and misleading; but if one tries to describe its 'real' significance, the grounds for doing so must be clearly articulated. It is then not enough to say that the documents 'speak for themselves'. To continue for a moment in terms of the dilemma thus posed: to take the material at its face value commonly leads on to a form of content analysis. But it may be protested that the objectivity claimed for this approach is in fact misleading, since by choosing the categories for analysis, we are in practice imposing our own meaning structures on to the material. If however, one advocates the second approach, the meaning of the material is no longer 'obvious'. On the contrary, one is led on an elusive search, which one expects to be only partially successful. Thus, as Cicourel has observed in a more general context:

> A newspaper article, public document, radio news story, or television commercial may be written under the editorial guidance of many persons with a variety of differing intentions. The ways in which such communications are perceived and interpreted by an audience can vary with the audience and communicator's normative conception about their environment at the time of communication; with different social types of actors who may be in different structural and locational arrangements in society and oriented to the communication according to their social identity and official and unofficial statuses and roles.[1]

Moreover:

> The intentions according to which the communication is produced

[1] Aaron V. Cicourel, *Method and Measurement in Sociology* (Glencoe Free Press, 1964), p. 155.

can be independent of the social scientist's interpretation of it, and independent of the actors who are exposed to it (and who may ignore, misunderstand, distort, etc.).[1]

The dilemma posed need not, perhaps, be as sharp as I have expressed it, since there is often the possibility for content analysis to be undertaken in the light of an interviewing programme or experience as a participant observer.[2] But if I have drawn attention to the problematic character of description, I have by the same token, shown why explanation in social research is not a matter of simple inference from 'the facts'. Some of the ramifications of this for the study of strikes and their social causation will, it is hoped, be brought out in the remainder of this chapter.

B. *A Note on the Concept of an Industrial Relations System*

I should like to suggest that the notion of an industrial relations system, used as an heuristic device, can facilitate the analysis of industrial conflict. The notion has been used and elaborated particularly by John Dunlop.[3] He defines an industrial relations system in the following way:

> An industrial relations system at any one time in its development is regarded as comprised of certain actors, certain contexts, an ideology which binds the industrial relations system together, and a body of rules created to govern the actors at the work place and work community.[4]

In Figure I, I have spelt out the main elements of the system and the environmental features, or contexts to which Dunlop draws attention. The broadest contextual category is clearly the locus and distribution of power in the wider society. It is the power context which is seen as defining the status of the actors in the industrial relations system. Hence, in empirical terms, this is an invitation to examine the prescribed functions and interrelations of workers' organisations, management organisations, and government agencies relevant to the conduct of industrial relations. This may well throw light on the ability or rights of

[1] ibid.
[2] In Chapter 5 of this volume I have made one such attempt.
[3] John T. Dunlop, *Industrial Relations Systems* (Holt, 1958).
[4] ibid., p. 7.

FIGURE I

THE CONCEPTUALISATION OF AN INDUSTRIAL RELATIONS SYSTEM

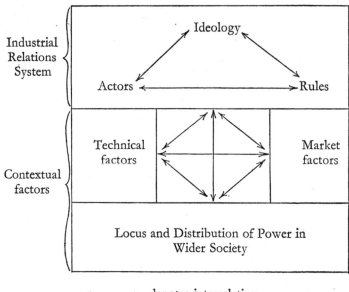

← ──────→ denotes interrelation

management and workers to be involved in strikes and lock-outs and on the kinds of procedures which exist for settling disputes. In analysing industrial conflict one may choose to begin by looking at shifts in the status and power of the actors in a country's industrial relations system over a period of time, or one may wish to compare the industrial relations experience of different countries with reference to the power context since, in Dunlop's judgment, it is in the rules most directly derived from the power context that there exist the greatest differences among countries.

The technical and market contexts are more readily applied to analysing industrial relations in particular industries or plants, rather than national industrial relations systems as such. The technical context is in fact concerned with delineating the type of work place and the type of work performed by the actors in the system. There are here a whole cluster of potential differences between systems and also in the same industry considered over a period of time. There may, for example be differences in the size of work places, which can commonly lead to a growing complexity and formality in the rules governing industrial relations conduct and, in consequence different patters of social relations between the actors. Or again, different forms of work operations may differentially affect the vulnerability of enterprises to production losses in the event of industrial stoppages. Thus, as is well known, small groups of workers in car delivery firms or producing components for the car industry are strategically in a very strong position, since a stoppage can affect thousands of workers in the car industry. The efficiency of the car industry is based upon low-cost, tightly knit specialisation – which, at the same time, is the source of its vulnerability.[1]

Considerations relating to the market context have two basic dimensions. The first concerns the impact on the industrial relations system of the product market (or, in the case of government-owned or subsidised industries, not directly exposed to the market, budgetary constraints). The second refers to conditions in the factor markets and, particularly, labour markets. Attention is drawn to such considerations as the following:

Different product market competitive conditions may be reflected in different wage rates for comparable occupations in a given area.

There are many instances in which firms, faced with identical or closely related product markets share common rules regulating the behaviour of the actors. They may form in consequence distinctive, or closely related, industrial relations systems, or form a recognisable sub-system in a multi-product industrial relations system.

The social characteristics of the labour force may affect in various ways the rules which are formulated in the place of work. Ethnic, religious and cultural divisions within the work force are all relevant considerations here. Of particular interest for our purpose is Dunlop's comment that:

Some communities are noted for a high degree of tension and conflict and for a high propensity to feuds, violence and radicalism. Whatever the social relations and experiences which have created such

[1] See A. Silbertson, 'The Motor Industry 1955–64,' *Bulletin of Oxford University Institute of Economics and Statistics*, Vol. 27, 1965, pp. 253–86.

communities, these features are likely to be reflected within the work place. Special rules respecting discipline, slowdowns, and work stoppages may arise to constrain this state of affairs at the work place.[1]

Now although I have advocated the use of the concept of an industrial relations system as a helpful analytical tool, it should be made clear that I am not attempting to smuggle in any assumptions about a system necessarily striving to perpetuate itself. There will be patterned expectations between the actors, wherever work is actually being produced, but the range, specificity and stability of those expectations is a matter for inquiry. In sociology, the sources of conflict and co-operation, order and instability must have an equally valid claim to problem status. It is perhaps necessary to underline this since Dunlop's definitional statement, that it is the ideology which binds the industrial relations system together, might give the impression that the systems are 'naturally' stable and integrative. Ideology (a much over-worked term by any count) refers here to the 'body of common ideas that defines the role and place of each actor and that defines the ideas which each actor holds towards the place and function of others in the system'.[2] The extent to which such common ideas actually exist is, in a sense, a reflection of the extent to which the system may be regarded as legitimated. It is appropriate too, to observe that even where there are widespread shared understandings between the actors in an industrial relation, these may embrace the notion of legitimate conflict and even, in certain circumstances, striking. Thus, in the British system of industrial relations it is widely accepted not only that conflict be regulated as far as possible through institutionalised settlement procedures, but also that in the event of failure to agree, after these procedures have been exhausted, the strike is a legitimate weapon. Thus, although the government was clearly disturbed about the probable effects of the 1966 seamen's strike in aggravating Britain's balance of payments problems, its legitimacy was not denied. Mr. Wilson could portray the seamen's leaders as wrong-headed, but not as wrong. In this sense, therefore, there may be certain built-in tolerances of conflict within the existing system. In this way felt grievances

---

[1] Dunlop, op. cit., p. 86.
[2] ibid., pp. 16–17.

and tensions arising from inconsistencies in the system may be 'managed'. Such 'management' does not of course imply that there is subsequently a restoration to the status quo, rather there is a shift in the 'tension balance' of the actors on the industrial relations scene. Further, tension is not always 'managed' in this way, since it remains possible for disputes to arise over the basic organisation of the existing industrial relations system.

What the concept of an industrial relations system does minimally is to remind us of a whole range of considerations to bear in mind when trying to explain strikes. The character of the interrelations, both within the system and with the environmental features impinging on and interacting with the system, is a matter for investigation, but their existence is a warning against single factor explanations of social phenomena. Further, not only may reference be made to such a conceptualisation in comparative studies, trend studies and case studies, but one may always recognise that different kinds of explanation can be handled and assessed within this rubric. Thus some explanations may stress the motives, others the goals of actors. Other explanations may focus on the social constraints and the room for manoeuvre which they do, or do not, allow the actors. The ways in which these kinds of explanations may be mutually supportive is, perhaps, best explored by the use of case studies. But, since striking may have different meanings attached to it in different situations, it is likely that we will also have to look for more than one bundle of such mutually supportive explanations.

C. *Strikes and National Industrial Relations Systems*

The major study to be discussed in this section is Ross and Hartman's *Changing Patterns of Industrial Conflict*.

> We attempt to establish and explain the general trend of strike activity in the non-Communist world; and to explore differences in trends and in the meaning of strikes between one country and another.[1]

The authors looked at strike data for fifteen countries and, as far as the available material permitted, covered the years 1900–56. Some six measures for comparing strike activity between countries

[1] Ross and Hartman, op. cit., p. 8.

Explanations of Strikes

and within a country over a period of time were utilised. Two of these measures were given prominence in the analysis 'because they appear to reflect most sensitively the institutional and historical forces at work'.[1] These were:

(a) The membership involvement ratio. When applied to a country this refers to 'the sum of all workers involved in all strikes during a year divided by the average number of union members during that year'.[2] Table I summarises the experience of the fourteen countries, which could be looked at individually over the whole period.

TABLE I

MEMBERSHIP INVOLVEMENT IN STRIKE ACTIVITY

	1900–29 %	1930–47 %	1948–56 %
Denmark	6·3	2·4	1·4
Netherlands	7·0	2·6	1·3
United Kingdom	16·1	6·4	5·9
Germany	14·2	3·7	2·6
Norway	27·0	6·8	1·2
Sweden	22·7	3·0	0·3
France	27·1	29·0	62·4
Japan	30·3	39·0	21·5
India	—	102·2	37·2
United States	33·2	20·3	15·4
Canada	14·7	13·3	6·3
Australia	18·2	14·8	25·2
Finland	24·5	9·0	13·9
South Africa	24·4	3·9	1·4

Source: Ross & Hartman *Changing Patterns of Industrial Conflict.*

(b) The strike duration ratio. At a national level this ratio is constructed 'by dividing the number of workers involved into the number of working days lost (through strikes) for the particular year. In other words it shows time lost per striker'.[3] Again this ratio could be applied to fourteen countries over the whole period and the findings are summarised in Table II.

The general picture which emerges is of a gradual decline in the proportion of union members going on strike during the

[1] ibid., p. 13.
[2] ibid., p. 11.
[3] ibid., p. 12.

TABLE II

AVERAGE DURATION OF STRIKES

	1900–29 (days)	1948–56 (days)	1948–56 as per cent of 1900–29
Denmark	28·7	4·3	15
Netherlands	32·7	7·5	23
United Kingdom	23·0	4·3	19
Germany	15·6	9·9	63
Norway	33·6	15·2	45
Sweden	37·1	22·6	61
France	14·4	2·9	20
India	26·6	8·8	33
Canada	27·1	19·3	71
Australia	14·2	3·2	23
Finland	36·0	15·8	44
South Africa	15·8	2·6	16

Source: Ross & Hartman *Changing Patterns of Industrial Conflict*.

period studied, in most of the countries, and a decline in the average duration of strikes in all the countries. We shall return to the explanations offered for these trends subsequently. However, the experience of each of the countries is by no means uniform. Taking the period 1948–56 as the point of reference, they look for differences and similarities between countries in terms of possible combinations of the two criteria of membership involvement and strike duration. Thus they classify countries according to whether they have a nominal membership involvement ratio (less than 3% annual average) a moderate one (over 3% and up to 16% annual average) or a high one (over 16% annual average). Similarly, they distinguish between countries having a low average duration of strikes (less than five days) and those having a high average duration (over fourteen days). Those falling between these two extremes are categorised as intermediate. On the basis of this exercise the distinctive combinations (Table III, following page) emerge.

This they treat, however, as a valuable clue to further inquiry. They ask essentially how far do these groups of countries embody industrial relations systems with shared characteristics. And upon examination they conclude that, with the exceptions of South Africa, Australia and Finland, the four groups of countries represent four patterns of strike activity which 'are associated with

Explanations of Strikes

TABLE III

DIFFERENCES AND SIMILARITIES IN
NATIONAL STRIKE PATTERNS 1948–56

	Membership Involvement	Average Duration	Country
A	Nominal	Low-Moderate	Denmark Netherlands United Kingdom Germany South Africa
B	Nominal	Long	Norway Sweden
C	High	Low	France Italy Japan India Australia
D	Inter/High	Long	U.S.A. Canada Finland

characteristic configurations of labour-management relations, political structure and government policy'.[1]

In discussing the factors which the authors suggest influence strike activity they emphasise that such influences must be assessed not as independent variables but in terms of the configuration in which it is located:

> When we say that a certain factor is conducive to industrial peace or to industrial conflict, we mean that it has this effect in combination with other influences which it is characteristically conjoined. The context is crucially important.[2]

Given that the context is crucially important in modifying or accentuating the role of particular factors, it is nevertheless possible to summarise the factors which Ross and Hartman utilise and to indicate the kinds of tendency statements which these embody in relation to industrial peace or conflict. I have spelt this out in the following manner:

[1] ibid., p. 28.
[2] ibid., p. 175.

FACTOR	TENDENCY STATEMENT RELATING TO INDUSTRIAL CONFLICT
1. Organisational stability	
(a) Age of labour movement	'Older movements are more likely to have completed their struggles for existence, recognition and security, and to be integrated into their national economics. Once this point has been reached, bargaining machinery can be developed to handle economic issues without frequent work stoppages.' (p. 65)
(b) Stability of union membership	'Pronounced fluctuations are generally conducive to industrial conflict as the unions strive to organise and absorb new members and to settle the most pressing grievances, or struggle to limit their losses and recapture their territory.' (p. 65)
2. Leadership conflicts in the labour movement:	
(a) Factionalism, rival unionism and rival federations	'The union structure most conducive to the elimination of industrial conflict is a unified national movement with strongly centralised control. Under these conditions the central leadership can consciously substitute other tactics for the strike and can restrain the exercise of power by strong subordinate unions.' (p. 66)
(b) Strength of Communism in unions	'Where the Communist faction has substantial strength in the labour movement, strike activity is usually stimulated – particularly the use of massive demonstration strikes.' (p. 66)
3. Status of union/management relations	
(a) Degree of acceptance by employers	Organisational conflict is minimised where 'employers and unions have attained an acceptable balance of power and prerogatives.' (p. 67)
(b) Consolidation of bargaining structure	'Multi-employer bargaining is conducive to industrial peace.' (p. 67) Where 'the labour market is regulated and disciplined as a whole . . . the strike is most likely to wither away.' (p. 68)
4. Labour political activity	
(a) Existence of labour party as a leading political party	Labour political action is 'a deterrent to strikes.' (p. 69)

FACTOR	TENDENCY STATEMENT RELATING TO INDUSTRIAL CONFLICT
4. Labour political activity	
(b) Labour party governments	'If the labour party comes into power the deterrent effect is even stronger.' (p. 69)
5. Role of the State	
(a) Extent of government activity in defining terms of employment	'Greater participation by government as entrepreneur, economic planner, guardian of labor, and supervisor of union-management relations has been partly responsible for the declining frequency of strikes.' (p. 69)
(b) Dispute settlement policies and procedure	'Labor protest against public employment policies or compulsory arbitration awards is more likely to take the form of brief demonstrations than actual trials of economic strength.' (p. 69)

In the light of these tendency statements, the significance of the four characteristic configurations, to which Ross and Hartman draw our attention, can more readily be appreciated. This is brought together in Table IV.

The explanations offered for differing strike patterns are in terms of differing clusters of interdependent factors. But what about the deviant cases? If one takes the point about tendency statements being appraised in their configurational context, they become less surprising. Thus 'normally' one would expect to find a country with weak and divided unionism, relatively little collective bargaining and a government hostile to labour, to have a high strike rate, yet in the context of the South African industrial relations system this is not so. Ross and Hartman explain this in terms of a different power structure existing in the wider society:

> It appears that the opposite situation in South Africa is explained largely by the thorough going repression of the non-white majority, and particularly by the government.[1]

Or again, given the tendency of strong labour parties to depress the level of strike activity in a country, why is this not so in Finland or Australia?

In the first case the economic environment has been too hostile for

[1] ibid., p. 159.

TABLE IV PATTERNS OF STRIKE ACTIVITY AND SOME ASSOCIATED FACTORS

Groups	Strike Measures (a) Membership Involvement	(b) Duration	Organisational Stability (a) Age of Labour Movement	(b) Stability of Membership	Union leadership conflicts (a) Factionalism	(b) Communist Influences	Status of Union/ Management Relations (a) Employers Acceptances of Unions	(b) Consolidation of bargaining structure	Labour Party activity (a) Labour Party important	(b) Labour Government	Role of State (a) Regulations of terms of employment	(b) Intervention in Collective Bargaining
A. North European I	Nominal	Low – Moderate	Old	Stable	Subdued	Weak	Widespread	Highly Centralised	Yes	Common	Limited	Active
B. North European II	Nominal	Long	Old	Stable	Subdued	Weak	Widespread	Highly Centralised	Yes	Common	Limited	Passive
C. Mediterranean Asian	High	Low	Young (or Reorganised)	Unstable	Marked	Strong	Uncommon	Limited Consolidation	Not Unified	No	Marked	Passive
D. North American	Intermediate – High	Long	Fairly Young	Fairly Stable	Subdued	Weak	Widespread	Decentralised	No	No	Limited	Mixed

successful reliance on the political mechanism and in the second case the constitutional powers of the federal government are too weak.[1]

Hence the relevance of the power context and the market context as delineated in Dunlop's scheme is illustrated. Indeed, in the case of Australia, its 'deviance' is also related to the character of its industry-mix – the technological context.

The converse consideration implied in this discussion of the deviant cases is the fact that the indices of strike activity – in this instance membership involvement and strike duration – even when they give similar readings as between countries, may not be endowed with the same cultural meaning. It is only as different industrial relations systems are shown to have shared characteristics, which are combined in similar ways, that one can have any confidence in suggesting that similar levels of strike activity in different countries mean the same thing.

To get at the question of the meaning of strikes involves a historical perspective. Ross and Hartman are aware of this, particularly when they examine trends of strikes in particular countries. They suggest that the decline in strike activity, as measured by their indices, particularly in Western Europe, reflects the fact that the meaning of the strike as a form of action has changed considerably:

> After the struggles for organisation and recognition had concluded strikes became trials of economic strength in disputes over terms of employment. But strike activity has tended to disappear as the labour market has been more tightly organised, union-management relations have become more solidaristic, and labour has directed its activities into the political sphere.[2]

In other words it is argued that the traditional goals of strikers have either been realised, or changed in the course of time. Where these goals have not been attained or where new goals are aimed for, it is suggested that these may now be more effectively met by other methods (notably representation in the political sphere).

In considering the adequacy of the Ross and Hartman approach there are a number of critical points which must be raised.

First, some of the tendency statements on which the study

[1] ibid., pp. 68–9.
[2] ibid., p. 176.

rests are at least problematical. For example, is it really the case that the consolidation of bargaining structures tends to reduce industrial conflict? Multi-employer bargaining may, in certain respects, be conducive to industrial peace, but not in all. Thus, the 1959 steel strike in the U.S.A. accounted for 42 out of 69 million man days lost through strikes in the nation as a whole for that year. Dubin[1] maintains that the severity of this strike is accounted for by the fact that, in power terms, the employers and the union were equally matched, whilst, at the same time, the issue at stake was a fundamental one. (A fundamental issue is here defined as one which cuts across or is not adequately incorporated into existing collective bargaining procedures.) In this instance the employers attempted to establish the contractual right to make changes in plant operations without the consent of the union, even though the employment opportunities of the union membership might be adversely affected. This was held by the union to cut across their idea of how a contract should be established and their view of the existing 'common law' agreements in the industry.

In an authoritative inquiry, directed by Robert Livernash into *Collective Bargaining in the Basic Steel Industry*,[2] the investigators comment explicitly on the role of strikes in an industry which, uncharacteristically for the U.S.A., is based on multi-employer bargaining:

> Most union officials consulted on the matter of single-company versus industry-wide strikes feel that the former are not feasible. Basic steel is not a consumer commodity and the source or brand-name of the product is of little concern to the purchaser. One industry executive expressed the opinion that his company would lose a large percentage of its customers if it were struck separately. A real fear of permanent loss of markets and jobs overhangs the union's policy in this regard. Despite certain tactical advantages it might enjoy from 'whip-saw' strikes, the union is deterred by the success of past practice in industry-wide strikes, the political considerations of placing the strike burden overwhelmingly on the same locals, and the strong possibility of some sort of industry mutual-aid plan reducing the pressure on the struck concern. . . . The potential

[1] R. Dubin, 'A Theory of Conflict and Power in Union-Management Relations', *Industrial and Labour Relations Review*, Vol. 13, July 1960, pp. 501–18.

[2] U.S. Department of Labor, 1961.

national crisis character of strikes in steel may well increase the effectiveness of industry-wide strikes in steel compared with other industries.[1]

Another tendency statement, which Ross and Hartman propound and which appears to me to be problematical rather than axiomatic is the influence of a strong Labour party, and particularly a Labour government, in reducing the level and severity of strikes in a country. They suggest, for example, that trade union officials would not wish to sabotage the plans of their own government by sanctioning strikes. Commenting on this supposition in the context of the U.K., H. A. Turner observes:

> It is true that the incidence of disputes (having risen during the war) declined somewhat under the post-war Labour administration and rose again after that government fell from office. But this last change was largely due to events in mining. Outside the coal industry, the third Labour government's defeat was followed by no immediate change in the incidence of strikes, which has only risen conclusively in the latter four years of the Conservative regime. So if that rise is at all connected with national politics, it must rather be as an effect of the government's actions than as a reaction to its complexions.[2]

And as one turns to the experience of the present Labour government, one finds that the seamen were not deterred from entering on a long and costly strike, when the Prime Minister personally appealed to them not to do so. Further, one may wonder whether the 'shake-out' of labour in the summer and autumn of 1966, with the widespread redundancy which has resulted was any more acceptable because it was inaugurated by a Labour government. The picketing of the Labour Party Conference at Brighton appeared to be accompanied by much bitterness on the part of car-workers and the industry itself was the scene of long anti-redundancy strikes.

The underlying issue is raised in a slightly different way by Dahrendorf when he posits his theory of the institutional isolation of industrial conflict in modern industrial societies, such as the U.S.A. and the U.K. In particular he argues that:

> The notion of a workers' party (in post-capitalist societies) has lost its political meaning . . . In all post-capitalist societies . . . there is

[1] ibid., pp. 89–90.
[2] H. A. Turner, *The Trend of Strikes* (Leeds University Press, 1963).

a double tendency to establish the political independence of trade unions as interest groups in industrial conflict and to extend socialist or progressive parties as interest groups in political conflict beyond the boundaries of an industrial class to 'peoples parties' or 'mass parties'.[1]

Although at the time of writing Dahrendorf suggested that the trend was less evident in the U.K. than some other post-capitalist societies, it is perhaps gaining ground. Certainly it is not uncommon for political commentators to take the view that Mr. Wilson, both during the 1966 election campaign and subsequently, is making the bid for the 'middle ground' in the battle for electoral support. Insofar as this is happening, any identity of interests between Labour party economic and industrial policies and trade union policies could not be taken for granted. The furtherance of trade union interests becomes something to be fought for rather than assumed and the possibility of an increase in strike activity over particular issues remains.

Apart from questioning the validity of these two tendency statements, it is my view that the authors, probably in the search for clarity, are too ready to make statements about the changing meaning of strikes in particular industrial relations systems. They recognise clearly enough that 'the strike is not a homogeneous phenomenon but has different meanings in different parts of the world'.[2] At the same time there is a tendency to say of any given country that once the strike meant A and now it means B, rather than explicitly recognising that both meanings may be applicable at any one time. For example, it is said of the U.K. among other countries that 'the basic organising struggle is fairly ancient history'.[3] And so it is in many respects. Nevertheless, basic struggles for recognition still take place, not only among white collar groups and supervisory grades, but also among manual workers. The evidence given by both the Transport and General Workers Union and the National Union of General and Municipal Workers to the Royal Commission on Trade Unions and Employers Associations, bears upon this point. The N.U.G.M.W. report, for example, observes:

[1] R. Dahrendorf, *Class and Class Conflict in an Industrial Society* (Routledge and Kegan Paul, 1959), p. 275.
[2] Ross and Hartman, op. cit., p. 5.
[3] ibid., p. 48.

There is a widespread assumption that there is little resistance to trade unionism for manual workers among employers in manufacturing industry. Our experience of recruitment of members does not bear out this assumption.[1]

The union alleged that of 262 firms visited by union officials in a recruitment drive, 100 were anti-union in their attitudes, 65 were indifferent and 97 were co-operative. And the union goes on to make the stronger point that in the Ministry of Labour's own evidence submitted to the same Royal Commission, 'up to 30% of the differences on which Ministry of Labour conciliation takes place relate to trade union recognition'.[2] A similar kind of criticism may be made of Ross and Hartman's contention that in many countries 'the strike is no longer a sustained test of economic strength but a brief demonstration of protest'.[3] But again one must ask how valid is this observation when applied to the U.K.? There are two closely related points that need to be made here. The first is that tests of economic strength in the U.K. industrial relations field still take place. This is brought out in Chapter 4 of this volume. And the seamen's strike, mentioned above is a good example of its continued existence. No doubt such disputes are not so frequent as once they were, but that is another matter. Secondly, the impression conveyed by the Ross and Hartman observation is that short protest strikes are a recent phenomenon taking the place of the longer economic disputes. This is misleading since such protest strikes have been an integral part of the history of labour in this country, as has been well documented by G. D. H. Cole, E. H. Phelps Brown, H. A. Turner and others. It would be more accurate to say that what has happened in this respect is that the decline of wars of attrition between management and labour has exposed the rump of shorter protest strikes, which have been a continuing phenomenon.

The explanation of different national strike patterns in terms of differences in industry-mix is not given much prominence by Ross and Hartman. For the greater part of the study industry-mix is treated as a constant. Only in the case of Australia is it given much importance, where it is shown that the great bulk of

[1] *Evidence to the Royal Commission on Trade Unions and Employers' Associations* (N.U.G.M.W., 1966), p. 25.
[2] ibid., p. 26.
[3] Ross and Hartman, op. cit., p. 6.

strike activity was located in the coal and docks industries. It is to the exploration of inter-industry differences in strike proneness that we now turn. I have postponed until the next section also the Ross and Hartman thesis concerning the 'withering away of the strike'. I conclude this section by observing first, that the Ross and Hartman approach is a bold and fruitful way of organising a mass of data at the international level; secondly, that the configurational approach advocated for explaining differences in strike patterns is similar to the Dunlop scheme of delineating industrial relations systems with a (perhaps understandable) tendency to over-emphasise the power context, when explaining differences; but thirdly, that the approach is marred by some of the underlying assumptions as reflected in the tendency statements which have been discussed; and finally, that the historical perspectives provided to explain the changing meaning of strikes in particular industrial relations systems are too stereotyped to do the job properly.

D. *Inter-industry Comparisons of Strike-proneness*

I want to pay particular attention in this section to Clark Kerr and Abraham Siegel's study 'The Inter-industry Propensity to Strike – An International Comparison'.

The authors examined the strike records of a number of countries. Eleven were found to have relevant statistics for extended (but not identical) periods since the beginning of the century. Their research procedure can be broken down into the following stages:

(a) For each country obtain the number of man days lost by industry.

(b) For each country work out the percentages employed in each industry and, on that basis, construct an employment ranking.

(c) Classify industries for strike proneness within a country as follows:

High: Man-days lost rank substantially above employment rank.

Medium-high: Man-days lost rank significantly above employment rank.

Medium: Man-days lost roughly proportionate to employment ranking.

Medium-low: Man-days lost rank significantly below employment ranking.

Low: Man-days lost rank substantially below employment ranking.

(d) Make an international comparison to see if any industries commonly fall in one or another category.

(e) Attempt a theoretical explanation of the findings.

Table V, summarises the empirical findings of this international, inter-industry comparison.

TABLE V

GENERAL PATTERNS OF STRIKE PROPENSITIES

Propensity to Strike	Industry
High	Mining Maritime and Longshore
Medium–High	Lumber Textile
Medium	Chemical Printing Leather Manufacturing (general) Construction Food and Kindred Products
Medium–Low	Clothing Gas, water and electricity Services (hotels, restaurants, etc.)
Low	Railroad Agriculture Trade

Source: Kerr and Siegel, 'The Inter-industry Propensity to Strike'.

But how are these differences explained? The major consideration which the authors advance is that such differences should be related to 'the location of the worker in society'. Certain locational characteristics are specified. With this in mind, in Table VI

TABLE VI

LOCATIONAL CHARACTERISTICS AFFECTING STRIKE PRONENESS

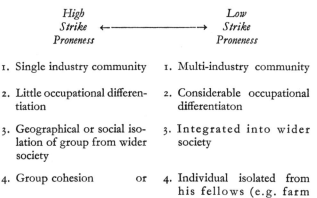

	High Strike ←————————→ Proneness	Low Strike Proneness
Worker's Location in Society	1. Single industry community	1. Multi-industry community
	2. Little occupational differentiation	2. Considerable occupational differentiaton
	3. Geographical or social isolation of group from wider society	3. Integrated into wider society
	4. Group cohesion or	4. Individual isolated from his fellows (e.g. farm workers)

I have summarised the polar positions making for high strike proneness and low strike proneness respectively; in part the locational characteristics are seen as determining the disposition of workers to strike and in part their ability to strike. Thus the shared and circumscribed life chances of workers in the 'isolated mass' results, it is suggested in strikes which are:

. . . a kind of colonial revolt against far removed authority, an outlet for accumulated tensions, and a substitute for occupational and social mobility. The industrial environment places these workers in the role of members of separate classes distinct from the community at large, classes with their share of grievances. These individuals are not members of the ubiquitous middle class but of their own class of miners or longshoremen; and they do not aim to be more considerate of the general community than they think the general community is of them.[1]

the ability to strike is seen as a function of group cohesion:

The capacity for group cohesion is dependent on the fairly steady contact of the members of the group, which in turn creates the basis for permanent organisation. . . . An isolated mass can be kept from internal solidarity not only by the turnover of its membership but also by racial, religious and nationality barriers.[2]

[1] Kerr and Siegel, op. cit., p. 193.
[2] ibid.

37

However, it is argued that the first three factors noted in Table VI at the high strike proneness end of the scale, typically provide the structural conditions which facilitate group cohesion. Thus the high strike proneness situation is appropriately described as a condition of *cohesive mass segregation*. But at the other end of the continuum, not one but two situations are identified. The first is the condition of *community integration*. The second is the condition of *individual isolation*. If the workers in a condition of cohesive mass segregation are both willing and able to strike, the community integration situation emphasises the worker's lack of desire or willingness to strike, whereas the individual isolation condition emphasises the powerlessness of the worker to strike effectively. What can be said about the character and validity of this explanation of strike differences? First, it is important to notice that as an explanation of inter-industry differences in strike proneness, it is indirect in the following sense. The major concern is to define the locational characteristics of the worker in society. It clearly remains a possibility, however, that workers in the same industry, but different countries, will not be identical in this respect. This indeed is to be expected in the light of the authors' own contention that in any one country the willingness or ability of workers in an industry to strike will change as their location in the social structure changes. Now in the case of coal mining, maritime and long-shoring work, their thesis is at its strongest, since these industries have, over an extended period of time, in different countries, contained workers who might reasonably be identified as being in a structural position of cohesive mass segration.

In other cases the picture is by no means so clear. The steel industry, for example, in six of the countries surveyed ranked low in terms of strike proneness, in three countries it ranked moderate and in one country (the U.S.A.) it ranked medium-high. In terms of the Kerr-Siegel thesis this must be because the workers in that industry are more 'integrated' in some societies than they are in others. The steel industry is perhaps a notably deviant case to use to make the point – so deviant that it is not even classified in Table V. But it is also the case that industries classified in that table in the middle range comprise, in fact, some which are consistently medium in all the countries analysed and some which vary from high to low as between countries. Examples of this latter group are printing, chemicals, and food and kindred products. With these industries therefore, one is only dealing with a statistical mean which can scarcely be said to offer an explanation of inter-industry differences in strike proneness. Only in a restricted number of cases can one agree with the authors that:

> Both the nature of the birth and the trend of development must be explained by some common causes, for both have been quite uniform for the same industry from one country to another.[1]

In the end, it is differences between the same industry in different countries as well as the similarities which have to be explained. Clues to these differences are, however, to be found in the Kerr and Siegel analysis. The marks of worker integration into the wider society, they suggest, are the acceptance of trade unions by employers, by the government and by the community at large. These broad status considerations are delineations of the power context, as indicated in the Dunlop industrial relations system. And we may notice also that they have much in common with the Ross and Hartman analysis, where these factors are seen as conducive to a reduction in industrial conflict.

It is interesting to observe that both Ross and Hartman and Kerr and Siegel comment on the declining rate of strike proneness in the western world. Kerr and Siegel say that this is because the process of worker integration into the wider society is becoming widespread:

> The 'homeless, voteless, womanless' worker is now the rare exception, and the workers and their institutions share now in the operation of society.[2]

For Ross and Hartman, the 'withering away of the strike' has occurred because:

> First, employers have developed more sophisticated policies and more effective organisation. Second, the state has become more prominent as an employer of labour, economic planner, provider of benefits, and supervisor of industrial relations. Third, in many countries (although not in the U.S.A.) the labour movement has been forsaking the use of the strike in favour of broad political endeavour.[3]

[1] ibid., p. 200.
[2] ibid., p. 204.
[3] Ross and Hartman, op. cit., p. 42.

There is, however, an element of industrial conflict which tends to be played down by the withering strike thesis. While strike proneness, measured in terms of average duration and man-days lost, may be declining, this does not give any indication of what is happening purely in terms of strike frequency. It is quite possible in that sense that the strike might be flourishing rather than withering.

The Kerr-Siegel thesis, as we have seen, in the discussion of high strike-proneness, lays great emphasis on the isolated homgeneous mass of workers as the source of such activity. The authors rightly point out that many general strikes in a number of countries have developed from groups such as miners, dockworkers and textile workers. In doing so they are stressing the severity of such conflict and, since the workers feel alienated from the values of the wider society, its revolutionary potential. But strike activity may be derived not so much from deep social divisions, but from groups of workers with more localised, albeit strongly held, feelings of relative deprivation. Thus we may find groups of workers seeking to challenge existing managerial prerogatives. The application or interpretation of particular work rules may be questioned, and changes in wage differentials between groups of workers may be seen as a threat to the existing status system in a factory and even regarded as 'unjust'.

This suggests that other considerations are necessary to fill in some of the gaps in the generalised statements of both Ross and Hartman, and Kerr and Siegel.

A slightly more elaborate measure of strike proneness, designed to bring out inter-industry differences, is used by Knowles in the context of the U.K.[1] Working on the Ministry of Labour's classification of immediate causes of strikes, he suggests that these causes may be fruitfully grouped into the following three categories:

1. Basic issues:
    (i)   Wage increase questions
    (ii) Wage decrease questions
    (iii) Other wage questions
    (iv) Hours of labour

[1] Knowles, op. cit., p. 309–10.

Explanations of Strikes

2. Frictional issues:
   (i) Employment of certain classes of persons
   (ii) Other working arrangements, rules and discipline
3. Solidarity issues:
   (i) Trade-union principle
   (ii) Sympathetic action

He then proposes that inter-industry differences in the propensity to strike be considered in these three dimensions. In making such comparisons, the relative propensity of strikers in a particular industry to be involved in strikes of one type of issue is expressed as a ratio between the percentage of strikers in the industry who came out on that issue and the percentage of strikers in all other industries who were so involved. As an example of this kind of approach, I have inserted Table VII.

TABLE VII

RELATIVE PROPENSITY TO STRIKE ON DIFFERENT TYPES
OF ISSUE 1927–36

Industry	Ratios illustrating relative propensity to strike on:		
	Basic Issues	Frictional Issues	Solidarity Issues
Mining and Quarrying	0·73	1·24	4·68
Textiles	1·51	0·57	0·10
Metal, Engineering and Shipbuilding	0·90	1·37	0·77··
Transport	0·51	2·51	1·07
Building	1·05	0·97	0·84
Clothing	0·74	1·08	2·46
Other industries and services	1·15	0·71	0·84

Note: The relative propensity of workers in a given industry to strike on a particular type of issue is indicated in the following ratio: the percentage of workers who struck on the type of issue in question divided by the percentage of strikers in all other industries who struck on the same type of issue.

Source: K.G.J.C. Knowles, ' "Strike-proneness" and its Determinants'.

41

This attempt to identify different dimensions in comparing strike proneness in different industries is, as Knowles himself is well aware, handicapped by two things. There is first the lack of a detailed industrial classification and secondly, the fact that it is derived from single cause Ministry of Labour tables. One might also question perhaps, whether all wage questions should be classified as 'basic'. Many wage disputes centre on methods of payment and their consequences for particular work groups and there is a case for suggesting that they might be classified as 'frictional' issues. But the point I wish to make particularly is this. The kind of strikes which are especially drawn to our notice in the Kerr-Siegel study of high strike prone situations are those which would be classified by Knowles as Basic or Solidarity strikes. This still leaves us with the frictional issues, which, as Knowles has ably demonstrated in the U.K. context, have tended to play a proportionately greater part on the industrial relations scene.

One study which does attempt to look at inter-industry differences in strike proneness, in a way which throws more light on frictional conflict (especially if we allow some wage issues to be frictional) is James W. Kuhn's study, *Bargaining in Grievance Settlement*. Kuhn is, in large measure, concerned to explore the dynamics of fractional bargaining. In the American context, in which the study was carried out, this means that, instead of the grievance procedure being accepted as a means of arriving at judicial settlements in the light of the previously negotiated management-union contract, the outcome of grievance problems is itself a matter for bargaining. The reality of such bargaining was illuminatingly described by a union local leader:

The realities of life do not always allow you to settle grievances peacefully and according to simple interpretations of the contract. The grievance process is year round, continuous collective bargaining. The contract is like a rubber bag. You probe it this way and that – what you need is leverage. The company doesn't view all the grievances judiciously because it cannot. Through its prerogatives and initiative it usually has more leverage than the union. We have to resort to undercover bargaining tactics to get any leverage to penalise the company. You've got to move the situation and you don't do it by being nice and talking sweet. I have always felt that the successful leader is the resourceful man who is able to find new ways to put the pressure on whenever the company is able to break the old.[1]

In such circumstances the strike may be one means used of deploying and demonstrating workshop power. As a tactical weapon such strikes are usually of short rather than long duration. There will be certain organisational pressures, if the strikes are 'wildcat', to keep them brief. These derive from the professional management and union negotiators who signed the contract. But of their frequency there can be no doubt. What is particularly interesting in the light of the withering strike thesis mentioned above, is Kuhn's observation that over the period 1941–59 there is no evidence of a long term decline in short strikes in the U.S.A. Short strikes here are defined as those lasting three days or less and involving six or more workers. But Kuhn also indicates that in the short term there was a tendency for these strikes to increase in periods of rising economic activity. This tendency was counter-balanced by the fact that longer strikes generally took place during periods of recession.

We may note in passing parallels with the British experience. Knowles, for example, has suggested that the tendency for strike frequency to increase when profits and employment are rising stems from the feeling that 'prospects of forcing concessions seem better, and possible penalties of failure seem less'.[2] But he also notes that:

> There is some tendency for big strikes to break out during downswings when the unions decide on full-scale resistance to money-wage reductions – until the deepening of the slump inhibits further action.[3]

And in a more recent study Turner and Bescoby have shown that this observation holds good for the British car industry.[4]

But if fractional bargaining is a reality of everyday life in the plant and if short strikes are an integral part of such activity very often, how are inter-industry differences to be explained. The

[1] Kuhn, op. cit., pp. 78–9.
[2] Knowles, op. cit., p. 310.
[3] ibid., p. 311.
[4] H. A. Turner and John Bescoby, 'Strikes, Redundancy and the Demand Cycle in the Motor Car Industry', *Bulletin of Oxford University Institute of Economics and Statistics*, 1961.

crucial variable for Kuhn is the technological context. Instead of the cohesive isolated mass of the Kerr-Siegel thesis, we have the cohesive work group as the source of strike proneness. Kuhn spells out the technological circumstances in which such a group is most likely to be found:

> The technology most conducive to fractional bargaining has the following characteristics: First, it subjects a large portion of workers to continued changes in work methods, standards, or materials as they work at individually paced jobs. Second, it allows workers a considerable degree of interaction with others in their task group as they work at their distinctive and specialised semi-skilled or skilled jobs. Third, it groups most of the work force into several nearly equal-sized task departments. And fourth, it requires continuous rigidly sequential processing of materials into one major type of product.
>
> The first and second of the above characteristics stimulate willingness of members of the work group to engage in fractional bargaining. The third tends to weaken the political authority of the local union over the work groups, and the fourth enables the work group to disrupt the plant's total production at a cost to itself which is small in relation to the cost it inflicts upon management.[1]

Kuhn's own fieldwork on which his conclusions are based is mainly centred on a comparative study of workers in the rubber tyre and electrical equipment industries in the U.S.A., over the period 1947-59. The far greater tendency of workers in the rubber tyre industry to participate in fractional bargaining activity, in his judgment, confirmed his thesis. In consequence he concludes that:

> Technology determines the ability of workers to press their demands and greatly affects their willingness to formulate demands.[2]

Now this explanation of industrial conflict pays more attention to the number of points of friction and hence is more concerned with strike frequency as such. In this respect it does seem to provide a valuable corrective to those who too readily propound the withering strike thesis. It is also important because one can more readily see that in certain industries, even if the worker can be shown to have become more integrated into the wider society

[1] Kuhn, op. cit., p. 148.
[2] ibid., p. 166.

in terms of the Kerr-Siegel thesis, the technology of the situation might still give rise to frictional conflict. And other industries which might not be characterised as highly strike prone at all on the Kerr-Siegel thesis, might score highly when analysed in terms of their fractional bargaining activity.

But if there are differences between industries in terms of strike patterns, there are also differences between firms in the same industry. As we turn now to consider these, it will become evident how, in some respects, they also compound the problem of explaining differences between industries.

E. *Intra-industry Comparisons of Strike Activity*

Kuhn, as we have seen, maintains that inter-industry differences in fractional bargaining activities are a function of the technological imperatives of the industry. But he has to admit that the incidence of such bargaining varies between firms in the same industry:

> Special circumstances may affect the particular incidence at any one plant but they are not the cause of the workers' use of non-peaceful tactics.[1]

The difficulty I find with this formulation is that it treats technology as the basic factor and other considerations are accordingly minimised. There are a number of specific points which I should like to raise in this connection, which, at the same time, throw light on possible differences in strike proneness as between firms in the same industry:

1. The technology of an industry may constrain but not determine the division of labour within a plant. There are at least two senses in which this is so. Firstly, in a number of situations, the organisation of the work flow may be organised on different structural lines. To take a well-known example, Wilfred Brown has distinguished between 'process organisation' and 'product organisation'.[2] The former term applies to an organisation in which departmental arrangements are that a departmental manager has control over a group of machines of the same type, or processes which involve common techniques. Product organisation

---

[1] ibid.

[2] W. Brown, *Exploration in Management* (Penguin, 1965).

refers to a situation in which, within a department, managers are responsible for co-ordinating interdependent machines or processes, which go to make up the completed product. In industries where this organisational choice is technically and economically feasible, differences between firms making similar products may be a reflection of different managerial beliefs about the 'right' form of organisation. Brown, for example, argues in favour of product organisation since:

> ... it is clear to me that a manager, placed in a job where the impact of the market bears directly upon his activities, is able to obtain a first-hand feel of the extent to which his work matches that market demand. Such a manager is in a position where he is much more likely to develop his work with requisite speed and objectivity than would otherwise be the case.[1]

But given the fact, which Brown acknowledges, that there has been insufficient analysis of the advantages of one form of organisation as against the other, one would expect different forms of organisation to co-exist between firms in the same industry. One might presumably argue that the different forms of the division of labour to which this gives rise should be subsumed under the heading 'technology' at plant level. If this is so, then explanations of inter-industry differences in conflict activity in terms of technology will be weakened where there is organisational variation in the division of labour between firms in the same industry. By equating a certain type of the division of labour with a certain type of technology, one may still postulate a technological explanation of conflict differences between firms in the same industry, or in the same firm at different periods of time. This appears to be the view of Leonard Sayles, to whose study, *The Behaviour of Industrial Work Groups,*[2] we will refer again below. Thus he argues:

> ... a division of labour which separates or eliminates workers doing identical tasks, reduces their tendency to engage in concerted activity. The number of problems on which there can be consensus has been reduced by the simple expedient of reducing the number of similar jobs, or so separating them in space that communications barriers are created among the job-holders.[3]

[1] ibid., p. 127.
[2] L. Sayles, *The Behaviour of Industrial Work Groups* (Wiley, 1958).
[3] ibid., p. 72.

46

Whether, therefore, one wishes to talk about this as organisational variation within the same industry, or different technologies in the same industry, it is clear that one cannot necessarily assume some 'normal' pattern of work organisation for an industry, as Kuhn seems to imply, and then explain intra-industry differences in conflict activity as due to 'special circumstances'. There may, in short, be a number of feasible forms of work organisation, with very different consequences for the kinds of bargaining activity pursued (although this, of course, may not be understood by the organisation planners).

A second, and related point to notice about the division of labour is this. Even when there are strong, or compelling economic arguments for a firm to adopt a particular form of technology, say, mass production assembly line work, within that framework there may still be differences in the way labour is actually utilised and deployed. The kind of possibilities I have in mind have been notably discussed in the work of Georges Friedman. In *The Anatomy of Work*,[1] he has described ways in which a number of British, American and European firms have reacted against the orthodoxy of Taylorian Scientific Management, and introduced schemes for their work forces involving job transfers, job rotation and job enlargement, to counteract the problems of worker boredom and monotony. Such schemes are clearly meant to increase job satisfaction and, indeed, productivity. I am not commenting here on their adequacy. Nor am I saying that such schemes will necessarily reduce management-worker conflict. After all, attempts to increase job satisfaction may have as a by-product an increase in worker solidarity and group cohesiveness. Hence, paradoxically, increased job satisfaction may be accompanied by increased pressures on the grievance procedure. This is simply speculation. But my suggestion is that, although no systematic evidence appears to be available to compare intra-industry conflict in this way, any explanations of the degree or intensity of conflict would have to take account, not simply of the type of technology, but also of the organisational style and the actual mode of the division of labour discernible in different firms.

2. Sayles, in *The Behaviour of Industrial Work Groups,* is im-

---

[1] G. Friedman, *The Anatomy of Work* (Heinemann, 1961).

pressed, as Kuhn is, with the influence of technology on the pattern of management-labour conflict. He suggests, for example, that:

> Plants which are primarily assembly or line operations or where crew activities predominate seemed to be very different in their climate of industrial relations from plants in which individual or batch operations were the dominant structure.[1]

But whereas Kuhn talks about differences in the incidence of conflict between firms with the same technology – implying that there is not much deviation from the 'normal' – Sayles makes clear that this is not necessarily the case. For example, plants based upon interdependent assembly or crew operations, and lacking strong individual work groups with some status in the plant, were found to comprise polar cases in his sample. That is to say, they contained firms with the 'best' and the 'worst' industrial relations records:

> These plants seemed to have more than their share of union-management co-operation and or complete absence of conflict, and also more than their share of situations where the union ran rampant, and where they were constantly threatened by irresponsible strike activity.[2]

Sayles suggests in the immediate context of the above observation that open conflict situations may reflect the inability of the rank and file to make themselves heard. In addition, however, he had noted in an earlier part of his study that:

> Interdependent work operations maintain a delicate internal balance; new members can 'quickly sour the whole bunch' . . . A really embittered employee can have a startling effect on fellow worker attitudes and behaviour in such groups, as can a highly satisfied worker with leadership potential.[3]

Hence, within the terms of Sayles' analysis, the paradox is explained as to why firms with similar technologies may in fact vary in terms of productivity, grievance pressure exerted and wildcat strikes. Indeed, by the same token, one might find variations within the same firm over a period of time.

[1] Sayles, op. cit., p. 113.
[2] ibid., p. 114.
[3] ibid., p. 91.

Applying the inter-firm comparison to the British car industry, here at least is a possible explanation as to why, for a long period, the industrial relations record of Vauxhall has been the envy of its competitors. But it would seem to follow from this that matters relating to union organisation, both on the shop floor and at district and national level, and managerial policies in relation to consultation with workers (both formal and informal) and in relation to negotiating practice and procedure, become variables in their own right.

Furthermore, the reorganisation involved as a result of company mergers, may affect the level of conflict activity within a firm. Thus the high strike liability of the Austin plant was passed on to other Nuffield factories following the B.M.C. merger. Bescoby and Turner suggest that this was not simply the fact of the merger, but the way it was handled, insofar as wage and labour policies were not co-ordinated.[1] The actual use of collective bargaining and consultation procedures – insofar as they condition how far managerial decisions are legitimised by the work force – is probably even more relevant than whether or not wage and labour policies are co-ordinated. What I have in mind is the fact that the earlier merger between Fords and Briggs had involved an attempt to standardise negotiating procedures, payments systems and conditions of employment, but this managerial initiative was rewarded with a period of prolonged labour unrest. Indeed, the new Paint, Trim and Assembly Building, which was created as a consequence of the reorganisation and which, it was hoped, in the light of standardisation of work rules 'make it possible for the men from Fords and Briggs to mix with the minimum of friction, misunderstanding and controversy, became the main source of subsequent industrial relations difficulties'.[2] Here again the objection was not to the changes as such, but mainly to the way in which they were implemented.

What I would wish to argue, therefore, is first that the Vauxhall case suggests that there is genuine freedom of manoeuvre for the

[1] John Bescoby and H. A. Turner, 'An Analysis of Post-War Labour Disputes in the British Car-Manufacturing Firms', *The Manchester School,* May, 1961.

[2] *Report of a Court of Inquiry into the cause and circumstances of a Dispute between the Ford Motor Company Ltd., Dagenham and members of the Trade Union Side of the Ford National Joint Negotiating Committee* (H.M.S.O., 1963), p. 10.

involved parties, for firms sharing the same technological context; secondly, that, while the experience of B.M.C. and Fords is consistent with Sayles' point that 'interdependent work operations maintain a delicate internal balance', the actual handling of industrial relations is an important intervening variable.

In Sayles' own analysis, as we have seen, leadership of the work group in certain circumstances, can make dramatic differences to the degree and intensity of industrial conflict. This would seem to lead us away from the doctrine of technological determinism when discussing the question of strike-proneness as between firms. And it does not seem to justify the rigidity of Sayles' own conclusion on the matter, when he writes:

> This study suggests that the social system erected by the technological process is . . . a basic and continuing determinant of work-group attitudes and actions.[1]

The reaction against an over-emphasis on the technological determinants of industrial conflict has recently been taken further by John H. Goldthorpe in his paper 'Attitudes and behaviour of car assembly workers: a deviant case and a theoretical critique'.[2] The deviant case is Vauxhall and the question is why should it be so? Goldthorpe, in his exploratory paper argues that to explain this one must look at the orientation which workers have towards their employment (and hence, for our purposes, conflict and grievance activity). This orientation should be regarded as a 'crucial independent variable relative to what occurs in the work situation'.[3] For him technology and formal organisations are treated:

> . . . not as the direct determinants of shop floor attitudes and behaviour but rather as constituting a set of limiting factors, the psychological and social implications of which will *vary* with the significance which workers attach to them.[4]

The investigation of the varieties of meaning attached to similar 'objective' factors involves, he suggests, looking at the

[1] Sayles, op. cit., p. 93.
[2] J. H. Goldthorpe, 'Attitudes and behaviour of car assembly workers: a deviant case and a theoretical critique'. *B.J.S.*, Vol. XVIII, Sept. 1966, pp. 227–44.
[3] ibid., p. 241.
[4] ibid., p. 240.

non-work aspects of the social lives of workers involved. The precise influence of these non-work factors have still to be described but he indicated that:

> . . . preliminary analysis of our data indicates that factors relevant in this connection may include, inter alia, these workers' experience of both social and geographical mobility, their position in the life cycle, and their present pattern of family and community living.[1]

The complexity of such an approach, derived from what Goldthorpe terms the 'social action' perspective can scarcely be over-estimated when it comes to making inter-firm comparisons. In principle, however, it should prove susceptible to multi-variate analysis and yield fruitful results.

3. Finally, one may observe that firms with similar technologies may be differentially affected in terms of management-labour conflict, as a result of union strategy, tactics and organisation. The use of 'key bargaining' tactics is a case in point. One firm may have to take the brunt of a union attack, with all the strike threats and possibilities which that involves; other firms in the industry may make peaceful adjustments in the light of the settlement hammered out. These pattern-setting firms are often the most efficient, since unions typically believe that this is the way to obtain better concessions and advantages in the industry as a whole. At the other end of the spectrum, firms which are marginal to an industry, in cost terms may be involved in conflict through their inability to keep pace. Clark Kerr has noted, however, that there may sometimes be situations in which union-management co-operation may occur in high cost firms with the aim of preserving investment and jobs.[2]

F. *An Examination of Three Case-studies*

There are surprisingly few good case studies of strikes. We have seen, in the preceding section, some difficulties in accounting for inter-firm differences in the level of strike activity. Certainly there is no simple explanation. But if one is to say more precisely how particular factors play their part, then there is no substitute for

[1] ibid., p. 241.
[2] C. Kerr, 'Industrial Peace and the Collective Bargaining Environment', in *Labor and Management in Industrial Society* (Harper, 1964).

the case study. In this way one is able to trace sequences of change in an industrial relations system over a period of time. By analysing strikes in this way, through the study of concrete social processes, one hopes, in particular, to know the part played by the different meanings which differently placed actors in the system attach to the changes that do occur.

The three American studies, which I now discuss, have enough in common to give them a family resemblance. But the similarities will also serve to throw into sharp relief some notable differences.

CASE I. THE LORAY TEXTILE MILL STRIKE, IN GASTONIA, NORTH CAROLINA, 1929

The Loray Mill strike is discussed in detail in Liston Pope's study, *Millhands and Preachers*.[1] In the context of the Southern textile mills of the U.S.A. during the 1920s, the ideology under-pinning the industrial relations system was one of paternalistic capitalism, in the mill villages:

> The capitalist did not merely provide capital, he also established the facilities and set the norms for politics, morals, religion, amuse-ment, and all other major spheres of culture. His control and his moral right to control had hardly been questioned. Regulation of his activities had been minimal. In short, Gastonia was a stronghold, relatively isolated and undisturbed, of paternalistic capitalism . . .[2]

Calculated benevolence was thought to be the managerial answer to trade unions. Thus the *Gastonia Gazette* pointed out in a report of the period:

> Employees of nine cotton mills in Gastonia are to meet in a joint community picnic . . . an old-fashioned all-day picnic such as the country churches still enjoy. . . . It will be held on the grounds of a suburban church. . . . There will be fried chicken, country pickles, pies and preserves. . . . The mills will furnish many substantial eatables and mill owners and superintendents will hobnob with operatives. . . . That is one of the answers of Gaston County to McMahon (president of the United Textile Workers) and his kind.[3]

The community values, since they were dominated by the

---

[1] L. Pope, *Millhands and Preachers* (Yale, 1942).
[2] ibid., p. 208.
[3] ibid., p. 199.

company interest and were defined in terms of 'what is good for the manufacturer is good for the community', reinforced the social controls exerted by employers over employees. And the mill village churches in particular, whose ministers were typically subsidised by the mill owners, preached the virtues of compliance with the existing system. Hence, the internalisation of the employees' willingness to work and obey managerial authority is to be found in the cultural milieu of the community. The 'appropriate' response to the benevolent mill owner on the part of the workers was gratitude. Since this response was typically internalised by the worker, the frowning providence of the manager was usually hidden behind the smiling face. Managerial power was such, however, that worker disobedience could lead to immediate dismissal and it was not always easy to find alternative employment.

How then is the Loray strike accounted for? If we take the Dunlop scheme for the analysis of industrial relations systems, the following inter-relation of elements may be traced:

1. A secular decline in the market for cotton textiles. The response to acute competition was:
2. Technological re-appraisal. This led particularly to the introduction of the 'stretch-out' (more machines per person to mind) an increase in the speed of the spindles, and a general managerial pre-occupation with 'efficient' methods of work.
This must be linked with:
3. Budgetary re-appraisal. The attempt was made to lower the costs of production by rationalising the industry. This involved mill mergers throughout the industry. These reflected changing conceptions of what constituted optimum size mills. There was an accompanying growth in the length of the management hierarchy and this increasing bureaucratisation of individual enterprises was accompanied by the development of absentee ownership. At the same time, budgetary re-appraisals led to the conclusion that:

> From the standpoint of immediate management economies, the most flexible item of production costs appeared to be labour. For the individual mill other costs tended to be relatively fixed. Though the percentage of manufacturing costs which went to labour was not unusually large, many managers attempted to effect economies on

this item. Three possibilities were open: direct wage cuts, location in a region affording cheaper labour, or a disproportionate increase in relation to wages of productivity per worker. Exploration of these possibilities provided the immediate background for a wave of textile strikes in New England, between 1926 and 1928 and in the Southern mills in 1929, of which the strike in the Loray mill in Gaston was one of the most spectacular.[1]

4. Changes in the power context. Traditionally, employers had assumed that they could impose their will on the employees in the South, because the workers were unorganised, inarticulate and compliant. However, compliance demands at least minimally, the fulfilment of certain expectations – in this case expectations about how a paternalistic capitalist should behave to his employees. The general bureaucratisation of the enterprises and the movement towards absentee ownership tended to make this more difficult. 'Welfare by proxy' was attempted in a number of instances as a functional equivalent of the old paternalism: the traditional paternal responsibility of the local owner being supplanted by the delegated responsibility of the social welfare workers. However, the growing impersonality of the welfare system did not correspond with the personal bonds which once existed between the owner-manager and the employee and on which the ideology of the industrial relations system was based. Hence the normative order was loosened at the same time as, and partly because of, efforts which were being made to tighten control over work arrangements.

At the same time, the National Union of Textile Workers was a union which could potentially make articulate the growing dissatisfaction of the employees in the industry. This shift in the balance of power, which the growth of the union represented, as between worker and capitalist, could potentially be reflected in individual mills if conflict broke out. Its very existence posed a threat to the paternalistic industrial relations model. The willingness to obey the employer, therefore, became less automatic as the employers showed themselves unable to conform to the industrial relations pattern they themselves had created, and the ability to disobey became a more effective option with the existence of union organisation.

If we turn now to a consideration of the internal elements of

[1] ibid., pp. 221–2.

the industrial relations system at the Loray mill, we can begin to see why Loray (rather than some other southern mill) became the dramatic flashpoint of strike activity. The atypicality of Loray as compared to the paternalistic-capitalist model of industrial relations, was reflected in a number of ways which served to reinforce each other:

1. It was a big mill by local standards, with some 3,500 employees in 1928.

2. It was characterised by a high labour turnover and frequent managerial changes.

If the first factor placed an inevitable strain on the paternalistic model of industrial relations, the second contributed further to the instability of the social relations in the mill.

3. Factors 1 and 2 both affected and contributed to the fact that the community was not tightly integrated in a way in which mill villages typically were. Hence the social supports for managerial values were greatly diminished. Norms emphasising the appropriateness of accepting managerial prerogatives and obeying managerial authority were not so universally internalised, since many of the employees felt no local loyalties to the community. They were often strangers – rootless and footloose.

4. Such loyalty to the company as may have existed among the 'locals' was further minimised by the fact that it was part of a Northern-owned syndicate of firms (Manville-Jencke) and structurally dependent on absentee-ownership. In consequence, the identity between community values and company values was not so clearly perceived or felt.

5. The mill was further atypical because it had been selected as a centre for union strategy. First, the United Textile Workers had supported a strike in 1919, as part of a campaign for recognition. This had been unsuccessful but the seeds of unionism had been sown. More immediately, the Communist controlled National Union of Textile Workers also selected Loray as a focal point, sensing that this was a good place to choose to canalise labour discontent and overthrow the existing system of industrial relations. Essentially this meant that the mobilisation of union resources was more likely in the event of overt management-worker conflict breaking out. It further meant that an otherwise anomic group of workers were provided with an organisation

which could command their loyalty, provide vigorous leadership, and challenge the existing economic order.

6. In the attempt to adapt the Loray mill to the wider exigencies of the textile industry, the Manville-Jenckes' management made certain policy decisions to cut the costs of production: the introduction of new equipment, a cut-back in the labour force accompanied by the introduction of cheap labour, a stretch-out policy for workers at the same time as wage cuts were introduced. These decisions were implemented by a new mill superintendent, who was brought in for the purpose and who made it his business to dismiss supervisors who were 'lenient'. Such local normative support as there was for the mill management was further diminished by the sacking of local men and supervision as part of the 'get tough' policy.

Management clearly felt impelled to make changes in the organisation of work on the grounds of economic necessity, but the manner in which they chose to implement their efficiency programme – through arbitrary, autocratic supervision – was based on the belief that their power position, vis-à-vis the workers was sufficient to enable them to steam-roller the changes through. However, in taking such action, they introduced an alien pattern of industrial relations in a plant where the normative order of the paternal capitalist system was already being undermined. But given the part which the United Textile Workers had elected to play at Loray, and the lack of other grievance channels through which workers might express their discontent, the strike becomes an all too understandable response.

These, then, were some of the discernible inter-relations of the elements of the industrial relations system, which may be said to have caused the strike. What do we learn from it about the character of social explanation? Mainly that various types of classificatory schemes used to explain the varieties of strike behaviour, may be as misleading as they are sometimes helpful. For example, it is sometimes thought worthwhile to classify strikes in terms of the goals of the actors. While one does not want to discount the utility of such a classification altogether, this strike does illustrate certain inherent difficulties. While many of the employees were concerned with the redressing of their economic grievances in a localised sense, the Communist union leaders were wanting to use the strike as the midwife of more revolutionary change. They had a vision of a new economic order, in which workers controlled and directed the means of production, and a new political order modelled upon the Soviet Union. But the strike itself could not in consequence be characterised exclusively as either reformist-economic, or revolutionary-political, since both elements were always present, although the latter came more to be emphasised as the strike proceeded and the union took control. The study of the union's role and policy, of course, does help to explain the way in which the workers' protest was canalised.

This brings us to a related consideration. Smelser has helpfully summarised some of the major explanations which are held to account for the sources of active unrest leading to strikes.[1] These are:

1. The 'economic advantage' school, which maintains that labour unions are 'in business' and attempt to maximise the wage gains of their members.
2. The 'job security' school which is a variant of the economic advantage school. It focuses on the desires of workmen to protect the conditions of their work in the long run rather than on short term wage gains.
3. The 'class warfare' (or Marxist) school which attributes worker unrest to the fact that the working classes suffer from systematic exploitation at the hands of the capitalists. This position has been stated in modified ways by various historians of the labour movement.
4. The 'political' school which emphasises political conflict between unions and management over the recognition of unions and collective bargaining, jurisdictional disputes among unions, internal leadership rivalries, and the influence of communism in unions.
5. The 'human relations' school, which is associated with the industrial sociology of Elton Mayo and his followers. Broadly speaking, this school traces basic dissatisfactions among labourers to the breakdown of primary groups among workers and the lack of communication and understanding between management and workers.[2]

Smelser goes on to observe:

Surely the appropriate strategy at this time is to abandon the almost ideological positions that have crystallised round these schools and

---

[1] N. Smelser, *The Sociology of Economic Life* (Prentice Hall, 1963).
[2] ibid., p. 52.

investigate the specific conditions under which *each* kind of cause is most likely to be active in the genesis of strikes.[1]

Smelser's statement tends to assume that the explanations are necessarily alternatives, whereas in some circumstances they may be complementary. One should not assume that any particular strike episode should fit any single type of explanation. In this case, for example, one can certainly discern elements of 'job security', 'class warfare', 'political conflicts' and 'human relations' difficulties.

CASE 2. THE YANKEE CITY SHOE INDUSTRY STRIKE, IN NEW ENGLAND, 1933

This strike, forms the subject of Warner and Low's study *The Social System of a Modern Factory*.[2] One of the central questions raised is this: why, in a community with a long history of industrial peace, did all the workers in the town's largest industry come out on strike in such a determined way? As with the Loray mill study, the answer is given in terms of the factors which led to the disintegration of a particular kind of industrial relations system, namely, localised, paternalistic capitalism:

> In the early days of the shoe industry the owners and managerial staffs of the factories, as well as the operatives, were residents of Yankee City: there was no extension of the factory social structures outside of the local community. The factories were then entirely under the control of the community – not only the formal control of city ordinances and laws, but also the more pervasive informal controls of community traditions and attitudes. There were feelings of neighbourliness and friendship between manager and worker and of mutual responsibilities to each other and the community that went beyond the formal employer-employee agreement.[3]

Essentially Warner and Low attempt to describe both the changes which took place in the social and economic organisation of the industry and the meaning which these changes had for the participants. Among the structural changes taking place may be noted:

[1] ibid., p. 53.
[2] W. L. Warner and J. O. Low, *The Social System of a Modern Factory* (Yale, 1946).
[3] ibid., p. 108.

1. A shift in the composition of the consumer market. No longer did the industry exist to meet local or regional needs: it was caught up in a national and international market structure. Factory output became heavily dependent upon large chain-stores for retail distribution.

2. The attempt to meet expanding market opportunities had originally been a source of stimulation among manufacturers to technological innovation. This had led, in the course of time, to the replacement of hand tool methods of work by machine tools and, ultimately, by assembly line techniques. Mass production both met and quickened the demands of the mass market. There was, in consequence, an erosion and virtual disappearance of traditional craft skills. Unskilled labour was sufficient to perform the repetitive monotonous tasks of the 'modern factory'.

3. However, the financing of a more capital intensive industry to meet these wider market demands became increasingly difficult for local capitalists to sustain. The advent of 'Big City' capitalism signified the advent of absentee ownership. And the local industry became just a link in the great chain of industrial ownership and just another member of a national manufacturers' association.

4. At the same time as the division of labour is simplified among the workers, it is diversified and extended among management. In order to cope with the complexities of marketing and distribution functional differentiation took place. Not only is the local manager in the community no longer the owner-manager, but also his direct relation with his customers disappears. The managers in direct contact with the market are to be found in the head offices at New York (Big City). The local manager is not master in his own house, he is an intermediary in the enterprise hierarchy with immediate responsiblities for production.

The bureaucratisation process is seen by Warner and Low, not only as changing the locus and distribution of managerial power but as creating a hiatus in the traditional pattern of authority relations. Absentee ownership symbolised absentee and alien power, which was not geared to serving, nor readily constrained by, the needs of the local community. Thus they observe:

> When a factory is locally owned the owner and supervisory staff are likely to be influenced in many of their decisions regarding factory policy by the broader community values to which they subscribe and by the fact that many of their employees are old acquaint-

ances and friends. But when a factory is absentee-controlled few or none of the workers are ever known to the higher officials and the latter do not feel the pressures that a local owner would feel to conform to the values of the community. Hence the absentee official can set factory policies more nearly in strict accord with the profit-making logic than a local owner, and to that extent the community loses control over the factory and becomes dependent on outside influences.[1]

The local managers at Yankee City, sons of the owner-managers of the previous generation, are portrayed as shorn of their effective power. They were stalked by the god-like figures of their dead fathers who symbolised the security of a community way of life which, to a large degree had been economically independent. Their awareness of their weakening power was indeed one factor which lowered the resistance of local management to the demands of the strikers. They also resented the over-riding dominance of the 'outsiders' and 'foreigners' in whose hands the uncertain destinies of the community now lay. To that extent the strike was not only a worker response but a community response to its growing dependence on the exigencies and complexities of the wider economic system.

By the same token, since the reciprocal ties and obligations, which once existed between local management and their work force, could no longer be sustained, because of the decline in local managerial power, then the authority of local management could no longer go unquestioned. But whose authority could be obeyed?

> It is certain that decisions charged with ruin or success for the economy of Yankee City and the stability of the lives of its people are made by men at the policy level of . . . international finance houses who do not so much as know the name of Yankee City and who beyond all doubt, do not care what happens to the town or its people.[2]

The strike was a sign of a lack of faith in an impersonal, distant, profit-oriented and unsympathetic power. When the depression, to which the industry was particularly vulnerable took place, the standardised response of the employers was to resort to wage-cuts. This became the immediate source of worker grievance. As

[1] ibid., p. 179.
[2] ibid., p. 156.

such the employers' action was a precipitant cause of the strike. But the question still remains, why was the grievance manifested in strike action as opposed to more amorphous and diffuse forms of discontent? What was it that made the work force both willing and able to strike? The answer lies in tracing out the meaning and consequences of the breakdown in the traditional craft system. It is the craft system which is portrayed as providing the mechanism for advancement of the individual worker. One aspired to become a master craftsman: starting as an apprentice and gaining proficiency in the basic skills, one moved onward and upward in the craft hierarchy. There was typically a close correlation between the age of a worker, his proficiency and skill level, his prestige and his pay. If age allied to skill was the basis of social differentiation among the work force, knowledge of the craft of shoe-making was something to strive for, and it provided the basis of one's own self-respect and respect for others in the shoe-making fraternity. Traditionally, one could, as a worker, entertain the hope of becoming one's own boss. In this sense the gap between worker and owner-manager could be bridged. By the same token, those who did become owners in this way could command the respect of their workers since, by definition, they knew what shoe-making was about. It is in this sense also that Warner and Low can say:

> Workers and managers were indissolubly interwoven into a common enterprise, with a common set of values. In this system the internal personal structure of workers and managers was made up of very much the same aparatus, and their personalities were reinforced by the social system of shoe-making.[1]

The changes in the industry, undertaken in the quest for economic rationality, served to destroy the sense of communality between managers and workers, the craft system itself and the career pattern and way of life which this embodied. But a new kind of work solidarity is created – a solidarity of the deprived and the downwardly mobile, who, by virtue of their new-found homogeneity, can more readily express a mass grievance. Furthermore, in such circumstances, the industrial union becomes an alternative and attractive source of allegiance and bargaining power. Indeed, the strike which began as a widespread but

[1] ibid., pp. 87–8.

relatively unorganised expression of worker protest against managerial behaviour, was taken over by the union and became, in addition, a battle for union recognition.

The Loray mill strike, after a period of bitter struggle, resulted in a victory for the employers. The Yankee City strike resulted in a victory for the workers in the sense that, not only did management agree to submit the wage grievances to an arbitration inquiry, but they also recognised the negotiating rights of the union from that time forward. The difference between victory and defeat in the two situations appears to be not simply a matter of luck. In the Loray situation, the union had been a revolutionary ginger-group, with an ideological commitment which did not dispose it to make compromise settlements. It effectively organised the workers' protest. But not all workers, as we have seen, shared the deep commitment to the Communist aims of the union. Hence as the strike was prolonged, doubt was cast on the instrumental value of the union to remedy grievances, and the more traditionally-minded workers were prepared to accept the discredit and calumny which was heaped upon the union's leaders. Disaffection set in and the strike was broken. By contrast, the industrial union to which the workers at Yankee City attached themselves, was, as Stein has pointed out, 'essentially a responsive counter-bureaucracy through which workers as a group improve their common lot'.[1]

CASE 3. THE 'GENERAL GYPSUM COMPANY' STRIKE, AT 'OSCAR CENTRE', NEAR THE GREAT LAKES, U.S.A., 1950

Alvin Gouldner's *Wildcat Strike* has already become something of a sociological classic. It is an attempt to describe and explain a strike which broke out at a gypsum mine in Oscar Centre (a pseudonym for a small community near the Great Lakes). Certain similarities as well as differences with the preceding two cases will emerge.

One important social process underpinning much of Gouldner's analysis is the shift in the character of management-worker relations from a 'leniency' to a 'stringency' pattern. Traditionally, within the plant certain expectations about how management

[1] A. Stein, *The Eclipse of Community* (Harper, 1964), p. 89.

should behave towards workers had been built up by the employees. These included not only the 'rights' of workers as written into the labour contract, but other matters of more tenuous legitimacy:

> Workers did not define 'leniency' as a management obligation. Instead leniency seems to refer to managerial compliances with workers' role preferences rather than role prescriptions. Furthermore, 'leniency' also involves managerial behaviour which is tempered by taking into account the worker's obligations in his other roles, for example, his obligations as a family member to maintain the family's income, to fix broken things around the house, or to leave work early to take 'the wife' on a special outing.[1]

Among the components of the indulgency pattern Gouldner cites, was the willingness to give workers a 'second chance' when they broke the company ruling on absenteeism or lateness, the permission given to use company materials and equipment for home repairs, and letting an injured worker come back on light duties before he was fully recovered, so that he might get more income than he could derive from accident compensation. Gouldner does not use the term 'paternalistic capitalism' to describe the ideology of the industrial relations system as Pope and Warner and Low had done, but he does stress in a similar fashion the personal ties that had characterised the social relations in the community. He suggests that the community embodied an egalitarian ethos, which reduced the potential social distance existing between men and management (and particularly between the men and first line supervision). The virtues of neighbourliness in a small community were carried over into the work situation.

What Gouldner attempts to do is to describe the way in which, on the one hand, the managerial interpretation of work obligations moves away from a position which has external support from the community at large, while, on the other hand, the cohesiveness of the community and its regulatory power of social control is itself diminished. These two social processes are seen as mutually reinforcing the other. But it should be noted that strains on the community value system were not solely generated from the company. Gouldner comments, for example, that 'with the

[1] Gouldner, *Wildcat Strike,* op. cit., p. 22.

transformation of farming into a business, class stratification in the area emerges more clearly, and intimate personalised relationships begin to wane'.[1] When it is said, therefore, that the strike is a symptom of social disorganisation, this disorganisation is of two forms: a growing discrepancy between the community value system and the value system detectable in industrial behaviour within the company; and the disintegration of the traditional value system of the community itself.

As with the other two case studies, we can see that part of the sequence of change leading to the strike was the changing market situation. The 'easy' war years of the sellers' market were replaced by the 'tight' post-war era of acute competition:

> For management rationalisation was a solution to a problem . . . how to retain its share of the market in the post-war period with its heightened competition and, ultimately, to expand the Company's position in the industry. The means management chose to employ were to cut unit costs and to produce more and better gypsum board.[2]

In seeking to make a more economical use of their resources, top management at the company's headquarters in 'Lakeport' initiated a policy of technical change – the introduction of new and faster machines. During this period they took the opportunity arising from the death of the old indulgency-oriented plant manager to replace him with an efficiency-oriented successor. Through him they carried out the strategic replacement of middle management and first line supervision by men who would more readily conform to the new policy requirements. This led directly to the closer supervision of work, a denial of the validity of indulgency expectations and a corresponding legalistic stress on the work contract. Impersonal, written rules were inflexibly applied and status differences in the plant hierarchy became a basis for managers and supervisors demanding deference from workers.

Now although the goal of rationalisation is increased efficiency, it is not necessarily achieved and in this case there were unanticipated consequences of the planned managerial action. There was a decline in work motivation as evidenced in a higher labour turnover, hostility to the new administration, apathy on the part

[1] Gouldner, *Patterns of Industrial Bureaucracy,* op. cit., p. 44.
[2] Gouldner, *Wildcat Strike,* op. cit., p. 85.

of some workers, more deliberate restriction of output on the part of others and, ultimately, the strike itself. The attempt to introduce even closer and stricter supervision to deal with the problem simply had the boomerang effect of lowering work motivation and increasing aggressive feelings still further. Management clearly thought, at the outset of its programme, that it had the power to implement its decisions, even if some of them might prove unpalatable to the work force. This was mainly based on their knowledge that there were few alternative job opportunities available at Oscar Centre. Indeed, they were even confident enough to re-route an important export order to Oscar Centre, from the strike-bound 'Big City' plant. This also had an unintended consequence. To the workers at Oscar Centre the re-routing episode symbolised the fact that the company's orders could be flouted and its power challenged. It reinforced grievance feelings on the grounds that 'we're not the only ones who feel this way' and helps to explain the timing of the strike and the fact that discontent was not simply expressed in more covert ways.

It was not only the management's ability to implement its rationalisation policy which was challenged, however, but more basically the legitimacy of its authority. The policy emanated, as we have seen, from the company's head office at Lakeport. This at one and the same time emphasised the fact of external control over the destinies of the work force resulting from absentee ownership and, by the same token, encouraged the workers to question the authority of plant management who were regarded as puppets.

The strike is defined by Gouldner in sociological terms as a 'breakdown in the flow of consent'.[1] The social disruption, which the strike reflected and symbolised, is seen as a consequence of trying to 'free' the labour contract from the social 'givens' which made it effective in the first place, namely, the shared traditional beliefs and values in the community from which workers had derived their complementary expectations. The attempt to sharpen the terms of the labour contract, with precise and often written statements about the duties and obligations of the worker, served to highlight the conflict between these legalistic demands and the traditional social supports which had sanctioned worker obed-

[1] ibid., p. 66.

ience in the first place. The conflict which emerged is an illustration of the fact that the 'non-contractual element of contract is . . . a system of common beliefs and sentiments' which forms 'an essential element in the basis of order in a differentiated, individualistic society'.[1]

How then could the flow of consent be restored between workers and management? Two kinds of answers were in evidence, classified as the traditionally-oriented and the market-oriented respectively:

> If the traditionalists sought to return to a relationship governed by 'trust', then the 'market-men' desired a situation in which trust did not matter; they wanted their prerogatives guarded by legal guarantee. If the traditionalists wanted to be able to return to the 'fold', the 'market-men' wanted to be 'taken into the business'. If the traditionalists wanted workers and management to be 'friends', the market-men wanted them to be 'partners'. In sum, the traditionalists wanted a return to the old indulgency pattern, while the 'market-men' were willing to set aside the informal privileges of the indulgency pattern in exchange for new, formally acknowledged union power.[2]

Both of these positions represent an attempt to put certain 'social givens' into the labour contract. The traditionalist hopes to restore the original social givens of the community norms and values. The market man sees in the emergence of collective bargaining structures a means of containing conflict and regulating the conditions of the 'effort bargain'. Given the economic and social changes that had already impinged on the community, the first response was ritualistic rather than realistic. The second aim was realistic in the context, but, given the fact that the labour contract was conditioned by changing market and technological forces, an element of instability is built into the system. Such frictional conflict as ensues may be regarded as a reflection of the politics of the work-place.

Unlike the Loray mill and Yankee City situations, the plant was already unionised. But the strike was a 'wildcat' – that is it took place without explicit union consent. Whereas in the Yankee City study we observed how the union was utilised as a counter-

[1] Talcott Parsons, *The Structure of Social Action* (Glencoe Free Press, 1949), p. 338.
[2] Gouldner, *Wildcat Strike*, op. cit., p. 63.

bureaucracy to fight the impersonal, bureaucratic power of management, in this instance the workers find themselves estranged from the counter-bureaucracy as well. While then, as we have seen, the strike symbolised a breakdown in the community-plant complex of norms and values, it also pointed to the felt inadequacy of the existing grievance machinery. A different kind of legitimacy crisis is implied:

> When the formal union leaders are oriented toward managerial expectations, and when they, therefore view certain of the workers' grievances as non-legitimate, they may actually impair upward communication.[1]

If the labour contract is subject to scrutiny and re-negotiation between management and labour, in the view of the market-men, so also is the contract binding the union and the rank and file together. What was once an acceptable grievance process need not always remain so.

But one thing stands out clearly. If we ask whether the strike was against management or against the union, the answer is that, for different reasons, it was against both.

---

[1] ibid., p. 102.

CHAPTER TWO

Unofficial Strikes

Some Objections Considered
CO-AUTHOR: G. C. CAMERON[1]

THE purpose of this essay is to discuss critically the bases on which objections to unofficial strikes are made. These we have classified broadly as sociological, administrative, economic and moral. Before embarking upon this, however, it is necessary to give an operational definition of what we understand by the concept of the unofficial strike.

One of the tersest definitions of the unofficial strike is that of Knowles:

> An unofficial strike is one which is not recognised by the Executive Committee of a Union.[2]

On the basis of Knowles' definition one may go on to distinguish between what may be called 'quasi-official' and 'pure unofficial' strikes. The former category would refer to unofficial strikes which at some stage, either before or after the event, would be regarded as justified by the official union hierarchy. The 'pure unofficial' strike would refer to those stoppages which, for one reason or another, do not have the support of the Union Executive. A distinction of this sort is sociologically useful in that we are able to get some indication of a union's actual policy towards unofficial strikes and some measure of the effectiveness of its social control over its members. At the same time, the mere fact that the membership of a particular union commonly participates in unofficial strikes is not a necessary sign of the union's lack of

---

[1] We are glad to acknowledge the advice given in the preparation of this essay by Mr. A. J. Odber.

[2] K. G. J. C. Knowles, *Strikes* (Blackwell, 1952), p. 30.

control. Mr. E. Hill, former General Secretary of the Boilermakers Society, for example, has recorded the view that:

> If a strike is on a question of wages we have got to support it. Sometimes it has got to be unofficial but if it is for the purpose for which unions were formed I can always find a way to justify it.[1]

Mr. Hill maintained his view even under the widespread adverse criticism he received (heightened no doubt because it was linked with an apparent condoning of ballot rigging in trade unions). Later the same month he indicated that the important distinction for him was not between official and unofficial strikes but between necessary and unnecessary strikes:

> We say we want to avoid unnecessary strikes. . . . But some of these strikes cannot be avoided and if we are going to protect our members we are going to support them.[2]

Quite where union officials draw the line between quasi-official and pure unofficial strikes is a question of tactics and traditions. B.I.S.A.K.T.A., for example, not only rules that 'it is not permissible for any member or members to strike his or her employment without the authority, and sanction of the Executive Council', but resolutely refuses to subsequently recognise as official, any such strike. Indeed, Branch officials who are involved in such behaviour are suspended from office for varying periods. At the Port Talbot works of the Steel Company of Wales, for example, in February 1959, an unofficial strike took place over the dismissal of a clerk. The Company argued that they were within their rights to sack the man. The men maintained that the clerk was not given sufficient dismissal notice. Following the strike action which was against the advice of the Divisional Organiser, five Branch officials were suspended by the National Executive.[3] Similar action was taken even in the case of the sympathy strike of bricklayers' mates (members of B.I.S.A.K.T.A.) at Port Talbot in the autumn of 1961. The bricklayers (organised by the Amalgamated Union of Building Trade Operatives) were in dispute with the Company and the 'mates' refused to work with 'staff' men who were doing the Bricklayers' jobs. This brings

---

[1] Report on the N.U.M. Annual conference, *Financial Times,* 5 July 1961.
[2] Report on the E.T.U. Annual conference, *Financial Times,* 20 July 1961.
[3] 120 Branch officials resigned in protest over this action.

out the rigidity with which the sanction against unofficial strikes is applied. In the context of this union there can scarcely be such a phenomenon as the quasi-official strike. By comparison, even the N.U.G.M.W., which can scarcely be described as militant, has had officials who have warned stubborn managements that unless a concession is made 'they cannot be responsible for the actions of their members'. As Clegg points out in his study on the General Union:

> On occasion, officers have been known to suggest to a shop steward that a demonstration of the validity of this kind of statement by their members would be of assistance in their negotiations.[1]

A very useful test enabling one to distinguish between the quasi-official and the pure unofficial strike is whether or not dispute benefit is paid. Payment of dispute benefit is the mark of ultimate justification. In the T.U.C.'s own report unofficial strikes were essentially regarded as those in which a dispute benefit was not paid.[2] One might also add, however, that there are cases where a dispute benefit as such has not been paid to strikers but an *ex gratia* payment has been given. In this way a union's policy about the non-payment of dispute benefit to strikes that take place without official union sanction, can be circumvented. Such strikes also are clearly quasi-official.

It is important to recognise that what we have termed quasi-official strikes are not always felt to be unofficial strikes. Thus W. Gallacher separated unofficial strikes from spontaneous strikes over trade union principles – 'such a strike is often necessary when something occurs leaving only the option of submitting or fighting'.[3] These might be described as 'perishable disputes', where speed of action is placed at a premium by the strikers. They might arise in circumstances where it is either impossible to contact the union official, or where it is felt that by the time the issue has gone through the negotiating procedure the battle will have been lost. Perishable disputes might arise in relation to such matters as the upholding of a closed shop principle, objections to manning arrangements or other conditions of work which were felt to be contrary to existing agreements

[1] H. A. Clegg, *The General Union* (Blackwell, 1954), p. 133.
[2] *T.U.C. Report*, 1961.
[3] Knowles, op. cit., p. 31.

and so on. Not all spontaneous strikes, therefore, need be regarded as wildcat strikes.[1]

A former Minister of Labour, Mr. Hare (now Lord Blakenham) showed that he was aware of some of the pitfalls that await those who try to define the unofficial strike. In the House of Commons on 21 May 1962, he pointed out that:

> There are difficulties in defining and classifying strikes as official and unofficial. . . . Some strikes start as unofficial and end as official. Some are official only when they are over. Some are official at district level and are repudiated at headquarters. It is difficult to give the breakdown.[2]

It is, however, a pity that only when specific questions are asked in the House of Commons, does the Government make any attempt to discover the incidence of unofficial strikes. It is now a decade ago that Knowles suggested that the Ministry of Labour improve its strike statistics by introducing a distinction between official and unofficial strikes.[3] He was thinking particularly of isolating the pure unofficial strikes, in order that the extent to which the unions used the strike weapon as an instrument of policy could be ascertained. Doubtful cases, he suggested, could be classified as such. Despite the difficulties which Mr. Hare outlined, it might still prove a rewarding and worthwhile exercise. In the House of Commons Mr. Hare revealed that in 1961, three million days were lost through all strikes reported to the Ministry of Labour.[4] Of these about 860,000 days were lost through strikes which were definitely stated to be official. On this reckoning 71% of time lost was through unofficial strikes. These would mainly refer to pure unofficial strikes because many of the quasi-official strikes would subsequently have been declared official.

The categories around which the following discussion is hinged are not regarded as water-tight. But they do provide a useful framework and should serve to reduce some of the confusion

---

[1] See p. 78 below for a discussion of the wildcat strike.
[2] *Hansard* (May 1962), Vol. 660, col. 8.
[3] op. cit., p. 305.
[4] These refer to strikes involving ten or more workpeople and lasting for one day or more. The aggregate number of days lost exceed 100. Countless small stoppages which characterise many unofficial strikes are thereby excluded.

that surrounds a rather controversial subject in which the emotions rather than the intellect are the first to be stirred.

Sociological Objections

A number of sociological objections to unofficial strikes are rooted in certain theories of conflict. In industrial sociology one form of this is to be found in the style of thinking which tends to assume that management/labour conflict can and must be eliminated by 'good' human relations. Writing on 'The Perspectives of Elton Mayo' Reinhard Bendix and Lloyd N. Fisher argue that:

> It is difficult to understand Mayo's work unless one realises how much he abhors conflict, competition or disagreement: conflict to him is a 'social disease' and co-operation is 'social health'.[1]

This, perhaps, does less than justice to Mayo's position but the statement illustrates the type of theoretical approach we have in mind. Landsberger[2] has reasonably noted that the epithet 'management-oriented' with which the Mayo school is dubbed is more readily applicable to the Michigan studies of supervision in industry and the Group Dynamics approach typified in Coch and French's 'Overcoming Resistance to Social Change'.[3]

But the existence of authority relationships both within and between particular social groups, which gives rise to real and perceived differences when the costs of prescribed courses of behaviour are evaluated, strongly suggests the inevitability of conflict both at the social psychological and sociological level. Certainly when one looks at the field of industrial sociology the power element is far more evident than in some other areas of sociological investigation. Yet, as John Rex has indicated:

> Anyone with experience of industrial relations knows that the actual relations between employers and employees are determined by a contract which ends a period of negotiations in which both sides are likely to deploy their powers in threatening strikes and lock outs. Yet very often industrial sociology ignores all this and discusses the social relations of a factory as though they were akin to those of

[1] R. Bendix and L. N. Fisher, 'The Perspectives of Elton Mayo', *Review of Economics and Statistics*, Vol. 31, 1949, p. 272.

[2] Henry A. Landsberger, *Hawthorne Re-visited* (Cornell, 1958).

[3] L. Coch and J. R. P. French, 'Overcoming Resistance to Social Change', *Human Relations*, 1948, I, pp. 512–33.

a village community, in terms of some sort of value framework which is supposed to be accepted by both sides.[1]

This statement acts as a useful bridge to a sociological objection which is rather more convincing. While strikes and lock outs have always been a feature of the industrial relations landscape, some observers are questioning whether they are a necessary feature. The international comparisons of Ross and Hartman in *Changing Patterns of Industrial Conflict*[2] show that in most countries there has been a reduction in the number of days lost through strike activity in the last 25 years. This trend provides grounds of hope for those who believe that the strike will become outmoded in mature industrial societies. B. C. Roberts, for example, argues that:

> The relative scarcity of major strikes will make the occurrence of small protest strikes of greater significance and will probably induce demands for some form of compulsory arbitration . . . when there are many strikes arbitration is impossible, but when there are very few there seems to be much less reason for letting them occur.[3]

It is not social conflict *per se* that is denied or abhorred, but social conflict that expresses itself in strike action. The regulation of conflict through collective bargaining procedures is advocated in order that the sharper forms of social antagonisms might be avoided, for, as Dahrendorf suggests:

> Conciliation, mediation and arbitration and their normative and structural prerequisites are the outstanding mechanisms for reducing the violence of class conflict. When these routines of relationship are established group conflict loses its sting and becomes an institutionalised pattern of social life.[4]

But it is precisely the normative and structural prerequisites that need to be established before the mechanisms of conciliation, mediation and arbitration are more acceptable to potential strikers than the use of the strike weapon. There would appear to be at

---

[1] J. Rex, *Key Problems of Sociological Theory* (Routledge and Kegan Paul, 1961), p. 111.

[2] Ross and Hartman, *Changing Patterns of Industrial Conflict* (Wiley, 1960).

[3] B. C. Roberts, *Industrial Relations: Contemporary Problems and Perspectives* (Methuen, 1962), p. 17.

[4] R. Dahrendorf, *Class and Class Conflict in an Industrial Society* (Routledge and Kegan Paul, 1959), p. 230.

least two presuppositions before the superiority of these mechanisms over the strike in general and the unofficial strike in particular can be admitted. The first presupposition is an acceptance in principle of the broad outlines of the existing industrial order by the major interest groups. Without this there will be an insufficient consensus of opinion for the collective bargaining procedures to work effectively. Where the legitimacy of an order is being questioned by any of the major interest groups, an appeal for industrial peace which would buttress that order can scarcely expect to be heeded. The strike weapon is held to be justified, in such a situation if it brings about the desired re-distribution of rights, duties and privileges. This is the source of the political strike. The Court of Inquiry into the Dispute in Civil Air Transport in 1958 admitted the possibility of the intrusion of political issues into the field of industrial relations. The Court deplored the use of industrial action for political ends, indicating that this was 'not compatible with the development of harmonious industrial relations and the smooth working of constitutional procedures'.

The second presupposition is that the procedures of conciliation mediation and arbitration are efficient, representative and in some meaningful sense 'fair'. Efficiency here refers to the speed at which decisions are taken and communicated back to the interested parties. Representativeness implies that, not only do the interested parties have someone to plead their case, but that the spokesman should understand the issues involved and be trustworthy in his conduct of the case. The cleavage between the style of life of the professional negotiator and the rank and file member of the trade union has not escaped the attention of commentators since the Webbs. This gives rise to a latent fear that the negotiator will join 'them' and sell his group 'down the river'. The need for constitutional safeguards to keep this fear in check is clear. Thus, Sir William Carron, at the annual conference of the A.E.U. in 1961, replying to a claim that the executive committee of the union had flouted a national committee resolution, maintained that:

> In this extremely democratic union all members can have redress by taking the executive to the final appeal court if it breaks the rules.[1]

[1] *The Guardian*, 28 April 1961.

The national committee here is the fifty-two man rank and file committee. The barbed retort of Mr. W. Fleming, one of the delegates, serves to illustrate the point that such constitutional safeguards must be properly maintained if the professional leaders are to be regarded as truly representative:

> The final appeal court is supposed to over-rule the executive, but when they over-rule them and the executive doesn't like it, the executive over-rules the final appeal court. So where are we? In Fred Karno's Army.[1]

The concept of 'fairness' is not susceptible to precise definition. But in broad terms we suggest that it implies that, under existing procedures, where gains and losses are involved, the parties concerned should have a roughly equal share of them. Where one union was constantly losing work as a result of decisions under demarcation procedures, for example, one might safely predict the advent of official or unofficial strikes. The concept of fairness is therefore, concerned with the distribution of decisions but it is also derived from the ideas of efficiency and representativeness. The expression of sentiments such as 'it's not fair that the men should be kept waiting,' or 'we shouldn't be kept in the dark about what's going on', or 'it's only fair that our point of view should be heard', illustrate this.

Apart from the sharing of gains and losses referred to above, it can also be maintained that there are situations in which the use of collective bargaining procedures leads to outcomes that are strategically preferable to all concerned. It is this kind of thinking, no doubt, which led Mr. Bertil Kugelburg, Managing Director of the Swedish Employers' Confederation to say:

> If you think of a negotiator, I think his first duty is to try to place himself in the chair of his opponent and try to find out what are the aims of the opposing party. What are their conditions, how do they work? If you do that and try to find a solution, even if you have strongly conflicting interests, I think it is possible to find a compromise which, to a certain degree, will be satisfactory to both of them.[2]

The actual evaluation of the costs involved, and hence of the

---

[1] ibid.

[2] Quoted in Jack Cooper, 'Industrial Relations: Sweden shows the Way' (*Fabian Research Pamphlet*, May 1963), p. 3.

superiority of the procedural methods to the strike weapon, is a matter for the parties concerned. But the empirical difficulties here for the student are considerable. Not only is it likely that the main interest groups will perceive the elements and issues of the bargaining situation differently, but the individual groups themselves are by no means homogeneous. In a trade union, for example, not only will there be differences potentially in the assessment of a situation as between the National Executive, the District Officials, the Branches, the Shop Stewards and the rank and file, but also between different skills and industry groupings as any dispute over wage differentials reveals.

Belief in the legitimacy of the industrial order, and the adequacy of the collective bargaining procedures are analytically separate propositions. But, as we have indicated, without the establishment of the first proposition, it is hardly likely that the collective bargaining procedures will work effectively. Similarly, if the negotiating procedures as laid down were constantly failing the tests of efficiency, representativeness and fairness, the legitimacy of the order would eventually be questioned.

Administrative Objections

The administrative objections to unofficial strikes arise in part from resistance to change which, to a greater or lesser extent is encountered in all bureaucratic organisations and in part from the dilemmas which the functionaries of the parties involved find themselves in as a result of such strikes. The position of minority groups is a perennial problem of democratic theory and highlights the issue of bureaucratic resistance to change. In industry, a group of workers who wish to transfer their allegiance from one union to another or to establish a new union, will meet the formidable opposition of the entrenched union and employers' bureaucratic structures. The employers and their Associations are reluctant to give negotiating rights to unions with which they are unused to dealing. The T.U.C. is likewise reluctant to recognise new unions and further holds that a union's right to retain its members is supreme over the member's right to change his affiliation, as the analysis of post-war jurisdictional disputes awards emphatically shows.[1] A small breakaway group does not easily gain control

[1] See S. W. Lerner, *Breakaway Unions and the Small Trade Union* (1961) Chapter 2, The T.U.C. Jurisdictional Dispute Settlement.

over the means of communication to present its point of view adequately to potential converts. When, therefore, the group draws attention to itself in the form of an unofficial stoppage, its leaders are likely to be described and dismissed as 'troublemakers'. Mr. Harry Douglas, General Secretary of B.I.S.A.K.T.A., speaking at the T.U.C. Conference debate on unofficial strikes in 1960, declared:

> The individual unions have set up a constitution democratically by their own elected members and then have come to this rostrum to support those who defy that constitution. . . . If self-elected dictators attempt to destroy the agreements democratically negotiated, they will just as surely destroy the Movement which negotiated these agreements.[1]

This is an expression of what Karl Mannheim in a more general context described as 'bureaucratic conservatism', the type of mentality which attempts to turn all problems of politics into problems of administration.[2] In its extreme form bureaucratic conservatism refuses to accept any revolutionary tendencies as legitimate and seeks to control industrial discontent by the manipulative techniques at its disposal. The moral objections to 'unconstitutional' behaviour, which we discuss separately, provide the ideological content and justification of bureaucratic conservatism.

Turning to the dilemmas which the functionaries of the parties involved find themselves in as a result of unofficial strikes, one can see that too many disputes when trade union officials are thin on the ground, makes it physically impossible to cope. The time and resources of the official may be stretched beyond endurance. In addition, there is the further dilemma of how to respond when an unofficial strike is brought to the attention of the trade union official. V. L. Allen has well illustrated this problem in connection with the dockworkers.[3] When strikes were being spread from port to port by unofficial strike leaders, the union officials had to try to get to the ports first. They then had to decide whether to hold their own properly constituted union meetings, with the risk

[1] Ibid., p. 351.
[2] K. Mannheim, *Ideology and Utopia* (Routledge and Kegan Paul, 1960), p. 105.
[3] V. L. Allen, *Trade Union Leadership* (Longmans, 1957), Chapter 12: (1) Dockworkers in the Union; (2) Union Leadership in the Docks.

that those they really wanted to be present would not come, or would even hold their own rival meetings, or to attend the unofficial meetings to put the official union view across. While the latter approach might appear to concede recognition to the unofficial group and certainly puts the union officials on the spot in a hotly dissentient atmosphere, on balance it appears to have been the most successful tactic in resolving the dilemma to the union's advantage.

It is what is commonly called the wildcat strike that gives rise to the union's administrative dilemma in its most acute form. The genuine wildcat strike is defined by Gouldner as:

> One in which the formal union leaders have actually lost control and the strike is led by individuals whose position in the formal structure does not prescribe such a role for them.[1]

Such strikes may give the appearance of being 'unreasonable' and apparently unpredictable, but Paterson who equates the wildcat strike to his 'operative variable' strike suggests that they are always preceded by changes in performance indices and to that extent can be expected.[2] They have, as it were, an internal logic of their own. It is a failure to read the signs embodied in an increased rate of accidents, work spoilage, labour turnover, psychosomatic illness and a lowered rate of productivity that gives the appearance of spontaneity. Contrary to popular notions, the wildcat strike is no new phenomenon. Writing of the nineteenth-century experience in *The Growth of British Industrial Relations*, E. H. Phelps-Brown observed:

> From time to time anxieties, grievances and vague resentments (regarding type of work, supervision, disruption of work groups, insecurity or technical change) seemed to cumulate and re-inforce one another . . . No issue had arisen of the kind with which union headquarters were used to dealing. So when strike followed, it broke out suddenly, men suffering from a real but undefined sense of grievance formulated some unreasonable complaint; a trivial in-

[1] A. W. Gouldner, *Wildcat Strike* (Routledge and Kegan Paul, 1955), p. 93. Gouldner distinguishes between the genuine wildcat and the pseudo wildcat strike, the latter being the situation in which the formal union leaders have employed concealed influence in sanctioning and leading the strike (p. 95). In our terminology this would be a form of quasi-official strike, whereas the former is pure unofficial.

[2] T. T. Paterson, *Glasgow Limited* (Cambridge, 1960).

cident precipitated an unofficial strike. The men felt they had to take action into their own hands because the union was no help to them. The officials at headquarters and the national executive were taken by surprise, and found fault with the men for breaking an agreement made in their name. The public blamed the leaders for being out of touch with the rank and file.[1]

It is not only the spontaneous element of the strike but the sense of alienation from the established union that characterises the wildcat strike. As far as the existing union organisation is concerned, the perishable dispute, which we noted earlier, is essentially defensive, whereas the wildcat strike is aggressive. ('The men felt they had to take action into their own hands because the union was no help to them.')

An administrative dilemma also confronts the Ministry of Labour in its conciliatory activities. Can it consult with the unofficial strike leaders without undermining the authority of the union officials and unjustifiably elevating the status of the strike leaders, thereby encouraging imitation by other potential strikers? Yet not to consult might only prolong the dispute. Michael Shanks has suggested that the official conciliation service should be separated from the Ministry of Labour.[2] but what it gains in freedom it might lose in authority for its own status would suffer by such a reorganisation.

Economic Objections

One of the most frequently stated views is that this country cannot afford unofficial strikes. Vigorous exponents of the attitude stress the disruption caused to industry by these disputes, and castigate the union leaders for not preventing strikes which hold back production, lose exports and reduce the national income. A motion in 1963 to the Central Council of the Conservative Party exemplifies this kind of thinking:

That this Council . . . urges Her Majesty's Government to provide further safeguards to workers, employers and the public against

[1] E. H. Phelps-Brown, *The Growth of British Industrial Relations* (Macmillan, 1960), pp. 331–2.
[2] In B. C. Roberts, op. cit. Chapter 9, Public Policy and the Ministry of Labour.

unofficial strikes and the disruption caused by individuals who neither represent, nor serve any national interest.[1]

More moderate opponents of unofficial strikes, including many prominent Labour Party leaders, argue that the unofficial strike is a 'luxury' which will have to be sacrificed if this country is to achieve a faster rate of productive growth. This attitude is clearly shown in a speech of Mr. Harold Wilson:

> We cannot afford unofficial strikes any more than we can afford tax avoidance or financial manoeuvrings that put quick profits . . . ahead of the national interest.[2]

Although it is clearly legitimate to argue that the economic costs of unofficial strikes are too high, this can never rise above the level of assertion unless precision can be given to the meaning and extent of these costs and to achieve this precision is a formidable task.[3] Initially there is the problem of data. Even if we can arrive at a workable definition of an unofficial strike, we have extremely inadequate statistics on the effects of such strikes upon production, earnings, revenue, consumption and exports. Moreover, these effects ought to be studied not only in relation to costs in the strike bound producing unit, but in units dependent for supplies upon the strike bound plant. Unfortunately the indirect effect of strikes are not taken into account in the official statistics, apart from estimates of the number of workers indirectly put out of work by the principal stoppages. Furthermore it is clear that the costs of unofficial strikes will vary from industry to industry in more ways than the loss of working days per employee. For example, an unofficial strike may cause the loss of an important order to a company, and yet the cost of this strike will be measured in terms of the loss of a certain number of working days, and this will take no account of the loss of 'future output'. In any case, the loss of working days ought to be weighed in some way to allow for varying economic conditions. For example, the loss of export orders due to unofficial strikes, at a time when a country faces a severe balance of payments

---

[1] Annual Meeting, May 1963.

[2] Speech to the Annual Conference of the N.U.R., 8 July 1963.

[3] The economic consequences of strikes are excellently analysed in Knowles, op. cit., pp. 262 ff.

deficit, is obviously more serious than any loss sustained during conditions of a favourable balance.

Our data on the after effects of unofficial strikes is similarly inadequate. By and large we do not know what happens to productivity after the completion of strikes, nor can we quantify the improvements in plant or material utilisation or from mechanisation, which management may undertake as a result of unofficial strikes. An insuperable problem also arises when we try to assess what would have happened to such things as earnings or output if the unofficial strike had not taken place.

The basic difficulty is that in trying to estimate the costs of unofficial strikes to the national economy, we not only have to weigh the gains of one group against the losses of other groups, but allow for the fact that the gainers may gain in one capacity but lose in another.

Bearing these complications in mind, we have attempted to estimate the loss of productive time and production itself as a result of unofficial strikes. Obviously this calculation will be affected by the definition of an unofficial strike and for this purpose we will consider only 'pure unofficial' stoppages and take these as covering approximately 70–80% of working days lost through all strikes. The loss of productive time can be measured by dividing the total loss of working days due to strikes by the total of potential working days, given the labour force and a standard working year.[1] A calculation of this kind for the decade between 1952 and 1961 shows that approximately one out of every 2,000 working days was lost through all strikes, and, as we have seen, this should be roughly deflated by 20–30% to give the percentage loss due to pure unofficial disputes alone. More recent figures tend to substantiate the general conclusion that the direct loss of working time due to unofficial strikes is extremely small. When he was Minister of Labour, Mr. Hare pointed out that in the first six months of 1963, out of 5,000 working days only one was lost as a result of strikes.[2] Even in the three most strike prone industries of 1962, the loss of working days due to all stoppages as a percentage of total working days, was less than one-quarter of one per cent in shipbuilding, just

[1] The standard working year is roughly equivalent to 294 days, i.e. 364 minus 52 days of weekends and 18 days of public and annual holidays.
[2] *The Guardian,* 22 July 1963.

over one-third of one per cent in engineering and less than two-
thirds of one per cent in the most strike prone industry of all,
the motor industry.

As we have already suggested however, the loss of working
days may not be an accurate measure of the loss of output, for
without consideration of a wider range of variables this measure
alone may easily over-state or under-estimate the actual loss of
output. In national terms, for example, it is conceivable that the
loss of output in strike bound producing units may simply be
off-set by the increase in the demand for output from plants with
spare capacity and similar products; or, in the extreme case,
national output may be maintained by the flow of goods or
services from producers who were on the point of destroying
their surpluses. Even if it is not possible to replace lost output
in this way, there is no certainty that the strike bound plant will
not be able to maintain normal output by using management
officials, office staff, new workers and even, in some cases, with
the aid of customers themselves. One interesting incident of
re-manning occurred in the 1961 strike of 150 seamen who
delayed the departure of their vessel in order to force the management to dismiss a bosun:

> The Canadian Pacific Company had recruited replacements from
> other ports, who travelled overnight to Liverpool. And in the
> November dawn, the vessel slipped quietly out into the Mersey,
> fully manned.
> The strikers, confident that they were going to achieve their object
> of either getting the ship's bosun removed or tying up the vessel
> indefinitely, were dumbfounded when they discovered she had
> sailed.
> 'Our Christmas money has gone down the Mersey' shouted one of
> the angry strikers who had previously rejected the advice of the
> General Secretary of the National Union of Seamen, to end their
> strike.[1]

Obviously, the ease with which strikers can be replaced will
depend on a host of factors – how many men are on strike,
whether their work is of a highly specialised nature whether the
safety of their replacements is imperilled by under-manning, and
whether non-striking workers within and outside of the plant
will work with the replacements. Of greater importance, perhaps,

[1] *Daily Telegraph,* 17 November 1961.

is the attitude of the strikers themselves to the use of replacement personnel, or in some cases strikes have been prolonged until 'black labour' was withdrawn.

It is considerations of this kind which result in a seemingly large loss of output in the shipbuilding industry. Figures given by the shipbuilding employers imply that over the three years 1958–60, an annual average loss of 4% was due to unofficial strikes. Here the strict demarcation of trades, and the assembly type of production dictate that each trade must wait its turn to start its work on the vessel, and this is complicated by the difficulty of not only finding replacement labour, but of persuading the non-strikers to work with these replacements.

The 1962 strike in the Wearside yard of J. L. Thompson is a good example of how the inability to replace a small number of strikers resulted in a general lay off and a considerable loss of output:

... The yard was closed (to 1,300 workers) because the absence of (ten) fitters meant that the cranes could not be serviced. The resumption of work has been made possible because two apprentice fitters have gone back to work. With the departmental foreman they have been checking the cranes, and as a result it is hoped that several hundred men will resume today with more to follow.[1]

On the other hand, employers may not always regret the loss of the workers' output, for the strike may enable managements to make improvements to plant lay-out. This may be particularly true of short strikes in 'round-the-clock' industries. A case in point has come to our attention in one such industry – steel rolling – where the management used a one day strike of maintenance craftsmen to try a new (and successful) method of changing rolls.

Even allowing for the fact that national output may be maintained by an increase in substitute output, by replacement workers, or in the long term by improvements resulting from the strike, it is clear that the loss of working days may, in some instances, understate the actual loss of production. This is most clearly seen when the actions of unofficial strikers in a few companies, deter overseas buyers from placing orders from all the companies in the country in question. The views of a leading Swedish shipowner, Mr. Tore Ulff are relevant when he said:

[1] *The Guardian,* 3 May 1962.

. . . there are things in British shipbuilding that are not at all satis-factory – the strikes and the threatened strikes. If it were not for the unfortunate effect of these disputes foreign owners would have more tonnage built in Britain – and they would have great confidence about the orders they placed . . . shipyard strikes on the continent are on a far smaller scale. Some countries just don't have strikes . . .[1]

'Future output' may also be impaired by the damage caused to plant and equipment as a result of a strike. If, for example, a steel furnace is left unattended during a strike, then there may not only be a loss of metal but damage to the furnace as well, which holds up production on the return of the strikers.

All of these factors suggest that the national loss of output from unofficial strikes can easily be exaggerated or minimised. This is also true of the loss resulting from the effects of strikes on other producers. Here three questions are relevant. First, does the producer possess a stock of products, or can he obtain stocks which can tide him over the strike? Second, are there any sub-stitutes which can be used instead of the 'strike product'? Finally, can consumption of the strike output be delayed tem-porarily? To take the last-mentioned it may be possible for a firm to do without its steel supplies for one day but not its supply of electricity to run the machinery.

The after effects of strikes on output are, as we have suggested, extremely difficult to estimate. Some writers consider that as a strike involves a rest from work, output is sure to rise when the workers return.[2] T. T. Paterson puts the strike in quite a different perspective when he argues:

The loss of coal output through strikes is comparatively small, the loss through bad performance is immense. And though miners may be castigated for striking, the real culprits are the agents who produce the frustrating and insecure situations . . . It might be the case in the coal mining industry that the 'wildcat' strike is 'good' for production (in the aggression causing environment) for the cathartic effect of the strike, 'It lets them get it off their chests', the recovery makes up part of the leeway lost in the approach to the strikes.[3]

[1] *The Journal* (Newcastle), 5 May 1962.
[2] Knowles, op. cit., p. 266 quotes a Ministry of Labour official as saying: 'Strikes are a form of rest and consequently beneficial to production.'
[3] Paterson, op. cit., p. 212.

What seems clear is that the after effects of the unofficial strike will vary according to the human and technical conditions within the plant. If the grievances which have caused the strikes are not removed then the cathartic effect which Paterson describes will soon be dissipated and output will fall again. Further, it may be a technical impossibility to get into full production immediately following a strike. The difference between re-lighting a blast furnace and switching on a machine in an engineering shop brings out this problem.

With loss of production may come increased operating costs and/or loss of revenue. Increased costs are often associated with paying premium (overtime) rates to workers to catch up on output, or there may be honorariums to pay to supervisory staff who have undertaken extra duties during a strike. Loss of revenue is extremely difficult to pin-point. If the factory is producing for stock then no loss of revenue may be incurred as long as the existing stocks are sufficient to meet current demand. Further, if consumption of the goods or service can be postponed, then revenue may be recouped at a future date. A one-day strike of barbers may simply result in twice the normal amount of work on the day following the strike. But a one-day strike in say electricity supply or rail transport will almost certainly mean that one day's revenue is lost to the generating company or railway company, since consumers cannot easily postpone their need for the services, and are unlikely to compensate by taking twice the amount of electricity or double the number of journeys on the following day. This loss of revenue may be especially high, of course, if the strike coincides with a peak in travel or in demand for electricity. Moreover, consumers may incur extra expense in substituting another service for the electricity or rail transport and this must be measured as a cost of the strike. On the other hand, their inability to have electricity or rail transport may induce them to consume other services which may prove cheaper and just as effective as the strike bound services. From the consumers' point of view then, this ought to be considered as a net advantage of the strike.

From these arguments it is apparent that the inadequacies of existing statistical data and the lack of detailed research, make it extremely difficult to arrive at any overall conclusions as to the economic benefits or evils of unofficial strikes.

Moral Objections

In a leading article of the November 1960 edition of *The British Manufacturer*[1] the following attack was made on the activities of the strikers in the seamen's and tally clerks' strikes of that year:

> To the informed and thinking man these strikes have been self evident examples of the wanton sacrifice of the national interest to private greed. Unfortunately, the public are not informed and seldom think, and the full moral obliquity of the men concerned has therefore escaped the general condemnation it deserved. . . . It is easy to say, and probably largely true, that the strikes were 'unofficial', which means that the men were not ordered out by their unions. It remains true that the strikers wielded the power they used so wickedly solely by courtesy of the established power of the unions.

Less strident and more reasoned objections come from writers who see in conditions of full employment a situation which makes both sides of industry willing to depart from agreements wherever some temporary advantage was thought to be attainable. B. C. Roberts, in his editorial introduction to *Industrial Relations* summed it up thus:

> Today, in national industry wide agreements are not looked upon either by employers or trade unionists as firmly binding the parties to their terms as they were in the past.

Referring to shop stewards Roberts continued:

> (They) think of the agreements negotiated by their unions at national level as no more than jumping-off points to be improved upon whenever possible by their own pressures. What is bad about this situation is that the demands of the stewards are often in breach of an agreement; it is no longer felt to be morally improper to make such demands and to back them up by actions that are a violation of agreed procedure . . .[2]

In the same volume Nancy Sear has this to say of the unofficial strike:

> In the British system of industrial relations in which agreements have no legal backing and are, therefore, valueless unless voluntarily

[1] Published by the National Association of Manufacturers.
[2] Roberts, op. cit., pp. 10-11.

86

honoured, even a small-scale tendency to treat them as scraps of paper can be seen as a serious threat not to be ignored.[1]

She realistically adds, however, that while the unofficial strike may weaken the official union hierarchy, as a bargaining weapon it is not likely to be abandoned cheaply, both because of its nuisance value in obtaining concessions from management and its prestige value to the shop steward leader.

What is made explicit by all of the writers quoted is the moral impropriety of the shop stewards, who in their pursuit of selfish, local ends, break formally and legitimately constituted agreements. Nevertheless, the second writer at least, accepts the fact that the present system of collective bargaining must be radically re-shaped if agreements are to once again command general acceptance by their signatories.

The danger of this kind of reasoning is that in accusing shop stewards and others who break national agreements of moral impropriety, whilst accepting that these same agreements may not be relevant to modern conditions, one is surely supporting loyalty to agreements for no better reason than 'all workers ought to be loyal to agreements'.

The stand of the two other writers may be even more difficult to sustain. In basing their moral attack on the sanctity of national agreements they make a basic assumption that these agreements are in some way the only agreements worthy of loyalty. Thus moral propriety is equated with supporting national collective bargaining. This attitude obscures the need for a precise and detailed investigation into the motives of shop stewards and others who break agreements. There seems little doubt that some plant leaders do exploit favourable local markets for labour, but the empirical question of how often in fact this 'exploitation' arises from the use of unconstitutional and coercive action by the shop steward or, instead, results from managements being pressed by the need to increase output in conditions of scarce labour is hardly ever asked. It is also possible that we have too often stressed the monetary selfishness of plant bargainers and failed to recognise the value of the increasing number of agreements on such things as redundancy, severance payments, sick pay and the like. There is the final point that with the multiplicity of national, local, plant and departmental agreements, some

[1] N. Sear in ibid., pp. 142.

formally drawn up, others informally accepted on both sides, there is a strong possibility that one agreement may overlap or even contradict other agreements. Consequently, when critics blame shop stewards for breaking agreements they ought first to establish to which agreement they are referring. Moral condemnation may not be so simple when it becomes apparent that shop stewards are obliged to break a national agreement forbidding strike action until the procedure has been exhausted, in order to defend a plant agreement which is being infringed by the plant management. Mr. C. Berridge, for example, a member of the A.E.U. Executive, has criticised the procedure for settling disputes in the engineering industry, as laid down in the York Memorandum, saying that it was responsible for many disputes because the employer was encouraged to adopt an inflexible attitude.[1] This also raises the question of whether stewards may be justified in 'unconstitutional action' if management refuse to put certain matters on the procedural agenda, since it is regarded as a basic management prerogative which cannot be the subject of negotiation. Stewards may be faced by a similar dilemma if they find that the national agreement covering the work of the plant is ambiguously phrased and leaves considerable scope for management to adopt an interpretation of the agreement which suits their purposes. An example of this is quoted by an engineer working at Ford's:

> Under the agreement the unions recognise the company's right to manage the job. But this means changing the speed of the plant line without consultation. We've had two big disputes in my plant where we got the national officers down to do something on this question of speeding up, but nothing came of it.[2]

We have also come across the case of an agreement covering steel workers which provided for consultation between management and unions over any change in the number of shifts to be worked, but, as one workers' representative put it:

> Consultation in this case simply means that we are called in by the management and told that shifts are going to be reduced next week.[3]

[1] See account in *The Guardian* of the C.S.E.U. Annual Conference, 29 June 1963.

[2] Peter Dunn, 'Behind all the trouble at Fords', *The Observer*, 3 June 1962.

[3] For further illustration of the ambiguities and problems surrounding the shop steward's role see Appendix D.

The T.U.C., in its report on unofficial strikes, maintained that the responsibility of employers for causing such stoppages is often minimised by the Press. In this connection it cited such issues as non-recognition, dismissal, out-dated claims of prerogatives by management and changes made in working conditions without adequate consultation. It went on to argue that:

> It may be formally correct to define an unofficial strike as one which takes place contrary to union rules and contrary to agreed procedures. But such a definition is not helpful. The strikers are automatically put in the wrong and the problem is therefore shown as one of 'how to persuade them to conform or force them to conform'. This leads to the proposal of simple remedies: for instance – the employers should stand firm, the unions should discipline their members, the Government should legislate.[1]

Finally, two empirical questions remain. How often in fact are national agreements broken, as opposed to being actually *enforced* by strike action, in the face of management infringement of these same agreements? Secondly, how often in fact do unofficial strikes break out when the whole of the procedure has been exhausted?

Answers to the points raised above may give us a clearer insight into the strike leaders' motives for breaking national agreements and remove some of the certainty on which moral condemnation of their actions is based. The attitude of Mr. George Woodcock, General Secretary of the T.U.C., is perhaps more in keeping with the complexity of the subject. He indicated that for him there are no ready-made rules or principles by which we can pre-judge every strike, be it official or unofficial:

> I do not like to hear of an unofficial strike but I do not immediately assume when I hear of one that there is no merit in the strikers' case or even that the strike is unjustified. Nor do I assume that workpeople are never selfish or that if a strike is official it is all right.[2]

Conclusion

It should be made clear that we have not presented an apologia for the unofficial strike, but rather we have attempted to examine

---

[1] *T.U.C. Report,* op. cit., p. 126.
[2] *The Observer,* 20 November 1960.

some of the assumptions on which objections to unofficial strikes are based. In conclusion it must be emphasised that the unofficial strike is a relative concept varying in scope, content and tactical significance as between unions, and within a union over time. Further, it is only one form of conflict which, in other situations, might give rise to go-slows, increased absenteeism and labour turnover and so forth (although, of course, these factors may co-exist with, as well as be substitutes for unofficial strikes).

Unofficial strikes need, ultimately, to be incorporated into a more general theory of industrial conflict. They may be seen as a particular expression of dissatisfaction with the existing rules of the industrial game (or a particular aspect of those rules). The rules, which are extensive and complex in modern industrial societies, are those which govern relations within a union organisation, between various unions, between the unions and the employers, between the employers and the work force – and all are influenced by social, political and legal sanctions exerted by the state. The same weapon, the industrial stoppage, may be used to express various forms of dissatisfaction with the existing 'reign of rules'. It may be an anarchical type of protest against the fact that there has to be a reign of rules at all. The work group becomes more than usually aware of the essentially coercive nature of the rules and rebels from a sense of oppressiveness. The unofficial strike then becomes a gesture of defiance against their industrial lot (although it may not always be consciously understood and defined as such). It may, however, be a protest against the fact that some other groups have broken the existing rules. This is a struggle for 'rights' as they are currently defined. Or again it may be used to point to existing anomalies in the rules and to demand that they be reformed and/or extended, either to cover adequately existing conditions, or, as the case may be, to cater effectively for changed conditions. Finally, the strikers may accept the necessity for a reign of rules, but wish substantially to re-model or revolutionise the existing industrial order.

Unofficial strikes may therefore, be evaluated at a philosophical and tactical level. At the first level, judgment will rest on whether we regard the goals of the strikers as legitimate. But such judgment may be modified by whether or not we regard the unofficial strike as tactically most efficacious, in the light of available alternatives, in achieving the stated goals.

CHAPTER THREE

The Demarcation Dispute in the Shipbuilding Industry

A Study in the Sociology of Conflict

THE shipbuilding industry in this country has long been a battlefield in which demarcation disputes have taken place. From the standpoint of the sociologist, one is concerned neither to condone nor condemn such behaviour in its various manifestations, but simply to try and understand it. This particular study has emerged, in the first instance, from field work conducted on the North East Coast, hence special attention will be given to that area.[1] However, this work is considered in relation both to historical and contemporary aspects of the industry as a whole. The description, analysis and interpretation of the demarcation dispute presented here is organised in four sections:

1. A discussion of the social sources and functions of the demarcation dispute in the industry.
2. A discussion of the changing frequency of demarcation strikes as reflected in the post-war experience of the North East Coast.
3. A consideration in terms of illustrative case material of the ways

[1] The field work was part of a D.S.I.R. research project, 'A Comparative Study of Industrial Relations in Three North East Industries: Steel, Engineering and Shipbuilding'. The interviewing material used at several points in the essay was collected by A. J. Odber, G. Roberts and the present writer. Particular thanks must be expressed to managers and shop stewards who took part in the interviewing programme and to some firms, who prefer to remain anonymous, but who generously allowed us access to documentary material relevant for the analysis of collective bargaining. The Newcastle regional office of the Ministry of Labour was of assistance in many ways, especially in checking and confirming our strike statistics, collected from newspaper sources, with their own records.

in which demarcation conflicts may be regulated by the use of procedures.

4. A consideration of the extent to which changes in the shipbuilding environment are undermining the raison d'etre of the demarcation dispute.

1. *The Social Sources and Functions of the Demarcation Dispute*

The demarcation dispute revolves round conflicting answers to the question 'who does what?' in relation to a particular work task. It is a form of conflict which arises when there is competition between occupational groups concerning the establishment or maintenance of job rights, as they perceive them. Where the groups concerned claim exclusive competence to the disputed work, the conflict is naturally more difficult to solve. In the shipbuilding industry, as we shall see, this has often been the case. But essentially it is a form of conflict arising from competition over a scarce resource, namely employment opportunities. It is a by-product of the search for job security.[1]

When the Webbs examined the demarcation dispute they paid a great deal of attention to the shipbuilding industry, where they found, 'the most numerous and complicated disputes about "overlap" and "demarcation" '. They noted, for example, that on the Tyne between 1890 and 1893, 'within the space of thirty-five months, there were no fewer than thirty-five weeks in which one or other of the four most important sections of workmen in the staple industry of the district absolutely refused to work' as a result of demarcation disputes.[2] In seeking to account for this, one may distinguish between certain factors which tended to charac-

---

[1] I have avoided the term 'restrictive practice' in discussing the demarcation dispute because of its emotive connotations and over-simplified usage in common speech. As against the easy utterances of politicians and journalists the cautious words of F. Zweig are still appropriate: 'A restrictive practice is a many dimensional phenomenon. It is like a sphinx with many faces, one face directed towards the past and others directed towards many interests of different orders. There is an element of equity and law and order in them, a human element and an element of social interest. It is easy to pass judgment on them if you limit your concern to one aspect only, but it becomes much more difficult when other interests are taken into account. not only purely individual but also long term industrial and social interests.' *Productivity and Trade Unions* (Blackwell, 1951), pp. 18–19.

[2] S. and B. Webb, *Industrial Democracy* (Longmans, 1920), p. 513.

terise the groups participating in such disputes, and certain environmental factors external to, but impinging upon, these groups.

The groups themselves were, of course, primarily craft groups. A whole range of trades was regarded as necessary for the building and fitting out of a ship: shipwrights, platers, riveters, caulkers, smiths, joiners, engineers, patternmakers, cabinetmakers, painters, drillers and so on. The social solidarity of these groups which is reflected in the tenacity with which they entered into demarcation strikes at this time may be seen as stemming from a number of inter-related group properties. There is first the actual pattern of recruitment to the group. It is traditionally the very nature of a craft to demand entry to the trade through apprenticeship. In this way the mystery of the craft is passed on from generation to generation. Tricks of the trade, standards of workmanship, pride in one's work, are the marks of such a sociological inheritance involved in the transmission of skills. This mode of recruitment makes for a clear social definition of group membership and a homogeneous group composition. The importance of group homogeneity, as Roethlisberger and Dickson, and Sayles have notably demonstrated,[1] lies in the fact that the willingness to exert pressure to achieve common group goals is not dissipated by internal conflicts of interest. Insofar as common norms and values are internalised through these patterns of recruitment and training, social cohesion within the group may be said to be culturally induced.

It may be inferred that membership of such an occupational group was of central importance in the life experience of the group member. Not only did his craft training implant in him a sense of exclusive competence in relation to a particular range of techniques, which members of the trade could undertake, but his work expectations were geared to that particular craft. To this extent he was a captive by his occupation and, upon the fortunes of his occupation in the labour market, hinged his own personal and familial security. Merton has argued that 'it seems likely that the greater the culturally defined degree of engagement in a group the greater the probability that it will serve as a reference group

[1] F. J. Roethlisberger and W. J. Dickson, *Management and the Worker* (Harvard, 1947) and L. R. Sayles, *Behaviour of Industrial Work Groups* (Wiley, 1958).

with respect to varied evaluations and behaviour.'[1] Hence the readiness to put up with some short term suffering in the form of a demarcation strike, when seen in the context of the longer term group interest, is not so surprising. Solidarity arises with the realisation that personal and group goals effectively depend upon the interdependent activities of group members for their achievement. To this extent social cohesion may be said to be organisationally induced.

This feature of organisationally induced social cohesion is underlined by the formation of craft unions. These unions were characterised by a high degree of completeness, to use Simmel's term. That is to say, the ratio of actual group membership to potential group membership was very high.[2] This enhanced the power of the union to act as an interest group. It must be pointed out, however, that in the late nineteenth century, there were different unions competing for the control of identical crafts. This was notably so in the engineering trades where the Amalgamated Society of Engineers competed with the Steam Engine Makers' Society, the National Trade Society of Engineers, the United Machine Workers' Association, and the Amalgamated Society of Metal Planers, Shapers and Slotters, to organise workers engaged in fitting and turning. Thus the demarcation question was overlaid with jurisdictional problems. The energetic pursuit of demarcation claims by the union could be regarded as at least one sign that they were looking after the interests of their members and thus could serve as a basis for recruiting new

[1] R. K. Merton, *Social Theory and Social Structure* (Glencoe Free Press, 1957), p. 311.

[2] The Boilermakers' Society was particularly successful in this respect, cf. H. A. Turner: 'It was, in fact, the unions that combined systematic collective bargaining with an exclusive restriction of entry that achieved by far the greatest solidity and effectiveness. Thus, the United Society of Boilermakers and Iron Shipbuilders was obliged, despite its membership's craft organisation, to undertake large-scale collective negotiation by the already-established system of piece-work sub-contracting in the shipyards, and to develop the office of full-time "District Delegate" to deal with the powerful local employers' groups. In consequence, however, perhaps only the Northumberland Miners' Association and the London Society of Compositors could approach the Boilermakers' claim to be the strongest major union of the period. Each of these unions, by the century's end, had virtually 100% membership of the workers with which they primarily concerned themselves.' *Trade Union Growth, Structure and Policy* (Allen and Unwin, 1962), p. 205.

members and maintaining the allegiance of the existing membership.

The distinction between culturally induced and organisationally induced social cohesion which we have utilised here, following Merton,[1] is particularly helpful since the former tends to stress the 'moral' aspects of group behaviour, while the latter tends to emphasise the 'expedient' considerations. Given the organisational possibilities outlined above, it may be suggested that a threat to certain patterned norms and values will give rise to the mobilisation of interest groups as a defence against such threats. This helps to explain both the tenacity of the disputants, but also the limitations which may be put on participation in such conflict. The point concerning group tenacity is well reflected in the sympathetic observation of the Tyneside shipbuilder John Wigham Richardson, commenting at the end of the last century on the protracted nature of demarcation strikes:

> Imagine what your feelings would be if you believed (as if it were the Gospel) that you had a prescriptive right to certain work of which you were being unjustly deprived . . . Unless you first realise that the men during a strike grow to look upon themselves as martyrs and to feel a martyr's exultation, you will never be able to understand how strikes last as long as they do, after the struggle is evidently hopeless.[2]

The willingness to embark on demarcation strikes would appear, in the first instance, to be limited by certain normative considerations. This comes out very well in a circular issued by the United Patternmakers Association, in 1889, justifying a strike:

> We are fighting this battle on the principle that every trade shall have the right to earn its bread without the interference of outsiders; a principle jealously guarded by every skilled trade . . . and one which we are fully determined shall apply to us.[3]

Explicit here is the recognition not only of one's own rights but also of the rights of others. One is not saying of course that an interest group, once it has realised its effective power, may not seek to extend its control over the work environment and ration-

[1] Merton, op. cit., p. 316.
[2] Quoted by E. H. Phelps-Brown, *The Growth of British Industrial Relations* (Macmillan, 1959), p. 160.
[3] Quoted by S. and B. Webb, op. cit., p. 514.

alise its behaviour in terms of the existing group morality. Ways in which this may be done and the circumstances promoting this form of behaviour will be discussed below.

Merton has also indicated that social cohesion in a group may be induced by the structural context in which the group finds itself.[1] It is basically the situation in which the group is bound more closely together in the face of threats to its existence or stability from environmental forces or groups. In the shipbuilding industry one may trace the nature of these threats to several sources. First the industry was subject to severe cyclical fluctuations. The insecurity which this bred was heightened by the fact that notice to quit the job could be given with less than a day's warning. It was further accentuated by the fact that employment opportunities outside the industry were usually very limited. If other industries existed at all in a shipbuilding town, they were usually heavy industries which endured slumps at the same time as shipbuilding and would probably have surplus labour of their own. In any case, many of the skills of shipyard workers were not directly transferable to other industries. There is, for example, nothing quite comparable to the shipwright's task of framing and fairing a ship. To exercise effective job control over a specified range of tasks was, therefore, to provide a cushion against shrinking employment opportunities in times of slump.

Secondly, one may observe that the industry was subject to technical changes that were continually upsetting any established division of labour. There were, for example, changes in the types of material used for ship construction, the most far-reaching of course being the change from wood to iron. The shipwrights, in consequence, found themselves working with the same material as the platers, and were correspondingly more vulnerable to challenges from them. At the same time, there was the ever-present need to cope with the additional features which came to be regarded as a necessary part of shipbuilding: refrigeration facilities, telegraph installations and the various luxuries associated with passenger liners. It has been fairly said, as far as demarcation disputes are concerned, that 'the industry had the misfortune to be the meeting ground of many well-organised crafts during a revolution in its technique, and to offer an expanding range of new jobs which lent themselves to much hairsplitting

[1] Merton, op. cit., p. 316.

debate.'[1] Apart from changes taking place that were new to the industry there was also the disruptive effect on existing work arrangements caused by a firm's decision to diversify its product, moving, say, from cargo ships and tankers to include passenger ships and Admiralty ships.

Thirdly, it was evident that different yards were in different stages of technical development as far as ship construction was concerned. This gave rise not only to different rates for the job as between yards (and hence provided a fertile ground for wage disputes) but also to different yard practices in the allocation of work. Shipbuilder John Price of Palmers, Jarrow, commenting on this state of affairs, observed:

> The principal difficulty in composing the disputes has arisen from the variety of practice in the different works and districts . . . Each society proposes to itself to have the largest possible number of its members employed at the same time . . . and to this end tries to secure the whole of the work it considers belongs to its members in accordance with usage and custom . . .[2]

When workers moved between yards, even on the same river, they were often confronted with situations that on the basis of their previous experience seemed to them anomalous. This could provide a source of discontent and friction when unfavourable comparisons were drawn with the rights of their particular occupation enjoyed in other yards.

Lewis Coser has suggested that one may use Simmel's differentiation between conflict as a means and conflict as an end in itself as a criterion by which one may distinguish between realistic and non-realistic conflict:

> Conflicts which arise from frustration of specific demands within the relationship and from estimates of the gains of the participants, and which are directed at the presumed frustrating object, can be called realistic conflicts, insofar as they are a means toward a specific result.[3]

Given the kind of environment in which different groups are

[1] H. A. Clegg, Alan Fox and A. F. Thompson, *A History of British Trade Unions since 1889*, Vol. I (Oxford, 1964), p. 128.

[2] Quoted by the Webbs, op. cit., p. 512.

[3] L. Coser, *The Functions of Social Conflict* (Routledge and Kegan Paul, 1956), p. 49.

competing for a scarce resource, namely, employment opportunities, the demarcation dispute may be described as a form of realistic conflict. To that extent it is clearly misleading to characterise all demarcation disputes as irrational. They may be dysfunctional as far as the needs of the industry measured in terms of optimum efficiency are concerned, but insofar as they are an effective means of achieving the stated goal of job security, they may be said to be a form of rational action, in the defence of particular group interests and the felt needs of the individuals composing them. Of course, in the long run such action may be self-defeating if it contributes to the overall decline of the industry, but this is not a problem which can be dealt with merely by exhortation and an appeal to the workers to refrain from 'irresponsibility'. When the interaction between group structure and function on the one hand and environmental context of the group on the other is drawn to our attention, then possible changes in group behaviour must be seen in the light of the industrial relations system of the industry seen as a whole. Some concrete ways in which a move towards the integration of this system in relation to the value of efficiency is currently taking place are indicated in the concluding section of this essay.

The great reliance on the strike as a means of settling demarcation disputes, to which the Webbs alluded, is of interest in itself. Since these were long drawn out affairs, they were inevitably tests of the economic endurance of the participants. It is a process of attrition through which one group can measure its own power vis-à-vis another. In this respect Coser's observation would appear to be pertinent:

> Since power can often be appraised only in its actual exercise, accommodation may frequently be reached only after the contenders have measured their respective strength in conflict.[1]

In the case of the shipbuilding industry, the matter may be put a little more precisely by saying that the strike as an overt form of conflict makes plain in a dramatic way the realities of power between the contending parties, but that it then becomes possible in ways which are discussed in more detail below, to build the realities of the balance of power into a normative system of conflict regulation. This balance of power may be challenged

[1] Ibid., p. 135.

RECORDED STRIKES IN MARINE ENGINEERING, SHIPBUILDING AND SHIP REPAIR IN NORTH EAST 1949-60

Year	Wages	Hours	Demarcation[1] (a) Horizontal	Demarcation[1] (b) Vertical	Redundancy[2]	Manning	Industrial Discipline	Other Work Arrangements and Rules[3]	T.U. Issues[4]	Total[5]
1949	—	—	1	—	—	2	—	—	—	3
1950	—	—	1	—	—	2	1	—	1	5
1951	4	—	—	—	—	—	1	—	1	6
1952	11	—	1	1	—	—	1	3	—	17
1953	5	—	1	—	1	1	—	—	—	8
1954	6	—	2	2	—	1	—	2	—	13
1955	3	—	—	—	2	1	—	1	—	7
1956	10	—	3	1	—	1	2	3	2	22
1957	8	—	2	—	—	—	3	2	2	17
1958	5	1	6	—	—	1	2	2	2	19
1959	1	—	2	—	2	—	3	—	—	8
1960	13	—	—	—	5	1	2	—	2	23
Total	66	1	19	4	10	10	15	13	10	148

Notes: 1. Horizontal demarcation = inter-trade disputes.
Vertical demarcation = trade versus non-trade disputes (i.e. 'dilution' disputes).
2. Redundancy includes disputes over short time working.
3. Other Work Arrangements and Rules includes disputes over working conditions and disputes over the employment of classes of persons.
4. T.U. issues includes disputes over trade union recognition, victimisation, and 'sympathy' strikes.
5. In this and subsequent tables, disputes lasting less than a day, or involving fewer than 10 workers (except where the total loss of working days exceeds 100) are excluded.

Source: Newspapers checked with Ministry of Labour.

from time to time and may result in strike activity, but what is suggested is that the frequency with which the strike is used is diminishing. A regional analysis of the North East Coast over an extended period provides some useful information on this and to that I now turn.

2. *Demarcation Strikes on the North East Coast in recent experience*

The Webbs' report of continuous demarcation strikes on the Tyne in the 1890–93 period contrasts markedly with G. C. Cameron's finding that in the period 1946–61 only two demarcation strikes took place on the river.[1] This in itself provides us with a valuable perspective, but there are a number of other questions which suggest themselves and on which it is possible to throw some light.

Taking the North East Coast as a whole (Tyne and Blyth, Wear and Tees) how significant are demarcation strikes compared with strikes arising from other causes? Table VIII provides some answers. The classification of strikes by immediate cause is a modified version of the Ministry of Labour's classification. The distinction has been introduced between horizontal and vertical demarcation strikes. On this Kate Liepmann has written:

> The device for preventing the inter-change of different trades is termed demarcation in current usage. For the measures taken to defend craftsmen's jobs against unapprenticed workers no term has yet been coined; they may be described as anti-dilutionism or as vertical demarcations.[2]

It is plain that by far the most frequent strikes are over wage questions, nearly 45% of them in fact. They are commonly a result of arguments over piece rates. Demarcation questions are the second most frequent cause of strike activity, but it will be noted that in percentage terms they comprise only some 15% of the recorded total strikes. The great majority of these demarcation strikes are 'horizontal' inter-craft disputes. Table IX illustrates how all the demarcation strikes, even those over 'vertical' de-

[1] G. C. Cameron, 'Post-war Strikes in the North-East Shipbuilding and Ship-Repairing Industry', *British Journal of Industrial Relations*, Vol. II, No. 1, 1954, p. 5.
[2] K. Liepmann, *Apprenticeship: An Enquiry into its Adequacy under Modern Conditions* (Routledge and Kegan Paul, 1960), p. 158.

The Demarcation Dispute in the Shipbuilding Industry

TABLE IX

UNIONS INVOLVED IN RECORDED DEMARCATION STRIKES
IN NORTH EAST MARINE ENGINEERING, SHIPBUILDING
AND SHIP REPAIR, 1949–60

Union	Horizontal Demarcation	Vertical Demarcation	Total
Boilermakers	13	3	16
Shipwrights	7	—	7
A.E.U.	—	1	1
A.S.W.	—	1	1
N.U.S.M.W.	1	—	1

Note: More than one union was sometimes involved in a strike hence the total of each category are not identical with the totals in Table VII.

Source: Newspapers checked with Ministry of Labour.

marcation, are carried out by craft unions. The identification of the unions involved also reveals that the great preponderance of demarcation strikes is to be found on the construction side of shipbuilding rather than the finishing side. It is the iron trades whose workers are more exclusively linked with the shipbuilding industry. Workers in the fitting out crafts can move in and out of the industry more readily. Approximately 88% of the strikes involved either the Boilermakers or the Shipwrights. Recent evidence of the Confederation of Shipbuilding and Engineering Unions to the Shipbuilding Inquiry Committee, 1965–6, indicated that the Boilermakers and Shipwrights as an amalgamated union, accounted for 33% of the total operative labour force in shipbuilding.[1] The A.E.U., the A.S.W. and the National Union of Sheet Metal Workers, on the same national check for the industry accounted for 9·6%, 7·1% and 2·8% of the total labour force, respectively. Each of these unions was involved in only one demarcation strike on the North East Coast during the 1949–60 period (each strike counting as just under 4% of the total number of demarcation strikes). It is also worth observing that the Amalgamated Society of Painters and Decorators, the E.T.U. and the Plumbing Trades Union, three craft unions which on the national returns accounted for 6·3%, 4·6%, and 3·6% of the total labour force respectively, were not involved in demarcation strikes as

[1] *The Geddes Report*, Cmnd. 2937 (H.M.S.O., 1966), p. 190. The figures in the remainder of the paragraph are, it will be noted, from the same source.

active participants at all during this period. And the two general unions, the N.U.G.M.W. and the T.G.W.U. which accounted for 15% and 7·3% of the total labour force in the industry as a whole, were likewise not active in demarcation strikes.

Since these figures were provided after the amalgamation of the Boilermakers and the Shipwrights' unions, no separate proportions of membership employed in the industry were given. To get a rough indication, however, I examined the occupational structure of a medium size yard in the North East and its fluctuations over the period of a year. During this time the trades organised by the Boilermakers outnumbered the trades organised by the Shipwrights by an average ratio of 2·75:1. One may use this observation simply as a bench mark to suggest that there is not much difference between the two unions, on a weighted sample, in the relative proneness to demarcation strikes.

Table X makes clear that there is a general tendency for all strikes to be settled in the first three days. This tendency is not

TABLE X

LENGTH OF STOPPAGE OF DEMARCATION STRIKES COMPARED
WITH ALL OTHER STRIKES IN NORTH EAST MARINE ENGINEERING,
SHIP REPAIR AND SHIPBUILDING 1949–60

Length of Stoppage	*Horizontal Demarcation* %	*Vertical Demarcation* %	*All Other* %
1–3 days	42·1	75	68·8
4–7 days	31·6	25	14·4
Over 7 days	26·3	—	16·8
Total	100	100	100

Source: Newspapers checked with Ministry of Labour.

found in the case of horizontal demarcation strikes. Nearly 58% of them took longer than three days to settle. By contrast, vertical demarcation strikes are not only less common than the inter-craft disputes, but there was also a tendency for them to be settled far more quickly. None of them lasted more than a week, and three out of four only persisted from one to three days. Cameron has noted this phenomenon and observes that these strikes tended to occur when local unemployment was very low. He suggests:

The Demarcation Dispute in the Shipbuilding Industry

It may be that managements were forced into attempts to employ dilutee labour because of the shortage of skilled craftsmen. This of course brought an immediate craft response – particularly from the bigger trades such as the welders and the platers. It is noticeable that these disputes were short and this suggests that in conditions of skilled-craft shortage the employers were unwilling to antagonise the fully-skilled craftsmen, and consequently withdrew the dilutee labour.[1]

The relationship of horizontal demarcation strikes to the level of employment is far less clear, but, broadly, they took place when the level of local unemployment was high.

If one compares the number of men directly involved in demarcation strikes, as is done in Table XI, it is notable that while

TABLE XI

NUMBERS DIRECTLY INVOLVED IN DEMARCATION STRIKES COMPARED WITH ALL OTHER STRIKES IN NORTH EAST MARINE ENGINEERING, SHIPBUILDING AND SHIP REPAIR, 1949–60

Numbers Directly Involved	Horizontal Demarcation %	Vertical Demarcation %	All Other %
1–100	36·8	100	61·6
101–200	36·8	—	25·6
201–300	15·8	—	4·8
300 +	10·6	—	8·0
Total	100	100	100

Source: Newspapers checked with Ministry of Labour.

most strikes in the industry tend to involve less than 200 workers directly, this is not so in the case of horizontal demarcation strikes. This is a reminder of the solidarity of response, which is manifested when an inter-craft dispute takes place. But it also reflects the fact that it is the numerically stronger trades which tend to strike – platers and shipwrights in particular. By contrast, vertical demarcation strikes did not involve many men directly. These appear to have been very localised strikes against introducing dilutee labour into particular work situations.

What may be stressed here is that while the evidence from the North East Coast suggests that resort to the demarcation strike is not frequent (in eight of the twelve years there were two or

[1] Cameron, op. cit., p. 18.

less) and that they tend to be restricted to the platers and boiler-makers, nevertheless, when they do take place between crafts, they involve more men and take longer to settle than the average strike in the region's industry.

3. *The Use of Procedures in the Settlement of Demarcation Disputes*

I have already described the demarcation dispute as 'realistic' in Coser's sense of the word. One of the marks of realistic conflict is that the form which it takes will be assessed by considering the relative instrumental adequacy of the choices available. Trial by ordeal, in the form of a strike between warring unions, is a costly and painful affair for the participants. While such strikes may have lent drama to life, they could also bankrupt the unions involved. Once the balance of power between unions has been established by a process of attrition, the search for a functional alternative, which is less costly while meeting the same individual and group needs for security, is evidence of realism. The formation of the Federation of Engineering and Shipbuilding Trades in 1890, served to underline the fact that, while there could be real conflicts of interest between unions, there was also a community of interest, since they were all negotiating with the same employers on matters of wages and working conditions. In an attempt to minimise overt conflict, unions began to work out apportionments of work and to develop 'books of agreements' with each other. These were then given to the employers concerned and used as a basis for reference. For example, the ship-wrights and joiners of the Tees and Hartlepools wrote, as follows, to the employers of their District in March 1893:

> Gentlemen,
>   As various disputes have of late occurred in consequence of us not having a proper understanding as to the work belonging to each other as trades, in the construction of Modern Vessels, the Shipwrights and Ship Joiners have jointly drawn up the subjoined lists, which have been mutually agreed to.
>   Trusting thus to prevent any unpleasantness or dispute in the future,
>   We are, Gentlemen,
>   Yours respectfully,
>   The Joint Committee.

These kind of agreements served to facilitate the possibility of procedural settlements, by providing an agreed framework in which the debating of issues could take place.[1] As more disputes were discussed and settled, the books of agreements could themselves be added to and clarified. In this way the normative basis of inter-group relations could be systematised, so that, at the very least strike activity based on norm ignorance could be eliminated. Conflict rather tends to operate now on the basis of differing interpretations of normative principles, as I shall illustrate below. Before doing that however, attention should be drawn to the fact that there are now in existence a variety of methods by which demarcation disputes may be settled procedurally.

The Shipyard Procedure Agreement, provides machinery for the settlement of disputes other than wages and piece work disputes. There are four stages of procedure which can, if necessary, be utilised:

(a) yard meetings between the employer and a deputation of the men concerned; if this is unsuccessful,
(b) a further meeting at the yard attended by local officials of the employers' association and the unions directly concerned; if there is still no success,
(c) a formal local conference between representatives of the local employers' association and of the union directly concerned; and finally,
(d) a central conference attended by national officers of the employers' federation and the trade union concerned.[2]

An Arbitrator may be called in, if all else fails, but in practice this provision is not used and the decision of the central conference is referred back to the yard involved to implement. It should be noted that the Amalgamated Engineering Union and the Boilermakers section of the Amalgamated Society are not

[1] Obtaining the agreed framework was not always a straightforward operation. When in 1890, for example, Thomas Burt, M.P., at the instigation of the joiners, conducted an investigation into the existing points of dispute between shipwrights and joiners on the Tyne, the joiners themselves refused to accept his recommendations as binding and struck on that account. Appendix B is an example of a Demarcation Procedure and Apportionment Agreement made in 1914 between Engineers and Plumbers on the Tyne, which gives an indication of the detailed negotiations involved.

[2] As recorded in *Geddes*, op. cit., p. 107.

105

signatories to this agreement, but they are usually prepared to observe it.

Alternatively, on demarcation questions, resort may be made to the 1912 Demarcation Procedure Agreement. This operates in the following way:

(a) yard meetings between the employer and a deputation of the men concerned. The employer (or usually in practice, the Yard Manager) makes a temporary decision in favour of one of the parties (or, occasionally, that the work should be shared) without prejudice to the outcome of the final decision. If either of the parties wish to take it further then,

(b) the issue is referred to three representatives of the local employers' association and three representatives each of the unions concerned. The employers in this situation are 'neutral' in the sense that they do not come from the yard involved in the dispute. The decision here is made by majority vote and is to be accepted as binding by the parties concerned.

Again it should be noted that the Boilermakers and Shipwrights sections are not signatories to this agreement, but in the areas where the procedure is worked it is usually followed by these groups. However, as we have seen, these are the two groups which are most prone to demarcation strikes, and their refusal until 1966 to be formally bound by procedural agreements may reflect a consciousness of their power position, based on the strong social control which they are able to exert over their members and the centrality and essentialness of their work in ship construction.

Both these forms of procedure involve the employer. Indeed, the employer's role in the settlement of demarcation disputes under these arrangements is crucial, since he is left with the casting vote. But it is possible for demarcation disputes to be settled without involving the employer. Inter-union disputes may be brought before the T.U.C. Disputes Committee, which, since the 1920s, has operated to settle jurisdictional and demarcation disputes. Demarcation disputes may, of course, occur within a union. This has notably been the case as between the various sections of the Amalgamated Society of Boilermakers. These disputes may be settled internally within the Society, when the District Delegate may act as an umpire or, if necessary, the National Executive Committee intervene.

The Wear District on the North East Coast operates both the

Shipyard Procedure Agreement and the 1912 Demarcation Dispute Agreement. The following three cases, which arose between the years 1957 and 1961, illustrate both these procedures in use. They are chosen as case studies so that we may examine concretely the kind of criteria that are regarded as relevant in the presentation of evidence and judgments concerning job rights.

CASE I

> Item: The fitting of water ballast tanks and bilge suction pipes.
> Contending parties: Fitters (members of the A.E.U.)
> Plumbers (members of the P.T.U.)
> Procedure: Shipyard Procedure Agreement.
> Level Reached: Yard conference (second stage in procedure).

At this stage the trade union District Officials are called in for the first time. They join the shop stewards at a meeting chaired by the Yard Manager. The local employers' association sent along their Technical Delegate. The occupant of such a post is expected to have a wide knowledge of ship construction and of the existing union agreements and practices governing work arrangements.

The Chairman first formulated the problem. He acknowledged that the arrangement of the ship differed from an ordinary cargo ship as regarded the job in question. A plan of the job was produced and it was explained that it involved 'a ring main going right round the ballast tanks in the double bottom and at each division of the tank there is a valve connected by a pad to the floor with a gearing rod connected going right up to the deck.' The Plumbers were in possession of the job as the Yard Manager believed this to be consistent with yard practice. The Fitters claimed that they should do the pipe work on the job. The A.E.U. representatives were accordingly asked to state the basis of their claim.

This claim was in fact based primarily on their understanding of the Book of Apportionment of Work existing between them and the P.T.U. The text cited comes under the general heading of Water Services and reads as follows:

> AE.U. fix, joint and strap complete all salt water services if of cast iron flanged pipes. If wrought iron or steel is used on this line for

filling oil cargo tanks for testing purposes these to be jointed by Engineers.

This clause to be applied to all deep tanks on merchant steamers if the pipe is six inches or over in diameter.

The supporting argument was based on custom and practice. It was said that it was the general practice of fitters to do all cast iron pipes over six inches in diameter. In this way, therefore, the Book of Apportionment between the A.E.U. and the P.T.U., and custom and practice were regarded as important criteria for judgment and the case was put in a manner which suggested that they were mutually supportive.

However, the P.T.U., the Yard Manager and the Technical Delegate each brought forward evidence and information which challenged the A.E.U.'s contention.

The P.T.U. considered the clause from the Book of Apportionment which the A.E.U. had quoted, to be irrelevant, since the Item from which it was extracted referred to Works Plant. Having examined the Book of Apportionment, my own view is that there was scope for confusion between the two unions because several subjects were dealt with under one Item. The first subject is headed Works Plant, as the P.T.U. noted but the immediate subject dealt with under the clause quoted is Water Services and does not appear to refer to Works Plant at all but to work on ships of a particular kind. It was the actual setting out of the Book of Apportionment that gave rise to a difference of opinion on this point. (Appendix B illustrates the way in which Apportionment Lists are set out.)

The Yard Manager's objection to the use made by the A.E.U. of the clause quoted from the Book of Apportionment was more substantial. He observed that the clause was inappropriate because in context it referred only to water services for tank testing. Further, he quoted from another Item in the Book of Apportionment, which, he maintained, was more directly applicable to the case in hand. It was headed Water Ballast Tanks and Bilge Suction Pipes. He said that it supported the Plumber's case since it was stated under that Item that their work included:

Cast iron flanged pipes complete on new and repair work except in boiler room, engine room and tunnel.

The Yard Manager went on to challenge the fitters' claim that the job was theirs by virtue of general practice. He pointed out that on an ore carrier built by a neighbouring firm on the river, the work in question was done by plumbers.

The Technical Delegate, for his part, supported the contentions of the Yard Manager. He added that the work on the ore carrier, to which the Yard Manager had referred, was on pipes that were nine inches in diameter. The A.E.U.'s claim to do pipe work over six inches in diameter was, in consequence, not beyond dispute.

It is evident that the criteria which the A.E.U. used to support their case – 'the book' and 'custom and practice' – are accepted as valid. What is questioned is the relevance, applicability and accuracy of the information brought forward by them to substantiate their case.

At this point a deadlock was reached and the A.E.U. announced that they would carry the matter further to the next stage of procedure. Essentially the technique employed by the Chairman to resolve the question was to widen the area of discussion between the two parties. The issue as defined in the debate so so far had referred solely to pipe work. However, there was still the question of deciding who should work on the valves mentioned in the description of the total job. The A.E.U. claimed that this too was their work on the grounds that 'the pad that has to be fitted to the floor is just as important as the pipe itself. It has to be machined in such a way as to take the valve in correct alignment'. When they had heard the claim put forward in these terms, the plumbers' contingent retired for a private discussion and, on returning, announced:

> We have considered this question very carefully and have arrived at the conclusion that it would not be right for us to claim this part of the work and that, in our opinion, it is rightfully fitter work.

Naturally, the A.E.U. representatives were very satisfied with this statement and their delegate reflected that 'it would be very pleasant if all questions of demarcation could be settled in such a manner.' The incident is a reminder to the onlooker that claims for work are not promiscuous or arbitrary, but are grounded in certain moral considerations. There is a recognition of one's own craft rights, but there is also recognition of the rights of other crafts and where those rights are felt to be unambiguous, there is no desire to infringe upon them.

At the same time, the plumbers' readiness to concede this issue without a fight was, in bargaining terms, an act of renunciation. This appeared to colour the thinking of the A.E.U. on the initial question of the pipe work. Certainly, although they formally referred the matter to their own District Committee, they conceded the pipe work without taking the matter further through procedure. In a sense, therefore, the plumbers' altruism was also tactical wisdom, whether conscious or not. Not only did they help to create a climate of greater flexibility in the bargaining situation, but also put the onus on the A.E.U. to settle in the same spirit. The employer, by taking the two issues separately, played his part in resolving the conflict. He did this first by extending the range of discussion beyond the immediate point in dispute. This in itself can often serve to reduce the fixity of the disputants' entrenched positions. Secondly, and related to the first point, the discussion of the two items helped to create a point of saliency around which a settlement could crystallise. It is no longer an all-or-nothing situation, but is so structured that both sides gain something and do not return to their members empty-handed.

CASE II

    Item: The caulking of elm doublings with oakum.
    Contending parties: Shipwrights (members of the Shipwrights' Union)
                Joiners (members of the A.S.W.)
    Procedure: Shipyard Procedure Agreement.
    Level Reached: Local Conference (third stage in procedure).

At this meeting, seven members of the local employers' association were present, including a representative of the yard involved in the dispute. The union district officials and the relevant shop stewards from the yard were also present. In addition since, as we shall see, the dispute involved a contracting firm from outside the District, they also were represented.

The contracting firm had put joiners on to this particular insulating work and the shipwrights were contesting the decision. Their claim was based on two considerations. First it was said that the 1891 Book of Apportionment between shipwrights and joiners allocated all caulking work to them 'whenever required'. Secondly, they observed that under the 1947 agreement relating to the recruitment and training of apprentices, caulking tools were listed as necessary for shipwright apprentices but were not mentioned so far as joiners were concerned. It was said that shipwrights normally did miles of caulking even before they finished their apprenticeship.

The joiners, in defending their right to continue with the work, based their case upon considerations of custom and practice. It was admitted that in other districts, shipwrights did the work now under discussion, but for seventy years joiners on this particular river had always done caulking work in insulated spaces. Their delegate proceeded to give many examples to support his own case and challenged the shipwrights' delegate to produce one example to the contrary. The shipwrights' delegate did try to meet this challenge, but was shown to be factually incorrect in that the work he cited was not relevant to the dispute under discussion. The Technical Delegate, however, who had heard the A.S.W. claims at an earlier stage in procedure, had investigated them thoroughly and they did not all stand up to his scrutiny. In one case, the ship in question had not been built in the year specified by the A.S.W. and it was found that the work in question was not in fact done by anyone, since it was not part of the specifications. In two other cases, the work was done by apprentice shipwrights. But, on the other hand, five of the examples quoted were verified.

The A.S.W. buttressed their claim by pointing out that the Technical Delegate who had preceded the present occupant of the post, had been a shipwright by trade, and he had never questioned the joiners' right to this work. Further, it was emphasised that not only the contractors involved in the present dispute but other insulating companies also, negotiated as a matter of course with the joiners and had produced a list of piece prices to cover all work in insulated spaces, including caulking. The fact that caulking tools were not mentioned in the apprentices tool list for joiners was not felt to be conclusive evidence against them, since the list was not exhaustive. In any case, it was said that shipwrights did many jobs for which they did not receive specific training.

The case, therefore, basically presented itself in terms of a conflict between 'the book' and 'custom and practice'. The employers, through their casting vote, awarded the work to the joiners: custom and practice thus won the day. It would appear that, in the shipbuilding context, rights have to be exercised if they are to be upheld against encroachment. Again, however, one must note that this was not necessarily arbitrary encroachment by the A.S.W. This union suggested that some seventy-five years earlier, shipwrights had done some caulking work in insulated spaces, but had chosen to exchange this for some work which joiners had hitherto done elsewhere. This would certainly help to explain the entrenched nature of the custom. It would also help to explain why a shipwrights' shop steward, during earlier informal discussions, had told the yard management that his union had no claim to the work. The dispute, however, was subsequently initiated by the shipwrights' District Delegate. Why?

It is perhaps significant that the dispute, which took place in 1960, was in a year which saw an average of 9·2% total unemployed for shipbuilding in the North East and 16·2% on the Wear, the river concerned. In both cases, this was a sharp increase on the previous year – 5·9% and 8·2% respectively. What this suggests is that the union delegate was increasingly preoccupied with safeguarding the security of his members as far as possible. Hence a demarcation question, which had been dormant for many years (or perhaps had been informally settled on the basis of an exchange of work) was now formally raised by the shipwrights' delegate in the interests of his members. It represents an attempt to re-build broken dykes to defend the occupation against the sharply rising tide of unemployment.

CASE III

Item: The erection of temporary pillars.
Contending parties: Shipwrights (members of the Shipwrights Union)
Platers (members of the Boilermakers Society)
Procedure: General Demarcation Agreement, 1912.
Level Reached: Local Conference (final stage of procedure).

The Demarcation Dispute in the Shipbuilding Industry

It will be recalled that under the terms of this procedure agreement the employer from the yard where the dispute has taken place is not permitted to be present.

The shipwrights, who had initiated proceedings, claimed the work in question on the basis of custom and practice. In the yard concerned, it was said, any pillar, whether fixed or portable, solid or tubular, round or oval, hexagonal or any other shape, had been erected by shipwrights on all ships. The only exception consisted of pillars that were of angle bar construction and these, it was admitted, had been erected by platers. But the pillars now in dispute were 15 inch diameter cargo hold pillars, octagonal in shape and portable, and, it was maintained, there was a clear distinction between these pillars and the angle-bar type erected by platers.

The boilermakers (platers) also claimed the work on the basis of custom and practice. Their delegate quoted the testimony of a Foreman in the yard, which he regarded as impartial and conclusive:

These temporary pillars were hinged at the top and were about 6 inches short at the bottom to be wedged up. I was surprised at the time that the shipwrights made any claim to them because all temporary or portable pillars in the yard had always been platers' work, such as pillars under winch decks, between decks and all pillars in connection with grain shifting boards . . .

The difference between the two unions was that in the case of the shipwrights the method of construction was put forward as the deciding factor, whereas, in the case of the platers, the purpose for which the pillars were used was held to be the significant consideration. In particular, by stressing the portability and temporary nature of the pillars, the platers were emphasising that the pillars had nothing to do with the alignment of the ship (which, had it done, would have provided an unambiguous basis for the shipwrights' claim). This explains the significance of the following exchange, which looks like the work of Lewis Carroll:

Boilermakers' Delegate: 'It is possible for these pillars, which are hinged at the top end, to be stowed under the deck and never used at all. Would they then be properly regarded as pillars?'
Chairman: 'They would certainly not be used as pillars while they were stowed in this way.'

113

However, the shipwrights, for their part, refused to accept the position that they could only claim work connected with the alignment of the ship. They had always fitted such pillars and felt that they should continue to do so. They discounted the testimony of the foreman, whom the Boilermakers had quoted, pointing out that all the previous examples he had referred to, related to pillars of angle-bar construction.

In this case then, both unions based their claim on considerations of custom and practice. In fact, the job concerned was new to the yard in the sense that tubular pillars had never been used before. It was probably this slight element of uncertainty arising from the innovation which caused the issue to emerge.

In the event, the employers' casting vote went to the shipwrights. It is interesting to notice how the Boilermakers' Delegate accepted the decision. He said that his members would accept the decision of the committee. He was satisfied that he always got a fair hearing and was firmly of the opinion that the procedure laid down in the 1912 Demarcation Agreement constituted a right and proper manner of dealing with these questions. In his opinion, the dispute affected three parties, two unions and the employers. He considered that it was reasonable that the employers should have an equal right with the two unions to take part in the discussions.

The use of procedures, such as those we have described here, indicates the possibilities of obtaining a working consensus between conflicting parties. In the light of these examples, one may suggest certain ways in which this consensus is developed and maintained.

(a) The introduction of order through the use of procedures tends to encourage a stylised approach to the problem under discussion. There is a definite arrangement as to who should be present at proceedings, who should take the chair, who should speak first (the chairman giving the aggrieved party the chance to state its case). At the end of the debate following the decision it is common for the rival claimants to thank each other and the employers for the way in which the meeting has been conducted. Even where quite harsh things are said by one party against another, the debating framework lends it the appearance of a set-piece in a drama, as though it is an expression of militancy or aggressiveness which, at that particular stage in the proceedings, is felt to be an appropriate step to take in the ritual performance. These patterned enmities may serve the function of setting boundaries between groups within the industrial relations system, but without the economic costs attached to the alternative mode of conflict, namely strike activity. One is reminded here of Erving Goffman's perceptive observation:

> An interaction can be purposively set up as a time and place for voicing differences in opinion, but in such cases participants must be careful not to disagree on the proper tone of voice, vocabulary and degree of seriousness in which all arguments are to be phrased, and upon the mutual respect which disagreeing participants must carefully continue to express toward one another. This debaters' or academic definition of the situation may also be invoked suddenly and judiciously as a way of translating a serious conflict of views into one that can be handled within a framework acceptable to all present.[1]

(b) The cases I have discussed draw attention to the employer as an impartial party to the proceedings and exemplified in his role as chairman. At the same time the employer's impartiality is not naïve in quality, since he is obviously seeped in a technical understanding of ship construction and on points of detail may be aided by the Technical Delegate. It is interesting to see that another multi-craft industry, building, also operates procedures in which employers play an active and informed part in the settlement of disputes. As B. J. McCormick observes:

> Employers, of course, have a stake in the settlement of demarcation disputes if only because present work can be speedily and harmoniously completed and future work not be subject to uncertainty.[2]

In the building industry, the employers are assisted in their efforts not only to be but to appear impartial by the existence of a uniform rate for all craftsmen. Thus they cannot, in any direct sense, be accused of choosing the cheapest way of doing the job, regardless of the justice of the claim before them. Objections which are sometimes heard to the employer's decisive role in

[1] E. Goffman, *The Presentation of Self in Everyday Live* (Doubleday, 1959), p. 10.
[2] B. J. McCormick, 'Trade Union Reaction to Technological Change in the Construction Industry', *Yorkshire Bulletin*, Vol. 16, No. 1., May 1964), p. 27.

demarcation procedures in the shipbuilding industry,[1] from the unions, perhaps stem in part from the fact that there is no such uniformity in rates as between crafts and it may be felt that his judgment rests upon expedient rather than moral considerations. However, Case 3 indicates that this fear is not always felt by the losing party.

(c) The use of procedural methods of settlement essentially implies the growing articulation of assumptions and principles governing inter-group relations. The kind of process involved is described very well by Durkheim:

> It is neither necessary nor even possible for social life to be without conflicts. The role of solidarity is not to suppress competition but to moderate it . . . Rules are a prolongation of the division of labour . . . [What the division of labour] brings face to face are functions, that is to say ways of definite action, which are identically repeated in given circumstances . . . [The relations] are certain ways of mutual reaction which, finding themselves very conformable to the nature of things, are repeated very often and become habits. These habits, becoming forceful are transformed into rules of conduct. The past determines the future . . . there is a certain sorting of rights and duties which is established by usage and becomes obligatory.[2]

In considering the use of procedures in shipbuilding, it is clear that the past determines the future in the sense that the folkways and mores of the various craft groups are codified. This in itself leads to a growing clarification of normative standards governing behaviour both within occupational groups and the relations between them. Thus the rights of the contending parties are scrutinised in the light of previous decisions made concerning their spheres of competence. At the same time, however, given the reality of technical change, it is equally clear that rights and duties can never be established once and for all (otherwise prerogatives would never be challenged). But the past determines the future in the sense that procedural methods provide a mechanism for sifting claims in the light of the available evidence. Once the principle of settlement by rule making has been conceded by the conflicting parties, it becomes possible to modify

[1] Geddes op. cit., p. 108.
[2] Emile Durkheim, *The Division of Labour in Society* (Glencoe, 1964), pp. 365–6.

old rules to deal with anomalies, but also to create new rules to cover new situations. Through the use of procedures also antagonistic groups grow to recognise their interdependence. Indeed, the very fact that the contending parties have to develop a professional expertise in the conduct of their cases before employers who are themselves technical experts, involves a sophisticated mutual recognition of each other's spheres of technical craft competence. This invites a growing awareness of a certain reciprocal co-ordination between craft groups, without necessarily challenging their separate identity.

4. *The Demarcation Dispute in a Changing Environment: Concluding Comments on the Current Situation*

> The use of labour in shipbuilding is wasteful; nobody who discussed the industry with us has challenged this statement. Partly this waste is due to shortcomings of planning and supervision, partly to the practices on which the unions insist and partly to the level of the response and application of the individual participant which is itself conditioned by the first two factors. The planning and organisation of work could be improved but a solution depends on a substantial improvement in industrial relations and a raising of individual morale.[1]

Management in shipbuilding may not always mobilise their resources in a way that achieves maximum efficiency. Indeed, their assumptions about what constitutes such a state may not always be correct. At the same time, it is clear that planning production in a multi-craft industry does give rise to some distinctive problems. This was well elaborated in discussion with the General Manager of one shipyard:

> Consider what happens when different trades are fitting some particular item. Trade 1 lines the thing up; trade 2 drills the pilot holes; trade 3 burns it larger; trade 4 dresses it; trade 5 puts the fitment in. And so it goes on with eight trades doing one job, for example, fitting a porthole or cover. Some estimate that there is a 10% waste of time; others say it is 20% . . . No one trade will give up a job if it means unemployment. Even if unemployment falls this remains true, because this attitude is bred in the bone. For example, at X Company, the fabrication sheds employ twice as many men as are needed: both boilermakers and shipwrights. This arises from

[1] Geddes, op cit., p. 110.

changes in techniques. This is a stupid mentality although work-sharing is an understandable reaction. But workers do not think of costs. They only think of whether action will keep bodies in employment . . . To try to reduce demarcation, we try to give shipwrights all the erecting and fairing jobs on the berth, but try to keep all prefabrication in the sheds or skids for platers. But if we have two lots on the same job, we find that we also have to have two lots of labourers, one lot standing and letting the other lot work . . . The tackers are supposed to help the people they work with but they don't. Any tradesman who wants a temporary job done should be able to do it himself. Even in shipbuilding, a plumber can weld pipes together and do final welding, but his is about the only trade which can. A plater who is assembling a bulk head, putting in stiffeners, or tack welding, has to get a tacker to do it. I think some tackers only do a few minutes work a day . . .

The fundamental objection voiced here is that increasingly it is wasteful to plan work such that it coincides with existing occupational boundaries. As one Production Manager put it:

The real trouble with demarcation is that time is wasted. The planning of jobs is increased by the existence of demarcation.

The argument is that over time job rights based on claims of exclusive competence have become increasingly artificial. Skill monopoly on an objective assessment may be regarded as more notional than real,[1] yet it is maintained through techniques developed by craft unions as interest groups: the maintenance of a closed shop and a strict regulation of conditions of entry to the trade.

It was the over-riding and understandable concern with costs

[1] See W. E. J. McCarthy: 'Although the opportunity for any skilled group to obtain a job monopoly by means of entry control and the pre-entry shop depends, in the first instance, of the existence of a *real* skill gap, and although any development undermining the reality of the gap is a threat to the group's job monopoly, the group itself may rebut the threat, even if the skill gap continues to narrow until it disappears. If it can match employer power sufficiently, and for long enough, any group can win recognition, however reluctant, for the *notion* of a skill gap.' *The Closed Shop in Britain* (Blackwell, 1964) p. 139. By an objective assessment of the reality of the skill gap I simply have in mind the fact that comparisons of work practices may be made not only with foreign shipyards but also between rivers and yards in this country, to reveal wide differences in occupational boundaries and job flexibility.

which lay behind the suggestions put forward by the Ship-building Employers' Federation to the unions in 1962. They proposed that shipbuilding workers should be classified into three groups: metal trades, fitting out trades and ancillary workers. Within these groups emphasis should be placed on the inter-changeability of labour. Training which would permit complete flexibility of labour between the metal trades was advocated. And, as a general principle, it was suggested that a worker should be able to use any tool necessary for the performance of his task, even if it did not 'belong' to his trade. The problem, as perceived by the unions, was that to allow too much flexibility of labour might jeopardise standards of craftsmanship, by making a man a Jack-of-all-trades and master of none; and, at the same time, the interests of particular union members might be jeopardised by increasing the potential labour supply available. These traditional concerns could not be swept aside simply by an employers' manifesto.

Economic reality is a more powerful stimulus to structural adaptation of interest groups than mere exhortation and in the shipbuilding industry that reality takes the form of a fierce and potentially annihilating competition from foreign shipbuilders. It is revealed with stark clarity in Table XII. There we see that the U.K. share of world tonnage of merchant ships, whether measured by launchings or completions has declined very sharply indeed over the period 1947–64. From being a dominating pro-ducer in the world market making over half of the world's merchant tonnage, the U.K. now only makes about a tenth. Previously, in the context of cyclical fluctuations in order books but in which the strong position of the British shipbuilding industry vis-á-vis its competitors was never in question, demarca-tion disputes symbolised an attempt by craft unions as interest groups to stabilise the situation for their members. But now the overall secular decline in the industry's fortunes affects not just the relative prosperity of one group in its struggles with another, but all groups including the employers. It is now a question of arresting the decline of the industry's fortunes and if this is to happen, adjustments all round are called for. Coser has argued that:

As long as the outside threat is seen to concern the entire group . . .

The Demarcation Dispute in the Shipbuilding Industry

TABLE XII

UNITED KINGDOM OUTPUT OF MERCHANT SHIPS 1947–64

Year	Number	Launchings 000 gross tons	% of world tonnage	Number	Completions 000 gross tons	% of world tonnage
1947	341	1,193	57	299	944	50·2
1948	340	1,176	51·1	345	1,213	48·9
1949	320	1,267	40·5	340	1,353	43·4
1950	275	1,325	38·0	319	1,389	42·7
1951	261	1,341	36·9	246	1,340	37·7
1952	254	1,303	29·6	238	1,264	30·0
1953	220	1,317	25·9	233	1,250	25·3
1954	253	1,409	26·8	242	1,496	27·4
1955	276	1,474	27·7	260	1,322	26·6
1956	275	1,383	20·7	291	1,457	23·2
1957	260	1,414	16·6	268	1,421	17·5
1958	282	1,402	15·1	270	1,464	16·2
1959	274	1,373	15·7	276	1,383	15·9
1960	253	1,331	15·9	263	1,298	15·5
1961	247	1,192	15·0	256	1,382	17·2
1962	187	1,073	12·8	204	1,016	12·4
1963	160	928	10·9	178	1,096	12·1
1964	179	1,043	10·1	152	808	8·3

Note: Figures include ships of 100 gross tons and above World tonnage does not include U.S.S.R., East Germany or People's Republic of China.

Source: Lloyd's Register of Shipping.

internal conflicts do not hinder concerted action against the outside enemy.[1]

This is a little optimistic, since it is assumed that internal conflicts can be suspended at the drop of a hat, whereas it often takes time to arrive at a modus vivendi. Because time itself is a scarce resource, the survival of the group against outside threats is not guaranteed, even assuming it has the latent power to meet the threat. In the case of the shipbuilding industry there is evidence to suggest that attempts are being made to integrate the logic of efficiency and the logic of security in the light of the external danger to the system as a whole.

There is first, a growing awareness among management in the

[1] Coser, op. cit., p. 94.

industry of the need to take into account the social consequences of technical change in the labour force. Since it is through technical change that existing patterns of work arrangements are disrupted, it is here that a sensitive managerial policy can help to reduce unnecessary conflict. This growing awareness is by no means omnipresent. In one firm, for example, which not infrequently found itself involved in demarcation disputes, observations such as the following came up in interviews:

> The extent of pre-fabrication is terrific now. We didn't foresee how big lifts would become. It has caused some demarcation problems (between shipwrights and platers). We were informed about crane and berth developments. But we were not informed how great pre-fabrication developments would be. We are not usually asked advice on changes. Management usually has its own ideas.
>
> (Shipwrights' shop steward)

> The work of installing engines has provided a revolutionary change in tank work for us. We were told in advance about this. The firm say they ask your advice. They do go through the motions but it is rather hypocritical because they have already made up their minds . . . Some of us were trained for this work but the firm didn't give special training. They just said: 'We're going to do engines now.'
>
> (A.E.U. shop steward)

In the same firm, the Yard Manager commented:

> We don't make a point of letting workers know in advance about technical changes. They get to know on the bush telegraph.

What is suggested by these comments is not so much a conscious policy of managerial secrecy, but rather a piecemeal, casual attitude towards the advent of technical changes in a yard. Workers accordingly live in a twilight zone, where some things are known, others half-known and rumoured about, where they are prepared for some changes but not for others.

This kind of attitude, however, appeared to be superseded in some yards, where systematic consultation before the implementation of technical change was regarded by management as an integral part of planning. In one large yard, for example, it was consciously recognised that the introduction of new techniques sets up stresses and strains in terms of industrial relations and that because of this 'you are bound to get problems'. Further, it was not always predictable where those problems would arise since there may be 'over a million parts on a ship', any of which might potentially cause a dispute (not simply demarcation, of course, but wages, manning or disputes about working conditions). Management claimed, and the claim was supported independently by the shop stewards, that thorough consultation took place well before changes were implemented. This involved, for example, in the case of the introduction of a computer profile burner, taking a shop steward and a shipwright to London to see the machine, some eight months before it was installed. A senior manager also described how, before the initiation of an extensive yard modernisation scheme, he spent six months meeting men and stewards in the canteen 'over beer and pies'. In this way plans were discussed and a book of settlements between unions worked out which provided, it was felt, a useful basis to work on. This management also took care to introduce changes in periods of expanding activity, so that any direct technological redundancy would be avoided. The clash between worker security and worker efficiency was accordingly minimised. This general attitude of short circuiting problems rather than floundering in them was summed up in one management comment:

> Management should iron these things out and not wait for the fateful day when production stops.

Certainly this yard was remarkably free of demarcation disputes. Indeed, management were at some pains to point out that, to some extent, the outside world had a misleading picture of the worker's attitude to technical change. In some cases, it was noted, the workers themselves press for new equipment when the old is not working properly.

In a small yard which was studied, the same readiness to consult the men in matters relating to yard reorganisation was also evident. A foreman plater, for example, described how the Yard Manager discussed the planning of a new pre-fabrication shed, first with supervision and then with the men:

> He showed us an open plan of the shed and asked our recommendations for the planning of it . . . He then brought in two established platers, one of whom was a shop steward and said: 'In times past you complained. Now let's have some bright ideas while the job's still on paper.' . . . In a small family firm you can do this. We have the types of chap you can trust and it's to our advantage anyway. We're not just being Father Christmas about this.

In the same firm, following consultation with shop stewards and at their suggestion, photographs were put up indicating the proposed changes involved in the yard modernisation programme. In this firm also demarcation strikes were very rare. There is secondly, a growing co-operation between yards concerning the deployment of labour. This has meant that on a particular river, security of employment has been enhanced not by a worker necessarily remaining in a particular job in a particular yard, but by being moved to other yards on the river as one job finishes and another starts. The merging of separate companies on a river to form a group, as envisaged in the recent *Geddes Report* and as already operating to some extent on the Tyne, Wear and Clyde, will facilitate this opportunity for increasing both the security and the flexibility of labour.

Thirdly, one may observe the growing rationalisation of trade union structures, particularly in the metal trades. The Boilermakers' Society represents a union which has developed from a single-craft to a multi-craft union. The amalgamation with the Shipwrights in 1963 meant that effectively, there was one union covering the whole of the skilled workers involved in ship construction. Demarcation disputes within a union can and do take place. However, in such eventualities the disputes are no longer prolonged and hardened by the vested interests of different unions. Rather the emphasis lies with the union to exercise its own mechanisms of discipline and settlement. Indeed, the significance of the amalgamation was brought out in a message from the executives of the two unions at the time of the merger, to Branch Secretaries. Stoppages of work on demarcation issues, it was said, 'will no longer be countenanced'. A combination of originally antagonistic interest groups may then seek to re-mould the cultural basis of group cohesion. New boundary lines are joined and new loyalties are fostered by those who are initiating these changes within the union.

It is clear that the Boilermakers' Society is now in a very strong position as a union vis-à-vis job control. This very fact makes it more possible for it to think about the possibilities of increasing the flexibility of the labour force. This, one suspects, is a key factor making it possible for that union to respond to management initiatives aimed at facilitating labour flexibility and interchangeability at yard and river level of negotiations.

The Demarcation Dispute in the Shipbuilding Industry

A number of yard agreements which were negotiated on the Clyde in 1965, have been noted by Keith Richardson.[1] For example, in Lithgow's, Scotts', Lamont yards and the Greenock Dockyard, welders, platers, caulkers, burners and riveters are now inter-changeable categories. This has meant that tack welding has become a superfluous occupation and the men concerned are being re-trained for other work within the metal trades. In the yards at Fairfield, Yarrow, Connell, Stephen and Barclay Curle, agreement has been reached in principle on the complete freedom of boilermakers and shipwrights to move freely within the whole range of metal trades. Certainly this was not simply an act of grace on the union's part. It involved what has come to be known as 'buying the book' – a bargain in which existing work practices are relaxed in exchange for an increase in wages. To the present writer the Devlin Committee's comment on this process in the Docks is equally pertinent to the shipbuilding context:

> It might be said from the employers' side that if men have created bad practices, they ought to be willing to give them up without being paid. But most of the practices have now persisted for a long time with the acquiescence, however unwilling, of the employers – most of them for so long that the men have in effect squatters' rights. Such rights, once acquired, have to be bought out and their origin is irrelevant to their price . . . Most employers, we find, are quite realistic about this and recognise that repeated statements that all restrictive practices are objectionable and ought to be abolished are not going to get them anywhere.[2]

Given these kind of developments, it is reasonable to assume that the union will be prepared to re-consider existing apprenticeship regulations and divisions. It is certainly not absurd to predict the emergence of a 'platewright' in the shipbuilding industry, since this is the logical development of job inter-changeability in an area of pre-fabricated units.

I have argued at various points in this essay that the demarcation dispute was a form of realistic conflict since it was a means to a particular end, namely job control and, through that, security of employment. Given the uncertain environment and the fact

[1] 'A question of demarcation', *The Sunday Times*, 12 December 1965.
[2] *Final Report of the Committee of Inquiry under the Rt. Hon. Lord Devlin into certain matters concerning the Port Transport Industry*, Cmnd. 2734 (H.M.S.O., 1965), p. 119.

that employment opportunities were a scarce resource, the problem facing the craft unions as interest groups, was at the level of deciding which form of conflict was instrumentally more adequate, the strike or the negotiated settlement. However, another mark of realistic conflict is that 'it will cease if the actor can find equally satisfying alternative ways to achieve his ends'.[1] Some of these alternative ways now appear to be open. If these ways are pursued, then we may witness not only the withering away of the demarcation strike, but also the very marked decline of the demarcation dispute.

[1] Coser, op. cit., p. 50.

CHAPTER FOUR

An Official Dispute in the
Constructional Engineering Industry

CO-AUTHOR: GEOFFREY ROBERTS[1]

ETWEEN October 1954 and March 1955 what can fairly be described as a war of attrition was waged between the Constructional Engineering Union and the Bridge Building and Constructional Group of the Engineering Allied Employers' Federation. One of the firms involved gave us access to documentary material, which throws a great deal of light on the issues involved and the problems which both employers and union faced. This material we have supplemented by consulting contemporary newspaper accounts of the events. Although the dust of this particular battle has by now settled, there are several reasons why we feel that a description and discussion of the dispute is worthwhile:

1. Considering the amount of comment and advice that is offered on the uses, abuses, causes and cures of strikes, there are very few 'natural histories' of them. The possibility of making generalisations based on empirical case material is surprisingly limited.[2]
2. Although the events described took place a decade ago, they have

---

[1] We should like to express our thanks to Professor H. A. Turner for his comments on an earlier draft of this essay.

[2] But cf. T. T. Paterson and F. J. Willett, 'Unofficial Strike', *Sociological Review*, XLIII, 1951; T. T. Paterson, Glasgow Limited, (Cambridge, 1960); and University of Liverpool Department of Social Science, *The Dock Worker*, Appendix I, (Liverpool, 1956) for instructive examples of work done in this country. In the U.S.A. the complaint of paucity of material is also to be found 'Unfortunately, since there are so few well-documented histories of strikes, it is difficult to ascertain their common social processes.' Miller and Form, *Industrial Sociology* (Harper, 1964), p. 417.

a certain contemporary relevance. In the first place, the Industrial Disputes Tribunal was used in an effort to resolve the conflict. The T.U.C. have recently made representations to the Government for the restoration of the system of compulsory arbitration which the I.D.T. embodied.[1] Since, as we shall see, the method of arbitration was singularly unsuccessful in ending the dispute, certain observations on the efficacy of the system are in order. In the second place, the dispute is a commentary on the way in which an unco-ordinated wages structure can lead to leap-frogging by an appeal to the principle of 'comparability' and hence may contribute significantly to the phenomena of wage drift.

3. Very little appears to be known about industrial relations in the Constructional Engineering Industry, by those not immediately involved in them. By focusing on what was clearly a severe conflict, one is able to throw some light on the sources of strain on the industrial relations system in that industry.

In this study, then, we shall analyse the way in which conflict between the two parties is generated, the tactics and stratagems by which it is sustained, and the pressures and constraints by which it is limited and, eventually, resolved.

The Organisational and Procedural Setting

Management and labour in the Constructional Engineering industry are, for procedural purposes, linked to the general Engineering industry. There the great majority of firms are linked to the Engineering and Allied Employers' National Federation, with a total of well over 4,000 members. The Federation is broken down into geographical regional groupings and these groupings are themselves composed of affiliated local associations. Clegg has argued that:

> The national federation and the associations remain the most important levels of authority, because they are centres of original power, and because they control the funds. Their importance is increased by the collective bargaining procedure of the industry which deals with disputes which are no longer entirely internal to an individual firm first by 'district' meetings (where the local association handles the employers' business) and then at national

[1] *See Written Evidence of the Ministry of Labour to the Royal Commission on Trade Unions and Employers' Associations* (H.M.S.O., 1965), p. 105, para 22.

meetings held at York where the federation represents the employers.[1]

Labour's biggest bargaining unit is the Confederation of Shipbuilding and Engineering Unions, with over 40 trade unions as constituent members. The Confederation negotiates general agreements concerning wages and working conditions in the industry. At the same time, individual unions (which, for manual workers, may broadly be divided into three categories: strict craft, e.g. Patternmakers, modified craft, e.g. A.E.U., and general, e.g. T.G.W.U.) can negotiate with the Federation separately, matters affecting their union alone. The following comment from the Ministry of Labour Handbook on Industrial Relations describes the procedural arrangement:

> These national negotiations are conducted on an ad hoc basis at special conferences. The practice is for the trade union organisation concerned to write to the Engineering and Allied Employers' National Federation requesting such a conference, at which they present their claim. It is considered by the employers and a reply is normally given at a further conference. Discussions continue until either agreement is reached, or the negotiations break down. There is no agreed procedure to deal with the latter eventuality and, should the unions decide to press the case, they may seek conciliation or arbitration, or take direct industrial action.[2]

It should be made clear that at national level, it is minimum wages and conditions that are established. Thus, in the engineering industry one may find district time-rates above the national rate, craft-differentials above the minimum skilled time-rates, additional 'merit' rates and of course, a wide variety of piece-work and incentive schemes established at the work-place, with no uniform relationship to the national time-rate, which, as can be seen, is a rather notional concept anyway.

Constructional Engineering, because of the distinctive problems created by site working, has given rise to the specialised Bridge Building and Construction Group within the Federation and separate but parallel collective bargaining arrangements exist with the C.S.E.U. and the individual unions. This Group is itself

[1] H. A. Clegg, 'Employers', in A. Flanders and H. A. Clegg, *The System of Industrial Relations in Great Britain* (Blackwell, 1963), p. 221.

[2] *Industrial Relations*, Ministry of Labour Handbook (H.M.S.O., 1961), p. 29.

divided into three sections, based on considerations of product differentiation:

(a) Steel work erection. This applies to men who erect steel frames for buildings, bridges, conveyors, etc. The C.E.U. signed an agreement with the Federation covering wages and working conditions on 1 January, 1947. The N.U.G.M.W. and the T.G.W.U. signed a similar agreement subsequently.

(b) Water tube boiler erection. Those who are concerned with the site erection of water tube boilers for land installations, including the erection of boiler framings, conveyor supporting steelwork and the lifting into position of the boiler drums, operate under the Water Tube Boiler Erection agreement of 17 April, 1947, which the Federation concluded with the C.E.U., T.G.W.U., and N.U.G.M.W.

(c) Steel plate erection. Work covering the site erection of gas holders, storage tanks, blast furnaces, hoppers and similar vessels involving steel plate construction is bound, not by a national agreement, but by a Code of Practice based on the Steel Work Erection and the Water Tube Boiler Agreements.

It may perhaps be noted at this point that in both the general engineering industry and the constructional section of it, there are firms which are not members of the Federation. The significance of non-membership may vary: it may be because the firm is not willing or able to pay the national minimum federated wage rate; more likely it is because the firm wishes to be free, in conditions of labour scarcity, to bid up the price of labour; in still other cases the non-member behaves, so far as wages and working conditions are concerned, as though it were a member, by simply following the federation's lead.

At the time of the dispute the C.E.U. had approximately 22,000 members. Of these some 12,000 were steel erectors. About 8,000 of these 'spidermen' were employed by firms who were affiliated to the Federation.[1] The remaining 4,000 were employed by non-federated constructional engineering firms, and by firms which were classified as members of the civil engineering industry and the building industry, and were subject to the separate terms and conditions laid down for those industries.

[1] See *The Times*, 6 November 1954, and 4 March 1955.

The Dispute: Claims and Counter-claims

In May 1954, the C.E.U. applied on behalf of their members in the Steel Work Erection section of the Constructional Engineering industry, to the Federation for 'increased rates for the steel erector in order to bridge the gap between the qualified Steel Erector's Rate and that of other craftsmen in the building industry, advancing the other differential between the erector and other grades accordingly'. Other grades in this context referred to the following occupational groupings: Riveters, Riveters' holders up, Sheeters, Sheeters' holders up, Riggers, Crane Drivers, Welders, Burners, Rivet heaters, Erectors' helpers. What was the gap to which the C.E.U. referred? The current rates for steel erectors in all three sections of the Constructional Engineering Industry at that time were:

(a) The London rate – for those working within a 16 mile radius of Charing Cross – 3/7¼d. an hour.
(b) Other districts – 3/6¼d. an hour.

The rates for craftsmen in the Building industry, with whom parity was sought, were:

(a) The London 12 mile radius rate – 3/10½d. per hour.
(b) The London 12–15 mile radius rate – 3/9½d. per hour.
(c) Other districts – 3/9d. per hour.

The claim was effectively for an increase of 3¼d. per hour for erectors in the London area, and an increase of 2¾d. per hour for those working elsewhere.

It is perhaps not surprising that the claim originated from the Steel Work Erection group, since it clearly has closer affinities with the Building industry than the other two sections. However, the adjustment of the alleged anomaly would have been at the expense of the creation of another, in the sense that differential rates would then exist between workers in the same occupational grouping employed in different sections of the same industry. To cope with this internal difficulty, the union repeated their claim in July at the same time extending it to cover all three sections. Thus Steel Work Erection is for the union the key group through which the principle of comparability may be invoked and a general increase in the industry justified in the name of equity. In attempting to apply this principle for bargaining purposes, the union were making two basic assumptions: first, that it was legitimate to claim the status of craftsman for the steel erector, and secondly, that it was appropriate to link a wage claim to what was going on in the Building industry. Each assumption could be used to justify and support the other.

At the July Conference with the Federation the C.E.U. expressed particular concern that the employers did not regard steel erectors as skilled men. Probably the strongest ground of their claim lay in their appeal to an agreement reached in 1947 with the employers. Provision was there made for the category of improver, who, as either youth or man served for three years before graduating to the job of erector. In the agreement also the words 'qualified' and 'trade' are used with reference to the occupation of erector. In addition certain de facto arguments were advanced. It was said that there was hardly any difference between the rates of steel erectors who worked in the Building industry and the rates of craftsmen in that industry (which position had no doubt arisen through the narrowing of differentials as a result of flat rate increases that were commonly granted during this period). It was also argued that the steel erector commonly works with craftsmen in the Building industry on an equal footing and must, therefore, by extension, be regarded as a skilled man.

The employers, for their part, maintained that, while they did not dispute the importance of the work which erectors performed, the occupation could not be regarded as a craft 'in the accepted sense of the word' since its members served no recognised apprenticeship. The improver's training was presumably not an acceptable substitute since it only lasted for three years. Now, while the employers' position is understandable and, in the bargaining context, predictable, it does lead to an interesting paradox. By adopting the criterion of apprenticeship to define the skilled worker, they are in fact sheltering behind an institution to which, in other circumstances, employers frequently and vociferously object. It is objected to on the grounds of an unnecessary length of training time – 'You don't need five years to learn a trade, when Battle of Britain pilots learned to fly in six weeks' – is not an uncommon jibe. More soberly, a subcommittee of the National Joint Advisory Council observed, in 1958:

There are some occupations for which five years may not be too long; but we feel that with the adoption of up-to-date methods of training there are others in which the present period could be reduced.[1]

And apprenticeship, as an institution, is objected to when skilled labour is scarce and the union concerned does not permit dilution or upgrading of labour. Where both management and unions are prepared to by-pass or supplement the apprenticeship system, the craftsmen thus created become 'acceptable'. It is interesting to notice that the shorter training period and the possibility of training men of 21 and over for the job of erector provides the kind of flexibility that employers, in other contexts, exhort trade unions to permit.

The semantic difference implied in the use of the term 'skilled man' is perhaps best to be understood as a reflection rather than the basis of the disagreement between the two parties. It illustrates how men in different social positions, representing different interests, can impute different meanings to the same word and so talk past one another. One finds the same kind of thing happening when the employers challenge the union's assertion that steel erectors work with craftsmen in the Building industry. They argued that the steel frame of a building is usually in an advanced state before Building trade workers are brought in and that, furthermore, there are many types of erection work on which few, if any, Building trade workers would be employed. Without doubt there is substance in these statements. How then can semantic confusion arise?

To say that erectors work with Building trade craftsmen can be interpreted in terms of 'at the same time as' and/or 'in the same place as', and/or 'as part of the division of labour'. Clearly, there was some overlapping between erectors and Building trade workers in terms of time and place and certainly there was an element of co-operation between the two groups in relation to the finished product. The difference between the C.E.U. and the federation was in the significance attached to the area of overlapping. It is important to notice that the status grievance was more overtly expressed in the London area, where overlap between Building trade workers and erectors was more in evidence

[1] Ministry of Labour and National Service, *Training for Skill* (H.M.S.O., 1958), p. 23.

in the construction of office and shop blocks. One may notice in passing that where sites are more isolated from Building trade workers, the question of occupational status is not likely to be so pressing. Wage claims in such circumstances tend to be more ad hoc and take the form of claims for 'hot' money, 'dirt' money, 'wind' money, 'wet' money and other 'abnormal condition' payments, which are considered appropriate. The employers, for their part, could claim that the urban sites were given an exaggerated importance when seen in the context of the whole industry.

The difference in perception between the C.E.U. and the federation as to the 'right' skill grading of the steel erector raises a theoretical point relating to the nature of industrial stability, which merits elaboration. W. Baldamus[1] has distinguished 'occupational costs' from 'employment' as elements in wage costs. The former are connected with 'the acquisition of skill, experience, and occupational education and are reflected in, for instance . . . that component of wage structure which expresses skill differentials'. The 'decisive criterion of employment' is the compensation for 'effort'. He then goes on to make the following assertion:

> Everything that points to a 'harmony' of interests appears to be connected with the self-regulating mechanism of occupational costs and rewards within the institution of occupation. And the causes of recurrent disorganisation stem from an unbalanced and variable distribution of effort and effort rewards in the context of employment. The significance of this contrast can be seen at a glance from the fact that occupational costs are strictly determinate whereas effort is not.[2]

This attempt to identify the sources of industrial conflict and stability seems to us to be an over-simplification of the matter. It is certainly the case that much industrial conflict centres on what has come to be known as the 'effort bargain'. Indeed in the present dispute, some arguments we have not yet noted were put forward by the C.E.U. in justification of their claim, which might be subsumed under this heading. For example, the C.E.U. claimed that the use of machines had speeded up the pace of

[1] W. Baldamus, *Efficiency and Effort* (Tavistock Publications, 1961).
[2] Ibid., pp. 9–10.

work and that a high accident rate in the industry and the intrinsic dangers of the job merited a higher wage in compensation. To this the employers replied that these things had been taken into account in the existing wage payments. But central to the dispute was the disagreement over the status of the erector.[1] and where such conflicts occur it cannot be said that occupational costs are strictly determinate. In so far as occupational costs are linked to status considerations, conflicts over status ranking introduce an element of indeterminacy into the discussion of occupational costs. Indeed, one suspects that difficulty of resolving many conflicts between management and labour arises because at the same time there are differences of opinion on both the 'effort' and the 'occupational costs' axes. This is perhaps notably the case in arguments over wage differentials in which arguments about the reward for effort are inevitably comparative and introduce status elements into the discussion. Just as the concept of effort lacks an 'objective' frame of reference by which rewards can be agreed upon by all the parties concerned, so too may the concept of occupational costs.[2] And since they may be interacting rather than separate features of the industrial conflict situation it is misleading to apportion 'harmony of interests' to the alleged self-regulating mechanism of occupational costs and rewards, and to attribute 'conflicts of interest' simply to disputes over the reward for effort.

In order to justify the wage increase it was necessary for the C.E.U. not only to establish the skilled status of the steel erector, but also the relevance of the comparison with the Building industry. Conflict over the legitimacy of the comparison highlights the essential boundary position of the Constructional Engineering industry. Not only was it linked procedurally with the general Engineering industry, but in many cases constructional engineering was a branch or section of a general engineering firm. There were, therefore organisational and procedural ties to that industry.

[1] For an account of a similar type of disagreement over welding in the U.S.A. see Herbert J. Lahne, 'The Welder's Search for Craft Recognition', *Industrial and Labor Relations Review*, July 1958, pp. 591–607.

[2] cf. T. H. Marshall, 'It is ... possible by deliberate action to raise the social status of an occupational group, partly by altering the objective character of the job, and partly by changing the attitude towards it.' 'The Nature and Determinants of Social Status', in *Sociology at the Crossroads* (Heinemann, 1963), pp. 206–7.

At the same time, however, Constructional Engineering shares necessarily the technological context of constructional work. Some of the more important technological characteristics have been summarised by John Dunlop:

> Work operations on a particular site are characteristically of a short duration; at times they may only last a few hours or days; on other sites they may last some months or even a few years. Some projects have a large number of separate enterprises and workers; others may involve only a single enterprise and a single worker. The size and craft composition of the work force is likely to change markedly in the course of construction. Sites tend to be geographically variable; some are isolated from urban areas. A number of operations take place out of doors, and the weather has a significant effect upon the regularity of these work operations. The technology of building . . . requires a very wide range of different skills of a high order, many of which may be necessary on a single project, such as steam generating plant, or only one of which may be used, as on a re-painting job. Construction operations as a whole are relatively hazardous, although not to the same degree as underground coal mining, as a consequence of heights, material handling, temporary installations, and the interdependence of workers of different contractors on a job site. There are very wide differences in physical working conditions and in the technological characteristics of different construction sites and operations; the wide variety of sites poses special problems in rule-making designed to cover such diverse conditions.[1]

Hence, within this frame of reference it is clearly meaningful, if not desirable from the Federation's point of view, for the C.E.U. to link its aspirations to the Building industry. If one asks why they had not done so before, the answer is very simple: there was nothing to be gained. The dispute was prompted by the fact that, for the first time since the war, the rate of pay for Building craftsmen had gone above the Engineering rate of pay, to which the steel erectors were tied.[2]

In order to bolster its claim further, the C.E.U. applied the principle of comparability in yet another way. The union asserted that in both the Building and the Civil Engineering industries, men had a greater opportunity to work under incentive schemes

[1] J. T. Dunlop, *Industrial Relations Systems* (Holt, 1958), pp. 201–2.
[2] See *The Times*, 28 October 1954.

than in the Constructional Engineering industry. As an expression of dissatisfaction, this statement might be used to put pressure on the employers to jack the rate up. Essentially, however, it was a different issue. This is not to deny its importance since it bears directly upon the subject of earnings opportunities and actual take-home pay. It is also the kind of statement which, in principle, is open to investigation. In the interim period between the July conference with the C.E.U. and the convening of the Industrial Disputes Tribunal in December, the Bridge Building and Constructional group of employers undertook an earnings inquiry among members of the Federation. The picture that emerged for July 1954 was as follows:

	TIME WORKERS		INCENTIVE SCHEME WORKERS	
	Hours worked per week	*Gross Earnings*	*Hours worked per week*	*Gross Earnings*
Local Men (60% of total employed)	54·7	£11 15 1d.	52·3	£13 18 2¼d.
Away men (40% of total employed)	57·6	£12 9 1½d.	54·9	£14 1 11¾d.

The earnings figures do not include a radius allowance of 13/– per week average for Local men. Nor do they include a lodging allowance of 56/– per week average for Away men.

It is interesting to know that Away men tend to work longer and earn more than Local men, but basically as an inquiry this is disappointing since some of the most pertinent questions remained unanswered. While average earnings for these two groups are presented, no attempt is made to indicate the range as between, say, sites or districts. Neither is there any attempt made to indicate the percentages of workers employed on a Time and Incentive basis. It is clear also that no attempt to compare earnings experience in Building or Civil Engineering was made. As evidence against the C.E.U.'s contention, it was certainly deficient.

Circumstantial evidence, however, strongly suggests that the C.E.U. was factually incorrect in its allegation. The Ministry of Labour collects material every two years to indicate the proportion of wage earners who are paid under payment by results systems. The following table gives the breakdown for October 1953 and October 1955 for the industries in question:

TABLE XIII

PROPORTION OF WAGE EARNERS PAID UNDER
SYSTEMS OF P.B.R.

Industry	October 1953 Men 21 and over	October 1955 Men 21 and over
Constructional Engineering	45%	48%
Building	16%	18%
Civil Engineering	17%	16%

Source: *Ministry of Labour Gazette* 1954, p. 115, and 1956, p. 121.

This table includes those paid wholly or partly under any such system. It includes piece work arrangements, output bonus schemes, or any other systems of payment which vary according to the output of individuals, groups or departments. The figures apply to the last pay week in the month.

The markedly greater opportunity for P.B.R. work in the Constructional Engineering industry, as opposed to either Building or Civil Engineering, prompts the observation that it is strange that the employers did not refer to the Ministry of Labour enquiry for 1953 in the arbitration proceedings. Could it be that they were ignorant of these official and easily accessible statistics? Or was it merely that they regarded the C.E.U.'s assertion as self-evidently wrong to all those concerned with the industry? In either case, their own earnings inquiry seems rather beside the point. One suspects that the C.E.U., for their part, were making generalisations on the basis of a few cases. Perhaps in the London area, where the difficulties first arose, there were particular sites where those employed in the Constructional Engineering industry had less opportunity for P.B.R. work. But on this we have no positive information.

Tactics and Policies prior to Arbitration

At a conference with the C.E.U. on 5 October 1954, the employers' federation rejected the union's claim for the wage increase. The formal collective bargaining procedure was thus exhausted. In rejecting the claim outright at this stage the employers knew well enough that this gave the C.E.U. the right to call an official strike if they so wished. In taking this position they were saying, in effect, that they did not believe in industrial peace at any price. The cost of a strike might, in the long run, be cheaper than the cost of a concession to the union.

The C.E.U. did not strike immediately, but spent the next three weeks making plain to the employers through the Press that they would strike, if no concession were made. The threat was presented in a way that suggested that the costs to the employers would be very high, whereas the costs to the union would be very low. The union adopted a position of intransigence by stating at the outset to the employers that it had no intention of taking the matter to arbitration. This implied its readiness to undertake a long strike. In order to convince the employers of the feasibility of its position, the union indicated in advance how it intended to conserve its resources. The tactic of the 'snowball' strike, it announced, would be used. Union members on selected sites would be called out and, if this was not successful, mounting pressure would be applied by calling more members out from other sites. This is a variant of the 'rolling strike' tactic, in which selected groups of workers are called out in turn to strike, while those still at work contribute to their support. This tactic has a long history and, as H. A. Turner has shown, was used with conspicuous success by the early spinners' unions in the nineteenth century.[1]

It is unlikely that the employers believed that the C.E.U. was bluffing, given its known militancy and conditions of labour scarcity. Nevertheless, the Federation still refused to make a concession. Overt conflict broke out on 26 October when 100 steel erectors walked out on indefinite strike from eleven large building sites in the City of London. The General Secretary of the C.E.U. made his policy quite explicit to a newspaper reporter of *The Times*:

> We have chosen the City of London for our strike demonstration because it is a compact area, easily controlled by our organising staff, and we believe that the eleven big building construction jobs which will be affected will hit the employers where it hurts. The strike will go on indefinitely until our men win a pay increase.[2]

[1] In *Trade Union Growth, Structure and Policy, A Comparative Study of the Cotton Unions* (Allen and Unwin, 1962). See for example, pp. 57, 76 and 371.
[2] *The Times*, 27 October 1954. The sites included new offices for the Bank of England, the United Steel Company, Lloyds Bank, and the Blue Star Line Shipping Company.

The following day two more sites were called out, making a total of 110 erectors on strike.[1] Clearly, the financial burden on a union with 22,000 in its membership, was minute, but the withdrawal of key men could greatly slow down or even bring to a standstill work on large sites. The claim that this would hit the employers where it hurt was not an idle one.

The Director of the Engineering and Allied Employers National Federation promptly convened a meeting of the Bridge Building and Constructional group members to discuss how they should deal with this development. The official view presented and impressed on the members was that to concede the C.E.U.'s claim for 'comparability' with Building craftsmen would involve a greater increase in wage costs than the alternative of rejecting the claim and upholding the traditional link with the general Engineering industry. This viewpoint was supported by the fact that the craftsmen in the Building industry had just presented their employers with a claim for an extra 4d. an hour.

The Engineering employers' readiness to battle for a principle was a preview, on a smaller scale, of their subsequent battle on a wider front with the Confederation, which resulted in the 1957 Shipbuilding and Engineering strike. Indeed, it pre-dates Clegg and Adams' comment that:

> By 1956, a majority of organised employers seem to have come to the conclusion that there was an even greater danger than industrial conflict – continuous inflation.[2]

The major decision which the employers took at this meeting was to formally report the existence of the dispute to the Minister of Labour and ask him to appoint a Court of Inquiry or to refer the matter to the Industrial Disputes Tribunal. Because of this decision firms were asked to take no counter-action against the strikers; but they were asked to give the Federation the names of workers on strike. In addition, a sub-committee was set up to consider what counter-action should be taken if attempts at conciliation or arbitration failed. The sub-committee was an advisory group responsible to the Management Board of the Federation.

It is when there are no further steps available for settling disputes within an industry that the Ministry of Labour's con-

[1] *The Times,* 28 October 1954.
[2] H. A. Clegg and R. Adams, *The Employers' Challenge* (Blackwell, 1957), p. 143.

ciliation service can begin to operate, if one of the parties chooses to invite an industrial relations officer in.[1] As far as the general public is concerned, these are the hidden men of the British system of industrial relations. They have no legal sanctions but operate typically in an informal way, meeting the parties to the dispute separately, finding out the salient issues which divide the disputants, seeking always for some kind of compromise which may be acceptable to both parties. They may be able to discern some difference between the public utterances of the parties involved and the private views expressed. In this respect they may act as an unofficial emissary between the parties filtering information about the 'real' state of the conflict, if they think it may lead to a resolution of the dispute. If necessary or possible, they may hold joint meetings between the parties and take the chair at them, but their role is always quite distinct from that of an arbitrator.

During the first two weeks of November 1954, the Chief Conciliation Officer of the Ministry of Labour met first the employers' federation and then the C.E.U. The union was still firm in its resolve not to accept arbitration as a solution. They expressed a preference for direct negotiations with the employers, whom they were prepared to meet. However, a certain ambiguity in the rationale of the union's position emerged which was to colour the employers' response. While the union reiterated its claim that the erectors should receive the building trade craftsmens' current rate, they added that they were not claiming that rates in the Constructional Engineering industry should move or be geared permanently to those of the Building industry. The union presumably took this attitude in the light of the new claim of 4d. an hour for Building trade craftsmen. The dilemma confronting the C.E.U. was that it could either add this 4d. an hour into its claim and lay itself open to the charge of making exorbitant and unreal demands, or take the course which it did and risk the charge of opportunism. It could perhaps be argued that a more effective union strategy would have been to take the former course, more particularly since the Confederation of Shipbuilding and Engineering Unions had also put in for a wage increase. Had the C.E.U. kept to its intention of linking its wage

[1] For the official description of the Conciliation Service, see *Industrial Relations*, op. cit., pp. 134–36.

rate to the Building industry, the extra 4d. being claimed there would be offset by the award they would have received from being a member of the C.S.E.U. To this extent their claim would not have been unrealistic and it would certainly have been more consistent with their declared policy. As it was, when the employers learned of the C.E.U.'s attitude, they were strengthened in the belief in the morality of their own stand. They inferred that the union was not interested so much in obtaining for its members the status and pay of building craftsmen, but rather in using the comparison as a convenient vaulting pole to secure a simple wage increase. In the light of this, they refused to agree to the C.E.U.'s suggestion that a further meeting be held, since they did not wish to imply by such a meeting, any willingness to make concessions. They decided instead to refer the dispute to the Ministry of Labour under the terms of the Industrial Disputes Order.

During this period of attempted conciliation, the C.E.U. strike continued to spread. The guerilla aspect of the strike activity was underlined by the comment of the union's General Secretary to the press:

> There will definitely be a spread, but nobody will know anything about it until it starts. It may be both in and out of London.[1]

Token strikes, as in the case of a day strike of erectors in Nottingham, were used in addition to the snowball tactic. Throughout this period (and subsequently) the union took care to call mass meetings of strikers (notably in London) to explain the purpose of the strike, to encourage the strikers and to obtain their support of the executive decision.

In the light of the C.E.U.'s rejection of arbitration as the appropriate next step, the Ministry of Labour suggested that a committee of investigation be set up to examine the sources of the dispute. This was used, apart from its intrinsic value, as a technique to take the steam out of the dispute, since the condition was that the strikers return to work. The union refused to accept the condition. By the end of December, when the matter was finally considered by the Industrial Disputes Tribunal, the union had some 298 erectors on strike on fifteen sites throughout the U.K.

[1] *The Times*, 6 November 1954.

An Official Dispute in the Constructional Engineering Industry

The Use of Arbitration Machinery

During the period 1951–59, under the terms of the Industrial Disputes Order, a modified form of compulsory arbitration existed in the British system of industrial relations. Either side in a dispute could voluntarily refer the issue to the Ministry of Labour for reference to the Industrial Disputes Tribunal. The consent of the other party was not necessary, for such a Tribunal to be convened, but the awards made by the Tribunal were legally binding on both sides. It was under this arrangement that the employers were able to take unilateral action.

The Tribunal met on 31 December 1954, over two months after the first strike action had occurred. The union carried out its threat to boycott proceedings, claiming that the employers had refused to consider the case on its merits before rejecting it. To refer the claim to arbitration in these circumstances was, the union leaders argued, to 'make a mockery' of the negotiating machinery and procedure.[1] The employers' federation, however, submitted evidence to the Tribunal. The federation also sent the Tribunal the documents it had received from the C.E.U. in support of the claim.

The award, published on 5 January 1955, was as follows:

> The Tribunal have given careful consideration to the . . . statements and submissions. On the evidence made available to them, they find that the claim made by the union has not been established. The Tribunal award accordingly.[2]

Here, of course, theoretically, the matter should have ended. In practice, this was very far from the case. As we shall see, the dispute was not finally resolved until March.

When in 1959 the Industrial Disputes Order was rescinded, the then Minister of Labour pointed out that as a system of compulsory arbitration, it had depended on the willingness of employers and unions to make it work.[3] Employers had become increasingly disenchanted with the system and, in the light of events such as those we are discussing, it is not difficult to see why. Where unions were strong, the results of such arbitration

[1] *The Times,* 14 December 1954.
[2] Award 660.
[3] See *Ministry of Labour Gazette,* November 1958 and January 1959, where employer dissatisfaction with the system is noted.

awards were not always heeded if they upheld the employers'
position. Where unions were weak they provided employees with
a resource which, so to speak, enhanced in an artificial way their
power position. In such a context it was an effective substitute to
a strike (which the employees may not have been well organised
enough to have called). Thus although the T.U.C. in its recent
representations to the Minister of Labour, has claimed that a
unilateral reference leading to compulsory arbitration ensures
that disputes are settled in situations where one of the parties is
reluctant to submit to independent judgment,[1] the employers'
criticism that in practice the system was one-sided, is not without
substance.

From the policy point of view, however, one may wish to
consider in what circumstances arbitration is likely to be effective
in resolving social conflicts. Sociological analysis may, perhaps,
make a contribution here. To illustrate, we will describe and
apply to our present dispute an approach outlined by David
Lockwood in his paper 'Arbitration and Industrial Conflict'.[2]

Lockwood indicates that there are two contrasting views about
the function of arbitration: the 'judicial' and the 'political'.

> The judicial view implies that there is some 'just' solution to the
> dispute possible, and that it is the business of the arbitrator to decide
> on the principles and facts involved . . . Political theory regards
> arbitration as an extension of collective bargaining and, of course,
> collective coercion. The arbitrator now becomes a kind of sensitive
> instrument which will accurately record the relative strengths of
> the parties and makes sure that the lion gets his share.[3]

In answering the question, 'how effective are arbitration procedures likely to be?', Lockwood notes that this will depend in
part on the way in which the arbitration function is viewed by
the parties and by the arbitrator. But it will also depend upon the

[1] See *T.U.C. Report,* 1965: 'At the Meeting with the Minister (of Labour)
. . . General Council representatives said that . . . any machinery which provided opportunities for peaceful settlement of disputes was beneficial and
that action taken by the Ministry's officers on reports made under the Order
had stimulated voluntary negotiations in that a number of cases were settled
voluntarily because employers were aware that otherwise they would be sent
to arbitration.' p. 147.
[2] *B.J.S.,* Vol. 6, 1955, pp. 335-47.
[3] Ibid., p. 336.

type of conflict under consideration. Here he distinguishes between 'institutional conflict', 'conflicts of interest', and 'conflicts of right'. The first refers to 'conflicts about the legitimacy of the institutional framework within which contractual relationships take place'; the second to 'conflicts about the establishment of terms of contracts'; and the third to 'conflicts about the interpretation of the terms of contracts'.[1] We may summarise his position on the effectiveness of arbitration procedures in the following chart:

HOW APPROPRIATE ARE ARBITRATION PROCEDURES?

Type of industrial conflict	*View of arbitration function*	
	Political	*Judicial*
Institutional conflict	Not appropriate	Not appropriate
Conflict of interests	Limited use	Not appropriate
Conflict of rights	Limited use	Very appropriate

Judicial arbitration, it is suggested is only effective in dealing with the interpretation of agreements. The rationale behind this is that organisational disagreements about the distribution of power by their nature rule out awards that describe one party as 'right' and the other as 'wrong'. Only at the conflict of rights level is there a sufficient degree of normative consensus between the parties presupposed to make arbitration effective.[2] Where there is disagreement about the establishment of the work contract, however, some form of 'political' arbitration (which is essentially a form of mediation) might be effective. The empirical

[1] Ibid., p. 338.

[2] We agree that the judicial arbitration function fits best at the conflict of rights level and Lockwood provides some empirical evidence for his contention from experience in the U.K. and the U.S.A. It is possible, however, that he underscores the bargaining element at this level. cf. James W. Kuhn, *Bargaining in Grievance Settlement* (Columbia, 1961). He notes that some unions reject the notion that the grievance procedure has any judicial aspect (p. 14) and comments that: 'Managers will usually tell an outsider that grievances are settled only on the basis of facts and the provisions of the collective agreement. If so, both the facts and the agreement are amazingly tractable. Union representatives daily convince managers that facts and agreements are not what they first maintained them to be.' (p. 78).

problem arising for the student of industrial relations is, of course, the identification of the type of conflict. One difficulty is that what appears to be a conflict of rights, and thus susceptible to arbitration, may disguise a latent conflict at another level. Possibly this is more difficult in the British context than in some others since the division between conflicts of interest and conflicts of right is not clear-cut in collective bargaining arrangements as it is in, say, the U.S.A. or Sweden.

As far as the case under discussion is concerned, we know that arbitration was not successful and with the kind of approach outlined by Lockwood it is not difficult to see why. A judicial solution was offered to what was essentially a dispute in which elements of institutional and interest conflict were to be found. Further, since 'the arbitrator tends to give greatest weight to arguments in terms of cost of living and relativities, and thus implicitly assumes that his duty is to maintain what exists',[1] whether one judges the C.E.U.'s claim as basically an attempt to raise the status of the erectors as an occupational group, or as simply an opportunistic attempt to get what they could, their refusal to accept arbitration was quite understandable.

What is perhaps implied, as far as conflict regulation is concerned, is that collective bargaining is more adequately supplemented by what Kerr has termed tactical mediation, than arbitration, where such conflicts of interest occur.

> The purpose of tactical mediation is to bring existing non-violent conflict between the parties to a mutually acceptable result so that there will be no need for it to become violent or to end violent conflict by agreement or by transfer to non-violent means.[2]

The role of the mediator is more active than that of conciliator, but less dogmatic than that of judicial arbitrator. He may be used, according to Kerr, to reduce the irrational and non-rational elements of the dispute, to assist the parties in their search for solutions and when there is a need for either or both of the parties to make a graceful retreat. If necessary he may seek to re-structure the situation so that the cost of conflict is raised, leading potentially to a re-appraisal of the situation by the participants.[3] The

[1] Lockwood, op. cit., p. 344.
[2] C. Kerr, 'Industrial Conflict and its Mediation', in *Labor and Management in Industrial Society* (Harper 1964), p. 180.
[3] Ibid., pp. 181–6.

ramifications of this cannot be entered into here, but we may note that the British system of industrial relations does not allow much scope for this kind of mediation. The logical development within the system is the extension of the role of the industrial relations officers of the Ministry of Labour. Although the British Employers' Confederation have recently expressed the opinion that the role should not be extended in this way,[1] it is perhaps a functional alternative to a system of compulsory arbitration, which both they and the trade unions would, in the event, find more acceptable.

Post-arbitration: The Continuation of Conflict

The C.E.U.'s response to the arbitration award was to step up the number of guerilla strikes and to impose a double levy on all its members. The union had already managed to pay the strikers £7 10s. a week and a £6 Christmas bonus. Clearly, the selective nature of the strikes made this high rate of strike pay possible. Those constructional engineering firms who were not affected by the strikes were, indirectly, subsidising their colleagues' strikers.

The C.E.U. also attempted to harass the strike-bound firms by offering their members directly to building contractors whose work was being held up by the freeze on steel work erection. The effectiveness of this move is not known but it posed yet another threat to the employers. Even if only partially successful the costs of the conflict would be raised for the employers at the same time as they were lowered for the union.

It was at this stage that the employers had to decide upon a policy to combat the continued C.E.U. militancy. The Federation proposed to its membership a three stage tactical campaign:

Stage 1. Firms should restrict their C.E.U. employees to a working week of 44 hours (the basic working week according to the agreements in the three sections of the Constructional Engineering industry) by stopping all week-day overtime and week-end work.

Stage 2. If Stage 1 is ineffective, then firms should reduce the working week of C.E.U. members to 34 hours. The timing of this move should be determined by expediency.

[1] See Confederation of British Industry, *Evidence to the Royal Commission on Trade Unions and Employers' Associations* (1965), p. 27, para, 133.

Stage 3. If Stage 2 is not effective, then firms should lock all
C.E.U. members out of erection sites.

The basic policy behind this campaign was to widen the battle
front in order to stretch the union's resources and cause dissatisfaction within the union membership by affecting their take-
home pay. The lock-out was in fact the classic response to the
'rolling strike' but it was most effective in times of high or rising
unemployment.[1] That was far from the case in 1955. The primary
step of the overtime ban, preceded step two of the partial lock-
out and step three of the total lock-out partly at least because the
employers wished to maintain their public image of constitutional
behaviour. Public opinion as mediated through the Press was
certainly consciously considered by the employers. Although an
intangible factor, if Press support is obtained it serves to develop
the morale of the group, while adding to the pressures on the
opposing group. Indeed it is noteworthy that the employers
decided to implement their overtime ban after a token strike
called by the C.E.U. They could thus present a picture of an
injured party hitting back only after extreme and continuous
provocation.

What should be stressed at this point are the inherent difficulties
in evaluating the costs to the parties or the consequences of the
kind of campaign outlined by the federation. There are several
clear reasons for this which may be enumerated.

First the Federation was faced with the internal problem of
maintaining cohesion among its membership. This was partly an
administrative problem. The sub-committee set up to suggest the
tactical campaign was permitted to handle the day-to-day running
of things – but a decision on when to move from one step to
another had to be taken by a full meeting of the members of the
Federation. Cohesion was also affected, however, by the fact that
employers were differentially hit by the dispute. Some who were
strike-bound would have preferred more drastic measures to be
taken straight away. Others, who had been able to continue
working, saw even the overtime ban as too costly. They were
conscious of client pressures upon them and, in some cases, felt
that they risked falling foul of penalty clauses in their contracts.
Some firms maintained that they were particularly dependent on

[1] See H. A. Turner, op. cit., p. 371.

week-end working. Those working on railway contracts were a case in point, since it was more convenient to do much of the work when railway services were reduced over the week-end. It was, no doubt, with such considerations in mind that the General Secretary of the C.E.U., when the overtime ban was announced, described it as 'a rather Gilbertian situation'. He believed that the employers' plan would in fact support the union and he noted that on some sites C.E.U. members had themselves imposed an overtime ban.[1]

The Federation attempted to deal with this problem of internal cohesion, by establishing a common rule to apply to all members that the overtime ban would only be lifted on member firms if the delaying of work gave rise to a clear safety problem. An Appeals Court was set up to decide when exemption could be granted.

Secondly, the Federation had to consider how non-member firms would behave in the situation. Would they actively support the policy? Would they tacitly support it by not employing labour from strike-bound firms? Or would they cash in on the situation by happily poaching labour?

The third imponderable was how would the C.E.U. react? Would they sue for settlement or would they develop their own campaign and attempt to raise the costs of the dispute for the employers yet again by the adoption of go-slows or work-to-rules?

Finally, in this respect, the Federation also had to consider the effect that its counter-tactics might have on other trade unionists and lead to the development of 'sympathy' strikes or other gestures of support for the C.E.U.?[2]

Given that the costs and consequences of such a campaign are based upon imperfect knowledge, there is an inevitable element of indeterminacy about such conflict. At best one can hope for a feed-back during the on-going process so that fresh calculations

[1] *The Times*, 13 January 1955.

[2] Here they predicted correctly that such support, if forthcoming at all would be very limited. The attempt to raise the status of erectors, could have the effect of altering the prestige hierarchy of trade union organisations. The enthusiastic support of the established skilled unions or the general unions who would, so to speak, be left behind, could hardly be expected. Nevertheless, the point remains that the employers could not be sure that the C.E.U. would remain without support.

can be made with the addition of new knowledge and, if necessary, modifications about the timing or implementations of the tactics may be made.

The employers' ban on overtime came into effect on 21 January 1955. Five days later the Federation asked the 250 member firms concerned to report the number of sites and C.E.U. workers affected and to indicate how the workers were reacting to the ban. Replies were received from 130 firms. Of these, 32 said they were not involved, either because they did not employ C.E.U. members or because they were not currently engaged in site work. The replies are summarised in Table XIV. The Federa-

TABLE XIV

SOME EFFECTS OF THE OVERTIME BAN IN THE CONSTRUCTIONAL
ENGINEERING INDUSTRY (JANUARY 1955)

Section	No. of firms imposing ban	No. of sites involved	No. of sites not involved	No. of C.E.U. members involved
Steelplate erection	9	69	76	374
Water tube boiler erection	12	77	53	1,146
Steelwork erection	77	694	32	4,789
Total	98	840	161	6,309

tion considered that the bulk of the firms which failed to reply were not committed to work on outside sites and that information had been received from all the important sites and from the major employers. Certainly a large proportion of C.E.U. members in the industry were affected by the ban.

In the week following the implementation of stage 1 of the employers' campaign, the C.E.U. announced its intention to extend the guerilla strikes and to introduce either a work-to-rule and/or a go-slow on further sites. Thus during February the union called 160 members out on strike at the Tilbury Power Station site. This brought the work of several federated firms to a standstill. Towards the end of February, the C.E.U. instructed strikers from some of the London sites (who had been out the longest) to return to work. They did this and then promptly began to work to rule. This infuriated many of the employers who argued that, to all intents and purposes, they were now paying the men strike pay. The C.E.U. had simply shifted the financial burden across to them. Such firms tended to anticipate stage 3 of the national campaign by closing down the contract. Thus a partial lock-out occurred in the industry, although it was not officially sanctioned by the Federation.

In the main, the members of the C.E.U. seemed to have maintained quite a high degree of solidarity during the dispute, but a number of minor exceptions were reported. Several small groups of C.E.U. men, working on sites when the overtime ban was declared, told their employers that they had resigned from the union. Their action appears to have been prompted partly by their resentment of the prospect of reduced earnings and partly by their disagreement with the way in which the union had conducted its case. The employers made an effort to keep these groups together and worked them as non-union labour throughout the dispute. They were not, of course, employed on jobs with union men. The general effectiveness of the overtime ban was, however, called into question by the following report:

The National Executive (of the C.E.U.) will meet on Sunday to consider their next step in the strike of steel erectors which has been going on for 18 weeks. The strike, which began at 11 building sites in the City of London, now affects 500 men at 24 sites.

There is no sign of any move for a settlement. The union say they are quite prepared to go on for another 18 weeks or more. The cost to their general funds is comparatively slight because it is mainly met by a levy on members who are working . . .

For the past 4 weeks the employers have imposed a ban on overtime. As a result workers have been inclined to leave them for non-federated firms, with whom they can still obtain overtime earnings. According to the union, some federated firms are paying bonuses to keep their workers, which make up their earnings to what they would have been if they had been working overtime. . . .[1]

The Federation tended to play down the extent to which bonuses were paid to workers as compensation for the loss of overtime, or to discourage go-slows and work-to-rules. Comment here, however, is bound to be conjectural, since the essence of such inducements was that they were concealed.

[1] *The Times*, 4 March 1955.

An Official Dispute in the Constructional Engineering Industry

Resolution of the Dispute: The 'Face-saving' Formula

It might at first sight be a cause for wonder that the employers fighting for a principle against a union pursuing an interest which was in direct conflict with that principle, could ever reach agreement. However, with the passage of time, the pressure on the parties to settle the dispute, increases.

To begin with, the fundamental problems of social control over the membership became greater both for the employers and for the union as the dispute became more protracted. The basic aim of the employers' federation was to maintain the status quo of the established bargaining relationships with the C.E.U. In that sense it was acting essentially in a defensive manner. Having initiated the policy of defence it then had to ensure that the policy was kept. It sought to do this by suggesting that the interest of one was the interest of all in the long run and that it would be to the employers' overall advantage to subordinate short term considerations for 'the common good'. However, short term considerations are by definition those which give rise to immediate concern. And these concerns were directly related to the contractual arrangements with clients, the penalties that might be incurred and the good-will that might be lost. The situation was not made easier by the fact that in a few instances contracts were lost to non-federated firms, as too was scarce labour. Such events serve as symbolic signposts, to use Coser's phrase,[1] and undermine the morale of the party affected more than the numerical significance of them might suggest.

Essentially, one suspects that the Federation did not have adequate knowledge about whether everyone was toeing the line, though it could send out morale boosting messages to the effect that this was the case. The geographical diversity of the sites and the possibility of paying concealed bonuses, made their task very difficult. Further, although it could and did attempt to mobilise the support of non-federated firms and circulated a black list of strikers' names to them, it had no sanctions that it could use to ensure compliance. Indeed, even against member firms the only real sanction was the threat of expulsion from the Federation. But

---

[1] See L. Coser on 'Terminating Conflict', *Jnl. of Conflict Resolution*, Vol. 5, December 1961. Reprinted in A. Inkeles (ed.) *Readings on Modern Sociology* (Prentice Hall, 1966), pp. 226–32.

that was very much a two-edged weapon in circumstances such as these. Some firms, dissatisfied with the Federation's policy were seriously thinking of leaving anyway. Non-membership posed a threat to the Federation of winning contracts, poaching labour and possibly bidding up the price of labour. To increase the number of non-members was to increase the threat.[1]

The C.E.U.'s policy was, as we have seen, essentially aggressive. Its wage claim was, at the same time coupled with an attempt to increase the status of the erectors. It is probably the case that the identity of interest between union officials and union members was more marked than that between the employers' federation and member firms. Nevertheless, there were certain basic problems of social control. The possibility of recruiting and maintaining union membership was hampered as a result of the high degree of casualisation of labour in the industry. As late as 1963, a Divisional Organiser of the union could still say that 'for every ten members we organise we keep two due to the instability of employment'. This agonising problem gives some scope to the employers to utilise replacement labour in times of dispute.

One of the dilemmas confronting the C.E.U. was that a period of full employment was a strategic time to call a strike, in the sense that employers were caught with full order books. It is also the time to make high earnings. Even with strike pay, the snowball strike seriously affected the potential earnings of C.E.U. members. It is significant that as time went on more reliance was placed first on guerilla strikes and then on work-to-rules and go-slows. These enabled the union to lengthen out the struggle, but they still were bound to have a disruptive effect on the earnings of the strikers in many instances. Hence it was not simply the financial cost to the union as an organisation which counted, but the economic loss to the strikers.

---

[1] cf. R. K. Merton: 'The non-members who actively avoid membership for which they are eligible, are, in the words of Simmel, those to whom "the axiom applies, who is not for me is against me." And, as Simmel has also implied, the eligible individuals who expressly reject membership pose more of a threat to the group in certain respects than the antagonists, who could not in any case become members. Rejection by eligibles symbolises the relative dubiety of its norms and values which are not accepted by those to whom they should in principle apply.' *Social Theory and Social Structure* (Glencoe Free Press, 1957), p. 291. It is thus the social power of the group that is directly affected by its lack of completeness.

An Official Dispute in the Constructional Engineering Industry

It is for reasons such as those we have discussed in the present case that the problems of social control get more acute when a dispute is protracted and solidarity begins, so to speak, to fray at the edges. Coser has observed that:

> Most conflicts end in compromise in which it is often quite hard to specify which side has gained relative advantage. Hence one must distinguish between the will to make peace and the will to accept defeat. Quite often the former may be present although the latter is not. The parties to the conflict may be willing to cease the battle when they recognise that . . . continuation of conflict is less attractive than the making of peace.[1]

This is so, but it does not of course prevent the parties from manoeuvring to obtain what advantages they can. And the willingness to make peace usually involves the search for a salient point around which a compromise can be agreed.

During the early part of February, the Ministry of Labour's industrial relations officers attempted to promote a settlement. For the first time the employers' federation showed some willingness to move. They indicated their willingness to consider an increase for erectors. But they argued that to consider an increase for all other grades was not possible because the C.S.E.U. had an all round wage claim which was currently being negotiated. The offer in this form was rejected but the absolute deadlock between the parties was broken. Towards the end of February, the C.E.U. also made a tactical withdrawal from its position. It withdrew its claim on the less important (in terms of numbers employed) steel plate and water tube sections of the trade and suggested that, so far as the steelwork erection group was concerned, it would be prepared to settle for less than the 3¼d. an hour originally claimed.

The employers decided that to set up differential rates between the three sections of the industry would be a tactical mistake on their part and create further possibilities for wage leap-frogging. The final settlement, for all three sections was agreed on 21 March 1955.[2] An offer of 1¾d. an hour increase for erectors was accepted by the union. At the same time, it was agreed that the system of qualification for the occupation through the employ-

---

[1] Coser, op. cit., p. 231.
[2] *The Times,* 23 March 1955.

ment of improvers would be examined at a later date, with a view to its possible revision.

Both sides managed in varying degrees to 'save face'. The employers had confined the union to 1¾d. an hour instead of the 3¼d. demanded. And they had not conceded at that time the claim of the erectors to a skilled status. The C.E.U. did not return to their members empty-handed and were thus not 'defeated'. Furthermore, these negotiations were concluded only a week after a general increase of 3d. an hour was obtained by the C.S.E.U. It is not unlikely that C.E.U. members would feel that the aggregate increase had been brought about by their own efforts.

CHAPTER FIVE

Industrial Relations in the
North East Iron and Steel
Industry[1]

THE history of industrial relations in the British iron and
steel industry has in large measure been the history of
industrial peace or, more accurately, of regulated conflict.
It has become fashionable to use 'technology' as the important
variable in accounting for the degree of friction in industrial
relations. There is reason, however, for caution when it comes to
applying this approach to the iron and steel industry. The reason
is to be found in Clark Kerr and Abraham Siegel's study, 'The
Interindustry Propensity to Strike – An International Comparison'[2] and it has been singled out for special comment by
Siegel subsequently:

> No generally valid explanation for the pattern of strike activity re-
> vealed in this international comparison (where the steel industries
> ranked 'low' in strike experience in six countries, 'moderate' in three,
> and in the United States would rank between 'moderate' and 'high')
> emerges from this study. There simply does not appear (as there did
> in the case of the coal-mining and long-shoring industries) to be
> any inherent characteristic of the industrial environment in iron and
> steel fabrication which tends to over-ride the effects of differences in
> national industrial relations systems, industrial collective bargaining
> history and machinery, or cultural contexts, and which bids fair to
> predominate in the shaping of employee-employer relations in the
> industry, whatever its industrial location. The basic environment

[1] Some of the material contained in this essay has been previously published
in my paper, 'Plant Bargaining in Steel: North East Case Studies', *Sociological
Review*, Vol. 13, No. 2, July 1965.

[2] In A. Kornhauser, R. Dubin and A. Ross (eds.), *Industrial Conflict*
(McGraw Hill, 1954), pp. 189–212.

involving the relationships of workers, work process, and employers in the production of steel does not *per se* lead toward industrial peace or industrial conflict. In short, the explanations for the historical experience in steel appear to be at best partial and are frequently combined with unique causal factors. Both the partially transferable and the unique factors appear to lie outside the characteristics of the industrial environment imposed by the technology of steel production.[1]

In this chapter I shall indicate some of the factors which have been held to account for the industrial relations climate of the British iron and steel industry and the North East sector of it in particular. I shall then pay particular attention to the post-war experience of industrial conflict in the North East sector of the industry. In discussing the extent to which and the ways in which conflict is contained within the industrial relations system, I will develop the theme that technological influences are more adequately seen as interacting with cultural, economic and organisational factors.

1. *The Social Sources of Industrial Peace*

In 1917, a Commision of Inquiry was evidently impressed with the state of employer-employee relations on the North East Coast. They commented:

> We are satisfied from our inquiries that so far as employers on the North East Coast are concerned, the idea of exploitation is foreign to their minds . . . the employers express their appreciation of the Unions generally and desire to see the efficiency of these Unions maintained in the best interests of industry. If the North East Coast were wholly independent of other fields of industry it might well be left to employers and employed to settle by themselves any differences which might arise . . . On the whole, we formed the opinion that unrest arising from delay in settlement of disputes is less evident in the North East area than it seems to be in other districts . . . The employees collectively do not advance any demands that are extravagant or incapable of being met by friendly co-operation between Employer and Employee.[2]

[1] 'Strikes and Industrial Relations in the Steel Industries of Selected Countries'. This is Appendix B of the U.S. Department of Labor study, *Collective Bargaining in the Basic Steel Industry* (1961). The quotation is from p. 313.

[2] Cmd. 8662 – quoted in K. G. J. C. Knowles, *Strikes* (Blackwell, 1952), p. 192.

And yet the curious thing is, as Knowles has observed, that South Wales historically has had an industrial structure very similar to the North East, but a history of industrial militancy.[1] Why this should be so has never been satisfactorily explained and indeed, Phelps-Brown has argued that since we are dealing with the inter-play of the contingent on the unforeseen, we must treat the difference as an accident of history:

> It did happen – we may suppose it was determined, but we only know it happened – that on the North East Coast men arose on both sides to counsel mutual respect, and reason in negotiation: Sir David Dale, Sir Benjamin Browne, Sir Andrew Noble; John Kane, Thomas Burt, Robert Knight. One man's initiative would be reciprocated by someone on the other side; no economic storm came to break up the arrangement they made between them; a tradition was established, and drew strength from its own success. Human relations build up like that, but in either direction. Started in the wrong direction, not by malevolence necessarily but perhaps by some twist of circumstance, they can generate ever new conflicts out of the bitter memories of past ones. Each friendly act is suspect as a trap, each unfriendly one is vital to self-defence; and all because that is how it was yesterday.[2]

This is a proper reminder of the complexity of the factors involved in the study of industrial relations, or any other social situation for that matter. But it is also by implication a statement which points to the inter-locking nature of those factors. And the picture drawn of human relations building up 'in either direction', is a good illustration of the mechanism which Myrdal has called 'the principle of cumulation'. This concept Myrdal applied notably to the study of race relations in the U.S.A.[3] He noted how White prejudice and low Negro standards of living tended mutually to 'cause' each other. If either of the two factors should change, a process of mutual interaction is set up, which reinforces the direction of the original change and creates a permanent shift in the alignment of forces within the system under study. In empirical studies the scientific ideal for Myrdal would involve not only defining and analysing the factors, 'but

[1] Knowles, loc. cit.
[2] E. H. Phelps-Brown, *The Growth of British Industrial Relations* (Macmillan, 1965), p. 157.
[3] See G. Myrdal, *An American Dilemma* (Harper, 1944).

to give for each one of them a measure of its quantitative strength in influencing the other factors, as well as a measure of ability to be influenced itself by outside forces'.[1] The ramifications of that statement need not be entered into here, but the fact that we inevitably fall short of that ideal in social research, explains why we are reduced at times to talking of historical accidents. At the same time, if the principle of cumulation is used as a guide, even if the connections are only imperfectly perceived, one does avoid the pitfall of looking for and seeking to identify the 'basic factor' in a social situation.[2]

When we turn to the iron and steel industry in the North East, we find that it both contributed to and was influenced by the industrial peace of the region. In 1869, The Board of Arbitration and Conciliation for the Manufactured Iron Trade of the North of England, the first in the industry was set up. This has been discussed in some detail by A. J. Odber in his paper 'The Origins of Industrial Peace: The Manufactured Iron Trade of the North of England'.[3] The first president of this board was Mr. (later Sir) David Dale, a director of the Consett Iron Company. He had been impressed by the effectiveness of the conciliation procedures already operating in the hosiery industry of the East Midlands and pioneered by A. J. Mundella, and advocated similar arrangements to his fellow iron masters in the North East, as a means of avoiding costly strikes. The cautious iron masters were gradually persuaded that this practical advantage, if it could be achieved, outweighed the fact that to adopt an effective system of arbitration meant recognising equality of rights as between the parties.

On the men's side, Dale found a kindred spirit in John Kane, who was President of the Amalgamated Malleable Ironworkers Association, 1862–67, and General Secretary of the National Amalgamated Association of Ironworkers, 1868–76. He had suggested arbitration as a method of solving disputes, several times before the Board was established, but at that time the employers would not accept it. He too, was impressed with

[1] G. Myrdal, *Value in Social Theory* (Routledge and Kegan Paul, 1958), pp. 203–4.

[2] cf. ibid.

[3] A. J. Odber, 'The Origins of Industrial Peace', *Oxford Economic Papers* (New Series), Vol. III, June 1951, pp. 202–20.
See also: Ian G. Sharp, *Industrial Conciliation and Arbitration in Great Britain* (Allen and Unwin, 1950), Chapter III.

Mundella's work on arbitration and conciliation and commented in the *Ironworkers' Journal*:

> The history of the trade disputes at Nottingham and their disastrous end – the loss to the men, to the manufacturers and the public generally has happily been brought to an end by the appointment of an independent Board of Arbitration. Surely, if it is possible for the hosiery trade of Nottingham to settle their disputes, where they have 6,000 different articles tabulated and requiring separate consideration, it would be an easy matter for the ironworkers and their employers to settle their disputes.[1]

The composition of the Board eventually consisted of one employers' representative and one operatives' representative from each of the member works. The operatives, who were elected annually to the Board by their fellows at the individual works, were not elected as trade unionists, but simply as operatives. But in practice the operatives were trade unionists and their side of the Board was dominated by the Ironworkers' Union (led first by Kane and after his death in 1876, by Trow). The Board elected annually its own President (an employer), Vice-President (an operative), two Secretaries (one employer, one operative), two Auditors and two Treasurers. Further, the Board appointed a Standing Committee – President, Vice-President and five members from each side. The function of the Board was to discuss general questions arising from changes in trade conditions, whereas the function of the Standing Committee was to discuss disputes which had arisen in particular works. When a deadlock was reached on the Board, provision was made for an independent arbitrator to be called in whose decision was final and binding.

Writing at the end of the nineteenth century, the Webbs describe the Board as 'the classical example of the success of arbitration'.[2] Resort had been made to arbitration on twenty occasions in the first twenty-eight years of the Board's life 'with regard to the settlement of future wage contracts; and on every occasion the arbitrator's award has been accepted by both employers and employed'.[3] The more detailed account of Arthur Pugh on the early history of the Board makes clear that this

---

[1] Quoted in Arthur Pugh, *Men of Steel* (I.S.T.C., 1951), pp. 34–5.
[2] S. and B. Webb, *Industrial Democracy* (Longmans, 1897), p. 231.
[3] Ibid., p. 232.

is something of an over-statement.[1] There were occasions when employers did not immediately implement the terms of an award, and other occasions when men struck when an award went against them. But the overall success of the system in terms of industrial peace was undoubted and gradually similar procedures were adopted by the industry in other parts of the country.

The Webbs were concerned to point out that arbitration procedures could not automatically be regarded as the antidote to strike activity. The effectiveness of arbitration depended on workmen and employers sharing common economic assumptions about how wages should be fixed and regulated. And it was precisely this common ground that existed in the North East iron trade, and, to a lesser extent, in the Northumberland and Durham mining establishments. In both cases the agreement was expressed in the form of a sliding scale relating wages to the selling price of the product. Given this degree of consensus between masters and men the Webbs observe:

> It will be apparent that arbitration on issues of this kind comes really within the category of the interpretation or application of what is, in effect, an agreement already arrived at by the parties. The question comes very near to being one of fact, answered as soon as the necessary figures are ascertained beyond dispute.[2]

The emergence of this institutionalised form of accommodation between masters and men may be seen as a mixture of 'interest' and 'value' considerations. Both sides could and did calculate that the arrangements were to their advantage. Industrial peace for the employers meant that they did not have to dissipate their energies and resources fighting strikes and, more positively, they were well placed to secure contracts during boom periods without the fear of labour disturbances. And the wage element in their costs was now a factor under their control. For the men the matter was well expressed by John Kane:

> For the first time in the history of the iron trade a basis has been laid down by which the wages shall rise and fall in accordance with the changes in the selling price in the market, and it must not be forgotten that the men have got more frequent and better advances than they have ever got at any former time by strikes. With arbitra-

[1] Pugh, op. cit., Chapters IV and V.
[2] S. and B. Webb, op. cit., p. 233.

tion and conciliation wages have been gradually advanced without a single child having to suffer the loss of food.[1]

The value considerations, to which I have alluded, are derived from certain relevant religious orientations. Dale himself was a Quaker and, as Odber noted, was interested in industrial peace for its own sake.[2] Without the practical application of his doctrine he may not have got very far with the employers. But it will be recalled that Darlington at this time was a flourishing centre for the Society of Friends and Dale was by no means the only employer attached to it. No doubt it provided a 'resonance effect' to much of Dale's industrial thinking, so that it would be misleading to think of him as a voice in the wilderness. In any case, the voice of the Quaker was the voice of conscience, but it was also the voice of successful business and therefore could claim the ear of the business world.[3]

The other nonconformist religious influence of significance here was Methodism. The part played by Methodists and particularly Primitive Methodists in providing active trade union leadership in the mining industry in the North East has been well documented.[4] Men, as a result of the theological stress given to the role of the laity in church affairs, became articulate as local preachers and familiar with administrative matters through the organisation of societies and circuits, and then applied their knowledge to the development of trade union organisation. But, while they were radicals, insofar as they actively sought to improve the working conditions of their fellows, they were not typically revolutionaries.[5] They were concerned that the owners

[1] Quoted in Pugh, op. cit., p. 46.

[2] Odber, op. cit., p. 207.

[3] Note also that the early iron masters were typically Puritan in religion. See T. S. Ashton, *Iron and Steel in the Industrial Revolution* (Longmans, 1924). Hence R. H. Tawney notes: 'It was not that religion was expelled from practical life, but that religion itself gave it a foundation of granite ... The good Christian was not wholly dissimilar from the economic man'. In such a context business enterprise became 'the appropriate field for Christian endeavour'. *Religion and the Rise of Capitalism* (Penguin, 1938), pp. 251 and 270.

[4] See particularly, R. F. Wearmouth, *Methodism and the Working-Class Movements of England*, 1800–1850, (Epworth, 1937); and John Wilson, *History of the Durham Miners' Association* (1907).

[5] The part played by Methodists in the country at large is, of course, a more complex question. On this the main texts to be consulted are: E. Halevy, *History of the English People in the Nineteenth Century* (Penguin, 1924);

of mines should be 'good' owners and not tyrants and oppressors.
The ownership of the means of production was not typically a
matter for questioning, rather was the attempt made to mitigate
the evils of the existing order by establishing the legitimacy of
labour to bargain over terms and conditions of employment.
Once the existing order was reformed in this way, compliance
with it was justified. Thus the Durham Miners' Federation
Executive Committee could comment in 1899:

> We have previously expressed the opinion that the steadier we can
> make our trade, and the more certainty we can infuse into our
> industrial relationship with our employers, the better it will be for
> the workmen; and there is nothing more calculated to foster this
> desirable condition than the principle of conciliation.[1]

The Methodist influence although not so clear-cut as in the
case of mining, can certainly not be discounted when we turn to
the iron and steel industry. John Kane himself came from a
Methodist background. James Cox, the third General Secretary
of the Ironworkers Union, was a Wesleyan Methodist from
Darlington. Arthur Pugh, commenting on this maintains:

> There was nothing unusual in the fact of the general secretary of
> the Ironworkers' Union being an active member of the Wesleyan
> Church. At least the majority of the men who became trade union
> leaders in both the iron and coal trades in the latter half of the
> nineteenth century in the English counties, were fervent Methodists,
> as were large numbers of the rank and file.[2]

One is not surprised to see embodied in the branch bye-laws
prohibitions against smoking, cursing, swearing and taking the
name of God in vain.

Social justice then, was seen as abiding by the rules of the
conciliation system. Since some employers were also professing
Christians, inconsistencies between their profession and their
industrial behaviour might be noted by the union leaders, in an
attempt to shame then and bring them into conformity. The

[1] Quoted in Wilson, op. cit., p. 295.
[2] Pugh, op. cit., p. 361.

E. J. Hobsbawm, Methodism and the Threat of Revolution in Britain, in
Labouring Men, studies in the history of labour (Weidenfeld and Nicolson, 1964);
E. P. Thompson, *The Making of the English Working Class* (Gollancz, 1965).

following comment is instructive in this respect, relating to a Darlington firm which had refused to pay a wage advance under the terms of a recent arbitration award in 1871:

> We should like to know by what right this Albert Hill Co., tramples on the rules of our board and the laws of our country, making reductions on whom and where they please and refusing the just advance to sections of the men who are expected to have no-one to look after them and no-one to protect them from this grasping system of avarice . . . There are other cases to which we could refer of gross injustice which is a scandal to the firm and disgraceful to the manager, who is an actor once a week in the Primitive Methodist pulpit. Such teachers are a living scandal on the character of Christianity; they give to Christ their profession and follow the example of Judas and Barrabas.[1]

The belief in the fairness and the utility of the conciliation and arbitration system on the part of the men's leaders meant that they were prepared not only to speak up against employers who did not honour agreements, but also to discipline their own membership if the need arose. Clearly, the stronger the union was as an organisation, the better position it was in to apply sanctions against any workers who did not abide by agreements reached between masters and men. Dale had recognised that a strong union organisation was an essential prerequisite to the effective working of the Board. Once this conviction came to be shared by other employers, this served to strengthen the union's own position. Essentially, a form of countervailing power was built into the industrial relations system. The point to stress here, however, is that many employers were still not enamoured with trade unions as such. They resisted the idea that trade unions as interest groups should each be represented on the Board. Since, as we have seen, the men's side of the Board was dominated by the Ironworkers' Union, countervailing power was vested in them. This did not necessarily mean that they ignored the needs of operatives who were not in their union, but it did emphasise their dominant position vis-à-vis other unions.[2]

Trade union power was consolidated and rationalised in the iron and steel industry in 1917 with the creation through

[1] Ibid., p. 47.
[2] See Odber, op. cit., pp. 219–20. The point is also made that contract labour was not represented on the Board, nor could it voice grievances to it.

amalgamation of various unions of the British Iron Steel and Kindred Trades Association.[1] Any understanding of industrial relations in the iron and steel industry, must recognise the dominating influence which this industrial union has traditionally had. It has been the pace-setter in terms of wage negotiations and other unions – the general and craft unions whose interests are not geared exclusively to the industry – have been treated by the employers in the perspective of these negotiations.

2. *Contemporary Dispute Settlement Procedures on the North East Coast*

I refer in this section to the arrangements for the settlement of disputes that have existed or emerged in the post-war period in the industry so far as they affect the North East Coast. The employers in this region form a Division of the national Iron and Steel Trades Employers' Association. The employment figures for the years 1949–61 are given in Table XV. It might be added that during this period the North East sector has accounted for 10–15% of the total employed in the British iron and steel industry.[2]

In discussing the bargaining groups with which the employers have to deal, it is useful to bear in mind a basic distinction between process, maintenance and ancillary workers.

The major union responsible for the organisation of process workers is B.I.S.A.K.T.A.[3] The branches of this union are plant based. Within any plant one will find a number of branches co-existing. A branch may cover a particular occupation spread across a plant (e.g. a crane drivers' branch) or a group of occupations in a specific location (e.g. a melting shop branch). Individual branches are autonomous in the sense that they have the right to negotiate as bargaining units with management. Matters concerning manning, rates, work rules and conditions may be raised in this way. They may arise from the grievance of a particuar branch member, or they may be issues which affect the branch

---

[1] Technical details of this amalgamation are to be found in Pugh, op. cit., and in B. C. Roberts, *Trade Union Government and Administration* (Bell, 1956).

[2] See *The Northern Region* (North East Industrial and Development Association, 1961).

[3] Known alternatively as the Iron and Steel Trades Confederation.

TABLE XV

IRON AND STEEL INDUSTRY – NORTH EAST COAST AREA

Employment at the first week in October for the years 1949–61

| Year | NUMBER AT WORK* | | | | Total Number on Payroll |
	Process Workers	General and Maintenance Workers	Admin. Technical and Clerical	Total at Work	
1949	23,640	14,450	2,110†	40,200	42,150
1950	23,410	14,530	3,520	41,460	43,650
1951	22,910	14,480	3,840	41,230	43,040
1952	23,380	14,540	3,910	41,830	43,940
1953	23,710	14,500	4,030	42,240	44,200
1954 (a)	22,460	14,410	3,950	40,820	42,750
1955	22,470	14,060	4,050	40,580	42,770
1956	22,350	13,670	4,100	40,120	42,700
1957 (b)	21,510	14,160	4,190	39,860	43,620
1958	19,480	14,750	4,370	38,600	40,860
1959	19,770	14,690	4,420	38,880	41,030
1960	21,650	16,040	4,930	42,620	45,020
1961	20,690	15,630	5,030	41,350	43,780

(a) Prior to 1954 the figures include General and Maintenance and Administrative, Technical and Clerical workers associated with Drop Forgings, Wire and Wire Manufacturers employed by companies also engaged in other Iron and Steel Processes.

(b) From 1957 onwards excludes Labour employed in the Production of Welded Tubes over 16″ o.d.

* Two part-time female workers taken as being equal to one unit. The number at work excludes absentees owing to sickness, holidays and other causes.

† Clerical workers only.

Source: British Iron and Steel Federation.

collectively. In addition, if an issue arises which is felt to affect all the branches, it is possible, within the terms of the union constitution, to arrange meetings of the joint branches in a firm.

In the event of a branch being unable to resolve a dispute,

The branch secretary shall. without delay report the whole facts of
the dispute to the divisional officer of the division in which the
branch is situated, and the divisional officer shall arrange for an
official of the Association to interview the employer or his representative and the representatives of the members concerned for the
purpose of effecting an amicable settlement. Failing a settlement by
this means, the divisional officer shall send a full report of the dispute
to the Central Office so that the matter may be placed before the
Executive Council, which shall decide what further action is to be
taken . . .[1]

The authority to call or terminate strikes at any stage resides
exclusively with the Executive Council.

The usual procedure, if an issue is not resolved at plant level,
is for it to be taken to a Neutral Committee. This committee
consists of two employers' representatives and two workers'
representatives. Their neutrality stems from the fact that they do
not belong to the firm where the dispute has arisen, although they
must be members of a firm which is in the relevant employers'
association. It is also essentially a lay committee in the sense that
none of the members are paid full-time officials of the employers'
association or the union. The committee listens to the evidence
of the disputants, calls any relevant witnesses and, if agreement
is reached, the decision is accepted by employer and union as a
settlement of the dispute. If no agreement is reached, the matter
may be discussed at national level at a joint conference between
the union and the employers' association. Provision is made at
this stage for the matter to be referred to arbitration if necessary.
Although one commonly thinks of the union as initiating proceedings, it is open to an employer to do so if he wishes and this,
as we shall see, does in fact happen. The only other point to note
is that sometimes, instead of a neutral committee, an Ad Hoc
Committee is convened. These appear to relate to issues arising
from the disciplining of individual workpeople, whereas neutral
committees tend to be concerned with issues which affect groups
of workers.

B.I.S.A.K.T.A. in the North East is responsible for organising
workers in the process side of the steel industry. The National
Union of Blastfurnacemen has a parallel responsibility for workers
in the iron section of the industry. Numerically they are much

[1] *Rules of B.I.S.A.K.T.A.* (1957), Rule 19.

smaller of course. But, apart from the fact that fewer branches exist in any one firm, the procedural arrangements are very similar to those operating in the case of B.I.S.A.K.T.A. and do not merit separate discussion.

When one turns to the craft workers, who are responsible for the maintenance and repair of plant and machinery in the industry, one finds separate arrangements for the settlement of disputes. In particular, mention should be made of the co-ordinated form of disputes settlement operating at Works, District and National levels in the industry and covering the following unions: A.E.U., E.T.U., Boilermakers, Patternmakers, A.S.W., Associated Blacksmiths, Forge and Smithy Workers Society, Amalgamated Union of Foundry Workers, Plumbers, Heating and Domestic Engineers, and the National Society of Painters. The National Craftsmen Co-ordinating Committee has been in existence since 1949, but an Allied Crafts Committee had been operating in the North East for some years before that. Although formal negotiating procedures are much more recent than on the production side, the influence of the practices which have evolved among process workers is evident in the arrangements that have been agreed upon. If management and union representatives cannot settle a dispute, officials of the Unions concerned and of the Employers Association may be called in. Failing settlement at this stage, a Joint Sub-Committee may be convened. This consists of two employers' representatives and two craftsmen's representatives, if one union is involved and four from each side if more than one union is a party to the dispute. They are joined by the Joint Secretaries (one employer, one trade union) of the District Joint Committee. As with the Neutral Committee procedure members of the Joint Sub-Committee may not be drawn from the firm where the dispute has arisen. A further similarity is that, where agreement is reached it is regarded as binding by the parties to the dispute. If the matter is not disposed of in this way, it goes before the Joint Committee for the District, which consists of an equal number of employers and union representatives. It is also the function of the Joint Committee to deal with disputes that concern more than one works. If the Joint Committee fail to agree on a question arising they may call in the services of a neutral conciliator. Failing agreement at this stage the District Joint Committee can choose either to refer the question to the

National Joint Committee, or agree to submit it to arbitration. Arbitration is regarded as final and binding on both sides. The National Joint Committee, if it fails to settle a dispute, may also refer the question to arbitration.

One craft union in the iron and steel industry not represented in these co-ordinated arrangements is the Amalgamated Union of Building Trade Workers. This union negotiates separately and has its own Joint Boards with the employers for the settlement of disputes, which are similar to those of the process workers. Another small craft union, the British Roll Turners' Trade Society, also negotiates separately with the Employers' Association.

Finally, we may notice that the two general unions, the T.G.W.U. and the N.U.G.M.W. have some workers employed in the industry. The latter does have a formal joint board with the employers to deal with disputes that go outside the firm.[1] In the case of the T.G.W.U., that union is divided into trade groups at regional and national level. The iron and steel industry is part of a composite trade group – engineering, railway shops, shipbuilding and repairing, and metal trades. The North East part of the industry is contained within the wider Northern region of the T.G.W.U. organisation. It will be seen then that, unlike the other unions discussed here, no procedural agreements exist that apply exclusively to the iron and steel industry. But shop stewards may call upon the services of their regional officers as and when the need arises.

We may conclude this short survey of dispute settlement procedures in the industry, by noting the general characteristics: a three-tiered division between works, district and national levels of settlement; the provision of neutral committees or their equivalent; the opportunities for arbitration. There is also agreement between employers and unions not to operate the procedures under duress. During negotiations strikes, lock-outs or other forms of interfering with 'normal work practices' by either side, are ruled out by mutual agreement. This is not to say that conflict of this sort does not occur, only that it is not formally permitted.

[1] The written agreement of 1925 covering both local and general matters between the N.U.G.M.W. and the I.S.T.E.A. is quoted in Sharp, op. cit., pp. 87–9.

3. The System at Work: Plant Bargaining

In order to examine the system at grass roots level I will do two
things. First, I give the results of a content analysis of a hundred
meetings between management and men in one steel plant.[1] These
were all the formally recorded meetings that took place in a six
month period, October 1962 – March 1963, and the analysis is
based upon documents which were verbatim reports of what took
place. The plant itself remains anonymous. Secondly, I shall bring
forward a number of case studies to illustrate, as I believe, some
of the salient features of the plant bargaining process.

The dimensions of the content analysis are summarised in
Tables XVIA, XVIB and XVIC. In Table XVIA I have first of
all distinguished between the groups engaged in discussions with
management. In all cases, except four, management met union
representatives. It is worth noting, however, that the system
evidently permitted individual groups of workers to discuss
grievances with management, if they wanted to. Thus frustrations
that could arise when a particular group of workers were not
being adequately represented by their union branch could be
minimised by allowing them to make use of the grievance
machinery, without seriously undermining the dominating
position of the unions as bargaining units.

The number of meetings with which the main bargaining
groups were involved must be seen in relation to the percentage
of the labour force which they represented. In the case of
B.I.S.A.K.T.A. it was 68%, in the case of the Allied Crafts 18%
and in the case of the A.U.B.T.W. 5%, so that (if one adds to the
Allied Crafts the issues raised by individual craft unions) the
number of meetings attended is very closely proportionate to the
size of the group memberships represented.

The calling in of the District Officer of the trade union may
be taken as an index of the severity of the issue. It usually implies
that previous meetings without him have failed to dispose of an
issue, although occasionally he is present on the first occasion a
matter is formally discussed. The tendency of union officials to be
present is expressed in ratio form in column (d). One may observe

[1] This does not include iron, hence the N.U.B. is excluded from this
analysis. But see Chapter 6 Redundancy Conflict in an Isolated Steel Community, in which the role of the N.U.B. is fully discussed.

TABLE XVIA

PLANT BARGAINING: A CONTENT ANALYSIS OF 100 MEETINGS

A. Groups participating

(a) Unions or groups involved	(b) No. of meetings attended	(c) No. of times District Official present	(d) Ratio (b) ÷ (c)	(e) Elements in discussion: No. of times present							
				Wages	Hours	Demarcation	Redundancy	Manning	Industrial Discipline	Other Work Arrangements	T.U. Issues
1. B.I.S.A.K.T.A.	70	15	4·7	46	3	1	4	24	4	24	3
2. A.E.U.	11	2	5·5	1	0	5	1	5	0	2	0
3. E.T.U.	1	0	∞	0	0	0	0	1	0	0	0
4. Allied Crafts	6	2	3·0	3	3	0	0	1	0	2	0
5. Total Crafts (1, 2, 3 and 4)	18	4	4·5	5	3	5	1	7	0	4	0
6. A.U.B.T.W.	8	3	2·7	4	3	0	1	2	1	1	0
7. Individual Work groups	4	0	0	3	0	0	0	1	0	2	0
Total	100	26	3·8	57	9	6	6	34	5	31	3

N.B. 1. B.I.S.A.K.T.A. represented some 68% of the labour force.
2. Allied Crafts represented some 18% of the labour force.
3. A.U.B.T.W. represented some 5% of the labour force.

a close similarity in this tendency as between B.I.S.A.K.T.A. and the total for the craft groups (excluding the A.U.B.T.W.). The A.U.B.T.W. which, as we have seen, operates under a separate negotiating procedure from the other craft unions, was more prone to have a District Official present. One must recognise that different unions may have different policies so far as calling in union officials is concerned, but given the general reluctance to call them in, this does suggest that the system of plant bargaining was under some strain at this point. I comment further on this below.

For the purpose of further analysis, I have distinguished eight elements, any one or more of which might make up the content of a particular meeting. The classification is derived from one used by the Ministry of Labour in its analysis of strikes. The categories are, in the main, self explanatory, but it should perhaps be noted that 'Other Work Arrangements' refers to problems arising from work load, organisation or conditions not wholly covered by any other element. And 'Trade Union issues' refers to matters affecting the status or perceived rights of a union (apart from a straight demarcation issue, which is treated separately). It is clear that in this kind of analysis we can only deal with the manifest elements in a discussion. The question of cause in any formal sense must lie in abeyance, since we cannot account for any underlying latent elements, which may have played a part in promoting the discussion in the first place. But, the manifest elements cannot in any case be discounted and by recognising that more than one element may be present in a discussion, we have not been obliged to 'fit' any meeting into a single category.

In quantitative terms the three most important elements making up the bargaining discussion, during this period, were Wages, Manning and Other Work Arrangements, in that order. However, when the craft unions are taken as a distinct group, the emphasis is slightly different: Manning first and Wages and Demarcation in second place equally. The Demarcation element stems from the meetings held with the A.E.U. There is also a slightly different emphasis of elements in the case of the A.U.B.T.W., where Wages, Hours and Manning are the three elements most frequently discussed.

In Table XVIB, I have indicated how far one element provided the topic of discussion at a meeting and how far it was combined

PLANT BARGAINING: A CONTENT ANALYSIS OF 100 MEETINGS

B. Elements under discussion: their frequency and mutual combination

Element	Number of times raised as 'single' element (e.g. 'Box 1') or with other								Total
	Wages	Hours	Demarcation	Redundancy	Manning	Industrial Discipline	Other Work Arrangements	T.U. Issues	
1. Wages	24	3	—	—	16	—	20	—	57
2. Hours	3	4	—	1	2	—	—	—	9
3. Demarcation	—	—	4	—	2	—	—	—	6
4. Redundancy	—	1	—	2	1	—	—	2	6
5. Manning	16	2	2	1	9	—	9	1	34
6. Industrial Discipline	—	—	—	—	—	5	—	—	5
7. Other Work Arrangements	20	—	—	—	9	—	7	—	31
8. T.U. Issues	—	—	—	2	1	—	—	—	3

N.B. It should not be assumed that in any one meeting only 2 elements at most were involved. In some cases we noted issues involving a cluster of three elements. These were: 'Wages, Manning, Other Work Arrangements' – 5 times: and 'Wages, Hours, Manning' – once.

with any other element. This helps one to see the extent to which particular elements were associated with each other. Again the main quantitative conclusions may be readily seen. Wages questions were very often self-contained, but where this was not so, they tended to be linked with Manning and/or Other Work Arrangements. This association of elements was clearly, in numerical terms, the dominant theme of plant bargaining during this period. It is also interesting to see, however, the variety of elements with which the Manning category was linked. This perhaps is a reflection of the fact that matters of custom and practice in the work place, when they are called into question or challenged, directly or indirectly impinge upon established Manning arrangements. By contrast one can see that the element Industrial Discipline is self-contained. If in fact one ranks the elements according to the degree of diffusion they have with other elements the picture is as follows:

Manning with five other elements. Wages, Hours and Redundancy with three other elements. Other Work Arrangements and T.U. issues with two other elements. Demarcation with one other element.

This kind of approach does then enable one to see the 'cluster' of elements, which are actually found in bargaining situations: the frequency and range of combinations. Given adequate empirical data to work on, the possibility of intra-industry and inter-industry comparisons looks inviting.

In Table XVIC, I have taken the analysis a step further. There I have shown, not only the frequency with which Trade Union officials were called in, but the extent to which they were called in when particular combinations of elements were under discussion. One important general point which emerges is that while, as we have seen, Wages, Manning and Work Arrangements elements were most frequently under discussion, it was when Trade Union issues, Demarcation and Industrial Discipline matters came up that the trade union official was most likely to be present. It may therefore be suggested that it is not simply the *number* of issues but the *kind* of issues which determines whether the industrial relations system is under pressure – and by this approach one is able to give more sharpness to that kind of statement. Indeed, having located these areas of conflict, the case

TABLE XVIC

PLANT BARGAINING: A CONTENT ANALYSIS OF 100 MEETINGS

C. The Presence of Trade Union Officials in Relation to Elements under Discussion
(expressed as percentage of relevant figures in Table XVIIB)

Element	Wages		Hours		Demarcation		Redundancy		Manning		Industrial Discipline		Other Work Arrangements		T.U. Issues		Total	
	No.	%	No.	%	No.	%	No.	%	No.	%	No.	%	No.	%	No.	%	No.	%
1. Wages	9	37·5	0	0·0	—	—	—	—	2	12·5	—	—	3	15·0	—	—	13	22·8
2. Hours	0	0·0	0	0·0	—	—	0	0·0	1	50·0	—	—	—	—	—	—	1	10·0
3. Demarcation	—	—	—	—	1	25·0	—	—	2	100·0	—	—	—	—	—	—	3	50·0
4. Redundancy	—	—	0	0·0	—	—	0	0·0	0	0·0	—	—	—	—	1	50·0	1	16·7
5. Manning	2	12·5	1	50·0	2	100·0	0	0·0	0	0·0	—	—	1	11·1	1	100·0	6	17·6
6. Industrial Discipline	—	—	—	—	—	—	—	—	—	—	2	40·0	—	—	—	—	2	40·0
8. Other Work Arrangements	3	15·0	—	—	—	—	—	—	1	11·1	—	—	1	14·3	—	—	4	12·7
8. T.U. Issues	—	—	—	—	—	—	1	50·0	1	100·0	—	—	—	—	—	—	2	66·7

N.B. Totals for elements 1, 5 and 7 take account of the fact that more than two elements might be combined to make an issue. Double-counting is therefore avoided.

studies which we present below, may be seen in that perspective. They are not chosen arbitrarily. They will serve to bring out the ingredients of conflict which the presentation of statistics alone cannot do. In order to make them more intelligible, however, one or two general observations on the steel industry in the North East must be made.

The North East sector of the industry has shared in the technical advances and modernisation schemes that have characterised the industry over the past decade or so. The new integrated steel plants at Dorman Long Lackenby and South Durham and the establishment of a new Plate Mill and L–D and Kaldo furnaces[1] at the Consett Iron Company, are among the most notable cases in point. Sociologically, the potential effect of technical change is to challenge established patterns of behaviour which have traditionally been regarded as appropriate. In the industrial setting these behaviour patterns have been hallowed with the phrase 'custom and practice'. To disturb custom and practice by innovation is to disturb the authority structure and the nature of role expectations. This is perhaps particularly true in the steel industry, where the social organisation of the work force has been relatively fixed. On the production side, a number of promotion ladders are established within particular departments. Once on a ladder, a man cannot transfer to another ladder without starting at the bottom. Well developed job hierarchies with seniority of service as the regulating principle of mobility have meant traditionally that age, prestige-giving occupations, status and pay have been closely correlated. The plant bargaining pro-

[1] A glossary of technical terms used in the iron and steel industry is to be found in the Iron and Steel Board Special Report, *Development in the Iron and Steel Industry* (H.M.S.O., 1964). In Appendix VII, the following definitions of L–D and Kaldo processes are given:

L–D. 'Oxygen is blown at high velocity on to the surface of molten iron in a converter held stationary in a vertical position during the blow. The initials originally stood for "Linzer Dusenverfahren" (Linz jet process) but are now more commonly interpreted as Linz Donawitz, which are the names of two places in Austria where it was first developed. The original L–D process could use only low phosphorous ore.'

Kaldo. 'This steelmaking technique uses a cylindrical vessel rotating on an inclined axis (rather like a cement mixer) in which oxygen is blown against the surface of the molten iron. It takes its name from the initials of Prof. K. A. Lling, who developed the process, and of the Domnarfvet works in Sweden where the work was carried out.' p. 168.

cess, as we shall see, reflected some of the stresses and strains that occur when these features move out of alignment.[1]

While the North East has shared in the technical advances of the industry, it has also shared in the general recession which beset the trade from late 1958 to well into 1963. The scrapping of old plant and equipment sooner than would have been the case in a sellers' market was one of the ways in which the industry tried to curb an embarassing amount of surplus capacity. One result of this was redundancy of labour. This was made more acute in the North East because the other traditional heavy industries on which the region is still greatly dependent, were suffering in the same recession and were in no position to absorb redundant labour from steel.[2] Another result was that changes in market conditions constrained the industry to look outside the home market and compete more actively in the world arena. There was a corresponding development of cost consciousness and stress on efficiency among management.

The plant whose bargaining processes we are here considering, serves as a representative example of the impact of technical change and recession on work arrangements and organisation.[3] Indeed, the predominance of Wages and Manning issues and the tendency for them to be linked together may be traced to the extensive technical changes and developments in the plant. For example, the laying down of new mills necessitated negotiations with the union branches involved. Here, as is usual in the industry, management had the established prerogative to decide on the initial manning arrangements, but from then on the seniority system of promotion operates for production workers. On the wages side in this situation, one must distinguish between initial rates, interim rates and final rates. In the early weeks on new plant the men are paid on a time rate, which is usually based on

[1] Cf. George Homans, 'Status Congruence', in *Sentiments and Activities* (Routledge and Kegan Paul, 1962).

[2] See, for example, J. E. T. Eldridge and A. J. Odber, 'When Shipyards Close', *New Society*, 18 January 1962.

[3] Representative, that is for the region during this period. But cf. *Steel Workers and Technical Progress: A Comparative Report of six national studies* (O.E.C.D., 1959) where the point is made that: 'The period of change was, in almost every case, during the first half of the 1950s and in consequence a time when there was no serious fear of unemployment for the workers concerned.' p. 16.

the average earnings of their previous job with the firm. This is partly done to ease the worker's transition from one job to another – since faced with the problem of adaptation to a new job, he may not be able to make an adequate wage, if his wages are related straight away to production. Or for that matter there may be factors outside his control, which impede production during the early commissioning of the mill. But this kind of wage arrangement may also be sensible at the very early stage since it is sometimes necessary for a new union branch to be formed before effective wage negotiations can be started.

The union branches then negotiate an interim rate for the individual jobs. This is composed of a base rate, a bonus related to tonnage output and a cost of living adjustment.[1] It is the proportion of bonus allocated to individual jobs that is the critical variable in determining the total wage. The higher up the promotion ladder a job is, the greater amount of bonus in relation to base rate that is permitted. Interim rates are established because it is realised on both sides that any new mill presents problems of adjustment to the men manning it and that there will be teething problems of a technical nature. In practice this means something like eighteen months, two years, or even longer, before rates are finalised. Once this happens the matter is virtually closed unless there is a major change of practice. The problem is one of getting an adequate wage structure, such that differentials between jobs supply sufficient incentive for workers to go up the promotion ladder (and not choose to 'stick' half-way up) and of getting an appropriate wage level. It is technical change which creates these problems, but it is recession that intensifies the difficulties inherent in the task of wage negotiations.

If a mill is opened in time of recession, nobody really knows what its full capacity is. Because the issue is so crucial to the whole pattern of wages in the mill over an extended period, the union is reluctant to accept management's forecasts on the subject, no matter how well-intentioned they may be. Both sides are liable to

---

[1] The selling price sliding scale which characterised the iron and steel industry for such an extended period was 'suspended' in 1940 during the Second World War, when increasing government control and a rising cost of living made it unrealistic. The melters' sliding scale was stabilised at a stated percentage and, at the same time, the cost of living adjustment was made. See Sharp, op. cit., p. 97.

be somewhat jaundiced in their approach to the whole question. During the recession, not only will total output be low, but the manner in which the output is produced is not likely to inspire confidence on the union side of management's forecasts. This is because the orders, when they do come, are usually smaller. This necessitates frequent roll changes which aggravates any teething troubles which the mill may be experiencing. Management, for their part, will be very much concerned at such a time with costs and are not, therefore, likely to be over-generous in their offers. This is even true for an industry like steel that is not labour intensive. In times of acute competition attempts are made to minimise costs wherever the firm has some control over them.[1]

Let us turn now to some specific case studies.

CASE I   A QUESTION OF INDUSTRIAL DISCIPLINE

In an industry as highly capital intensive as steel, the concern of management with the equipment and product is understandable. This concern can be and is translated into punitive measures against members of the work force who are deemed to have endangered either. For small matters, a fine will be deducted from a man's wages. More serious errors will lead to suspension or dismissal. The case discussed here concerns the suspension of a first hand melter for alleged negligence in the performance of his job. A first hand is in charge of a particular furnace and is directly responsible to the sample passer who has oversight for a number of furnaces. The status of the first hand has traditionally been very high in the steel plant. Management imposed three days' suspension on the man because, it was said, he had allowed an exceptionally high temperature on his furnace. This had caused considerable delay in the working of the furnace and was likely to have damaged the vessel. The union branch, however, protested to management, both on the grounds of the severity of the punishment and because it had been implemented before the branch had had time to discuss the matter with the management, as commonly occurred.

The management claimed that, had an immersion temperature been taken at the right time, the situation would not have arisen,

---

[1] See Allan Flanders, *The Fawley Productivity Agreements* (Faber and Faber, 1964) where the same point is made in the context of the oil industry, p. 67.

therefore the first hand must be held responsible. The union countered by pointing out that the only way an immersion temperature could have been taken at the required time was by taking an oxygen probe out of the furnace. This was because, while the oxygen was on, a visual check was not possible owing to the presence of brown fumes in the furnace. But the action of taking the probe out of the furnace at such stage *had never been done before*. Furthermore, they indicated that the check on oil fuel supply revealed nothing unusual and, in the absence of facilities for measuring furnace roof temperature on that particular furnace, the first hand had done all that could reasonably be expected of him.

Labour relations disturbances among melters as a group are very rare. It is all the more noteworthy that the melters in this case were prepared to withhold their labour for a shift against what they regarded as an unjust punishment. In the event the strike did not transpire, when the first hand's suspension was reduced to two days. But the strong reaction of the melters to the suspension was, perhaps, not wholly explained by a sense of injustice. The high status accorded to the melter and the authority stemming from this is based essentially on technical competence. There is indeed a considerable mystique surrounding the job of the first hand, which seems, mainly, to be based on the visual skills, that were of paramount importance in the pre-instrumentation days. Yet it was precisely the technical competence of the man that was called in question. It is not so surprising, therefore, that the defence which the union representatives employed was not just a plea for mercy (as, for example, it would have been for persistent lateness or absenteeism) but was based on technical considerations. It is but a short step to enquire how a man who is technically incompetent obtained the job. The established pattern of promotion by seniority is thereby jeopardised. Inasmuch as this principle of promotion was effectively operated by the union, the control of the union over an important area of the work situation was menaced. Further, this particular first hand was the most senior in the shop. The principle of automatically promoting senior first hands to the post of sample passer (which custom was a management not a union prerogative) could, by the same token, be called into question. The need to buttress the authority of the first hand and hence preserve the aspirations of the work group was perhaps all the more necessary at this time. The growing use of young men as shift managers provided an alternative focal point from which authoritative decision could be taken. The professional qualifications of these men implied superior theoretical knowledge of steel-making and the duties they were called on to undertake could over-ride the decisions of the first hand. Union strategy demanded that the melter's account-ability for matters within his control be upheld, in order to justify his place in the authority structure. Hence the technical considera-tions brought forward in his defence were an attempt to demonstrate that the particular incident was outside his control. What was also implicit in the union's defence was that manage-ment sanctions, which were used to penalise the melter who made a mistake on the job, were not balanced by a concern that such mistakes be minimised by appropriate training arrangements. Whatever the merits of the allegation, the point to be noticed is that only in the period of worker adaptation to technical change, can it be sensibly made at all. In this sense, therefore, the case may be said to be induced by technical change. Technical change, however, must be seen as a necessary rather than a sufficient cause of such conflict, since such changes may be handled in different ways by different managements; both in terms of the way in which labour is trained for new jobs and the way in which sanctions are operated when mistakes are made. In this plant it did appear that errors of judgment by workers, which affect out-put and damage plant, were the most likely to be punished severely.[1] A similar case on the mills side of the plant occurred when a Cogging Mill Manipulator Driver was suspended for stopping the mill for six hours by jamming the rolls. The union protested that it was unfair since this was the man's first error. Management withdrew the suspension by what they regarded as an act of grace rather than in terms of the merit of the case. But at the same time, they made clear their attitude on the whole question of industrial discipline, when they argued that they did not accept that a man should first have a warning and then a suspension and then be dismissed. On some occasions it would be preferable to give a man a warning but on others a dismissal might be called for. These managerial beliefs are not in any direct sense a function of the technology of the situation, although the

[1] Similar problems arose in another plant and are discussed in Appendix C.

application of such beliefs might be coloured by it, as appeared to be the case here.

CASE 2 'ABNORMAL' WORKING CONDITIONS

While, no doubt, the general statement that working conditions in British industry have improved with time, holds good, the impact of technical change on working conditions in specific situations is by no means clear-cut. In this respect benefits to one work group may be at the expense of losses to another. Where this is the case, it means that expectations about improved living standards, inside and outside the plant, are not fulfilled. Such a situation is likely to generate a sense of relative deprivation.

A case in point arose in connection with the maintenance work which had to be performed in and around the electrostatic precipitators. It was taken up by the Allied Crafts. The precipitators were used to extract dust arising from the smelting process on the steel plant. The extension of oxygen to the furnaces resulted in a marked increase of dust going through the precipitators, but at the expense of worse working conditions for the maintenance men. These men had to work in a polluted atmosphere with dust which was 95% iron in content, and sometimes at very high temperatures. The Allied Crafts put forward a claim for time and a half for all work done in and around the precipitators on the grounds that the conditions were abnormal. Such payment was regarded as compensation for the risk of injury to health. Claims for abnormal condition money have, of course, an implied conception of normality. In this case there seemed to be at least two ideas on the subject:

(a) Conditions in and around the precipitator deviated from conditions that one would normally expect to meet in the steel industry generally. Thus, the Allied Crafts claimed that working in the chamber on the top of the precipitator in 130 degrees Fahrenheit could not be normal steel-work conditions.

(b) Management argued that conditions in the precipitator must be distinguished from conditions in the surrounding vicinity. In adopting this position, management was drawing a distinction between jobs where it was and jobs where it was not possible to eliminate bad conditions. They pointed out that the only dust which could escape outside the precipitators and in so doing cause abnormal conditions was from the conveyors. They were trying to eliminate this problem. Unfortunately, however, as far as the boiler was concerned, it was not possible to improve the conditions. The men had to go in and carry out the necessary work. Management felt, therefore, that abnormal condition money should be paid only on specific jobs.

Management's conception of abnormal working conditions was more precise than the unions' and, in the event, they only conceded condition money on three specific jobs in the precipitator. The conflict arose, in part, because they opposed the paying of a general flat rate extra. They feared that such payments would be tied to nothing in particular and, once granted, would in practice be impossible to cancel even if conditions improved. In this way they would become an element in the wage drift. The unions could counter by pointing to the administrative convenience of a general payment of condition money, for if condition money were paid only on specific jobs then, while direct wage costs may have been contained, other costs might be increased. For example, individual claims have to be submitted on specific jobs to the engineer in charge. His time and the time of the man making the claim and possibly of the shop steward, is thereby being used, when they might have been working on the task in hand. This is debatable, but what is clear is that in defending their point of view, management's position was made more difficult by the fact that, on their own admission, conditions were not as good as they might be outside the precipitator. What was perhaps strange in the circumstances was that the Allied Crafts did not appear to insist on condition money on jobs where improvements were promised, even for an interim period, until the promised improvements materialised. Whether this was a lack of sharpness in bargaining tactics or a sign of goodwill is an open question.

Conventional wisdom tends to interpret the human problem of technical change as 'the problem of overcoming resistance to change', with the implied assumption that such resistance is irrational. In the light of the uncertain and uneven effects of technical change on working conditions, which this dispute illustrates, it is clearly most unsatisfactory to attribute resistance to change as necessarily exhibiting a reversion to the Luddite mentality. 'Real' losses can lead to 'real' conflict and 'real' claims for compensation. But, by distinguishing at the outset of a technical change as carefully as possible between the avoidable and the unavoidable losses, then, at least, the area in which conflict is likely to emerge can be more clearly delineated.

CASE 3 A QUESTION OF DEMARCATION

It is interesting to notice that even the participants in a demarcation dispute sometimes get to the point where they feel the matter has been 'magnified out of all proportion'. It is as though they feel ensnared in a situation not wholly of their own making. It is perhaps not surprising that the casual observer commonly succumbs to the temptation to cry 'a plague on both your houses'.

In one sense, the demarcation dispute may be regarded as the unintended consequence of a feature of industrial organisation that in other respects is regarded as 'desirable'. In times of organisational, technical and market stability the virtues of everyone knowing his own job are stressed. It is in times of change that the virtues, so to speak, become a liability, since the particular rights and duties which occupational groups have come to regard as theirs are questioned.[1] Occupational prerogatives may be scrutinised and challenged. But such prerogatives are not lightly given up since they represent the group's concept of work, and, as has frequently been observed, a threat to work is a threat to personal and familial security. The following example will serve to illustrate one way in which a stable situation in terms of social organisation became an ambiguous one. We will describe and analyse the demarcation dispute that ensued.

This episode is drawn from one of the mills in the plant.[2] In the mill was a guide shop which was manned by guide setters, and had been since the mill opened some four years previously. These were classified as production workers and hence were members of B.I.S.A.K.T.A. The crucial question, however, concerned who should assemble the guides. Guides are attached to

---

[1] Parallel considerations arise, of course, at managerial level. For an effective documentation of this point, see T. Burns and G. M. Stalker, *The Management of Innovation* (Pergamon, 1961).

[2] For the purpose of maintaining anonymity, the precise nature of the mill discussed here is not specified.

rollers and ensure that the stock enters the rolls at the appropriate angle. Hence the guides have to be set in relation to the thickness of the material being rolled. Initially this had been regarded as the guide setters' task – a pre-production preliminary, so to speak. The original guides had been fairly simple in construction and hence the skill involved in this was minimal. Management had sanctioned this situation since they had been responsible for the original manning arrangements. At the same time, any repairs to the guides which were needed were performed in the machine shop by fitters – skilled craftsmen, who were members of the A.E.U.

In the course of time, more complicated guide equipment was introduced by management into the department, with the intention of improving the quality of the finished product. The assembling of the roller guides became more difficult but it was still performed by the B.I.S.A.K.T.A. guide setters. Their right to do this was, however, challenged by the A.E.U., who maintained that a fitter should be employed in the guide shop to do the 'necessary' skilled work involved in assembling. In other words, it was claimed that the assembly work could no longer fairly be claimed as merely a pre-production preliminary: it was maintenance work.

Management, for its part, on examining the position, had come to the conclusion that the fitters' case was a strong one. They indicated to B.I.S.A.K.T.A. their belief that if a fitter was put into the guide shop it would improve the performance of the mill. They urged B.I.S.A.K.T.A. to accept this, arguing that if the claim went through the normal procedure, the decision would go against them in the end. This, it was said, would, in the circumstances, be fairer to the company which was the suffering third party in the dispute. B.I.S.A.K.T.A. was not to be dissuaded, however, from its resistance, and the matter was prolonged for another six months. High ranking union officials were called from the respective unions, together with the Director of the Iron and Steel Trades Employers' Association, following which a fitter was introduced into the guide shop.

This, in simple outline, is a description of the issue. One can, however, go on to consider the pattern of the conflict and the mode and significance of its resolution.

It is first of all important to stress that the matter was regarded by the guide setters as a threat to job security, but it was also regarded by their union, B.I.S.A.K.T.A., as a threat to union security. For the men it was the immediate issue which was at stake; for the union it was the more general fear that this was 'the thin edge of the wedge'. Both these fears were expressed openly to management. These fears were symptomatic of their awareness that modern rolling mills are becoming increasingly dependent upon engineering skills and technology for effective performance. The relative numbers of craftsmen and production workers are beginning to be affected in the industry generally (for the North East this is reflected in Table XV) and hence the bargaining power of B.I.S.A.K.T.A. as the union 'pace-setter' of the industry is being threatened. Hence, upon the resolution of small matters, such as the one we are discussing, wider implications may follow.

At the same time, it is clear that both the fitters and the A.E.U. representatives regarded the work of the guide setters, as encroaching on their monopoly of skill. Their fear was undoubtedly that the longer the guide setters were allowed to continue in the work, the more competent they would become and the weaker their own claim would be. Their indignation can well be imagined, when, during the period of the dispute, a firm that was delivering new roller guides sent a fitter to demonstrate to the guide setters how the equipment should be assembled! This was strictly correct since the procedure in the industry lays down that during the period of dispute the status quo shall be preserved, until a decision is reached through negotiation or arbitration. Further, the guide setters' assembly work was supervised by a trained engineer. This, in itself, was felt to be anomalous by the A.E.U. and, at the same time, undermining their skill monopoly.

There were certain symbolic features which highlighted this conflict between the two groups. There was, for example, the importance placed by B.I.S.A.K.T.A. on the geographical location of the job. B.I.S.A.K.T.A. men worked in the guide shop; A.E.U. men worked in the fitting and machine shop. This stress on territorial division was, of course, based on considerations of custom and practice. The longer they could maintain this division, the stronger their claim to continue in it: which was one reason why they chose to take the matter through the procedure to national level. Management, recognising the way in which the territorial division reinforced the B.I.S.A.K.T.A. case, and sympathising with the A.E.U. point of view, was attempting throughout the dispute to reorganise the department so that the guide shop and the fitting shop would not be physically separate. There would, in short, be a guide-fitting shop. In this way the boundaries would be blurred and the importance of the spatial symbol lost. All this, however, took considerable time and did not appear to have been completed by the time the final decision on the dispute was reached.

On the A.E.U. side, considerable symbolic importance was attached to 'the tools and skills of the job'. The critical feature for them was not the physical location of the job, but what tools were being employed on the job. It was pointed out that assembly work of the more complicated guide equipment involved marking off, tapping, drilling, turning, milling and planing, and that vernier gauges and surface gauges were required. The B.I.S.A.K.T.A. reply to this was to cast doubt on how essential the tools were for the job and to suggest that these operations were not in fact performed by their men. At the same time, they insisted that they had been doing the work of assembling and disassembling the roller guides to the satisfaction of management until the A.E.U. had challenged their right to the job. However, it is clear that B.I.S.A.K.T.A. was in some difficulty here. If they were performing the task efficiently, they were encroaching on skills which were not, so to speak, their property. If they were not using the appropriate skills and tools, they were not performing the task efficiently. In the event of the former, they incurred the displeasure of the A.E.U. In the event of the latter, they failed to satisfy management. In fact, they appeared, to some extent, to be falling between two stools: doing some tasks and using some tools which were not legitimately theirs, but not exhibiting the range of skills which management required, or, with the extension of the mill's productive capacity, would increasingly require.

One can now begin to see that there were in fact various forms and levels of conflict which inter-mingled to make the issue the complex matter it was – despite the wish of each of the participants for a simple solution. These may be summarised as follows:

1. An occupational conflict – guide setters versus fitters.

2. A union conflict – B.I.S.A.K.T.A. versus A.E.U. – the one an industrial union, the other a (modified) craft union.
3. A functional conflict – production versus maintenance.
4. A management/union conflict – the A.E.U. aggrieved that management permitted the anomaly to occur and B.I.S.A.K.T.A. dissatisfied with the proposal of management to change the existing practice.

These organisational conflicts of interest, in a sense, provided a framework for other forms of conflict inherent in the dispute.

5. Conflicts of rights:
   (a) Job security versus skill monopoly.
   (b) Union security (B.I.S.A.K.T.A.) versus union prerogative (A.E.U.).

These were reflected in:

6. Symbolic conflicts:
   (a) The physical location of the job (B.I.S.A.K.T.A.).
   (b) The tools and skills employed on the job (A.E.U.).

And also in:

7. Factual conflicts:
   (a) Were the changes in the guide equipment changes of kind or changes of degree?
   (b) Did the existing manning arrangements impede efficiency?
   (c) What tools and skills were necessary for the jobs of assembling and disassembling guide equipment?
   (d) What is production and what is maintenance work?

It will be noted that the conflicts which have been delineated in the above scheme are mutually reinforcing.

In discussing the phenomenon of social stability within a firm the point has been well made that the:

criss-cross of relations creates communities of interest which only partly coincide. Individuals are thus integrated and differentiated from one another. The result is not a dichotomous classification into office or shop workers, or into supervisors and non-supervisors. It is instead a complex configuration of relations in which different groups are separated out and yet tied together.[1]

[1] F. Roethlisberger and W. J. Dickson, *Management and the Worker* (O.U.P., 1939), p. 560.

Yet in the situation that I have been describing it is precisely the dichotomous elements that have been made to stand out in terms of organisation, rights and contrasting symbols as between the various interested parties. It is the B.I.S.A.K.T.A. guide setters, seeking to defend themselves against threats to job and union security, who appeal to custom and practice and symbolise this by stressing territorial differences between themselves and the challengers. They are arrayed against the A.E.U. fitters, who seek to maintain their skill monopoly and who appeal to the skill differential as symbolised in the type of tools used. Management, which would like to regard itself as an innocent and injured third party (if not impartial) finds itself accused by B.I.S.A.K.T.A. of having let them down, while A.E.U. members simultaneously accuse management of procrastination. Management is to be found, therefore, in the maelstrom of a power struggle.

The peaceful resolution of such a conflict occurs as the dichotomies are shown to be in some sense false (if that is possible) which is usually attendant upon some sort of package deal or quid pro quo. Management, by virtue of its position is able to take some initiative in this. Thus throughout the negotiations and included in the final settlement was the promise that no B.I.S.A.K.T.A. men would be made redundant if a fitter was brought into the guide shop. The clash between job security and skill monopoly was accordingly minimised. Similarly, it was made plain to the B.I.S.A.K.T.A. representatives that management was not prepared to let the A.E.U. use this case as a representative issue, as a result of which they could touch off a series of other claims. By containing and particularising the issue management sought to reduce the perceived polarisation of interest, between union security and union prerogatives. Management also, as we have seen, sought to make the change more palatable to the B.I.S.A.K.T.A. members by altering the physical arrangement of the work and attempting to create a guide-fitting shop.

The final settlement, which arranged for a fitter to go into the guide shop, also permitted the guide setters to do the final part of the assembly work, which involved pushing two rollers into each guide. This was accepted as a 'necessary' preliminary to their task as guide setters.

During the final meeting no additional factual evidence was presented, but the meeting was a reminder of the latent power which each side possessed. It was used, in effect, as a basis for re-affirming the legitimacy of each group to govern over specified areas. Thus the B.I.S.A.K.T.A. representative observed that his union appreciated the increased mechanisation of rolling mills and that there was no intention on the part of his organisation to impinge on the work of the A.E.U. They knew the feeling the A.E.U. had about the quality of work and skill required. It was in B.I.S.A.K.T.A.'s interest that this should be accepted. At the same time, he noted that guide setting and guide assembly work had gone on in the industry for many years and his union had to be very careful that the A.E.U. did not take over their work.

The A.E.U., for their part, having got a fitter admitted to the guide shop, were prepared to stress the virtues of team spirit and to point to the abnormality of such disputes with B.I.S.A.K.T.A. There were in fact prizes all round since, while the A.E.U. achieved its objective, B.I.S.A.K.T.A. were able to go back to their members and say that the guide setters could continue to do the work they had been doing for the last four years. The B.I.S.A.K.T.A. concession, then, was a moderate one and well illustrates the use of casuistry in smoothing the sharp edges of an issue. As Schelling puts it in *The Strategy of Conflict*:

> . . . when the opponent has resolved to make a moderate concession one may help him by proving that he *can* make a moderate concession consistent with his former position and that if he does there are no grounds for believing it to reflect on his original principles.[1]

It is clear, by contrast, that where such a face-saving formula cannot be devised; where, that is, there are 'real' losses attendant upon change, in terms of job or union security, the disputes are correspondingly more intense and intractable.

CASE 4   CONFLICTING PRINCIPLES OF LABOUR RECRUITMENT

The plant in which this dispute was located was not the only one owned by the Company. The conflict underlying this issue arose when the Company employed in the plant five men, from other plants in the combine. These men, it was alleged by B.I.S.A.K.T.A., were either out of compliance, or had not been

[1] Thomas C. Schelling, *The Strategy of Conflict* (O.U.P., 1963), p. 35.

associated at all with the union. The principle at stake was whether in compliance B.I.S.A.K.T.A. membership took precedence over the company service. This clash of loyalties which reflected different managerial and union perspectives was brought into the open by the fact of recession. It is at such a time that the union makes strenuous efforts to get its redundant members re-employed, when any job opportunities occur.

In this case the Company claimed that it was not binding on management to engage only B.I.S.A.K.T.A. labour and that, until there was some national agreement on the matter, they had a free hand in the recruitment of labour. The union claimed that they were acting on a resolution adopted by their national executive at the beginning of the year (1963). So sure was the branch of the orthodoxy of its position and so intense was the feeling of the membership on the matter, that the branch indicated to management that a request was being put through to the union's executive asking them to call an official strike. The use of this ultimate sanction against an employer is extremely rare for B.I.S.A.K.T.A. Just as in the earlier case we noted that the semantic argument over what constitutes normal working conditions reflected a genuine conflict of interest, so too in this case did arguments over the concept of seniority. Management indicated that they had some sympathy with the union view that only B.I.S.A.K.T.A. members should be employed, but added that it was difficult to see how to apply what the union were asking for without giving up fundamental rights of management in regard to the recruitment of labour. They agreed that the union had an obligation to its members, but pointed out that the Company also had an obligation to its employees when redundancy arose.

A peaceful solution was achieved because it was discovered that, in this case, there was enough area of overlap between these conflicting principles to make a face-saving solution possible. Three of the five men were made redundant on the grounds that one had no previous service with the Company and the other two had less claim to employment in terms of Company service than other men who had just been made redundant on another plant (and who were in compliance). In future, the Company agreed to give preference to in compliance B.I.S.A.K.T.A. men, but only within the Company, not the District. For its part, the

B.I.S.A.K.T.A. branch recognised the Company's right to operate a 'black list'. This consisted of men, who through misdemeanours of one kind or another, were not felt to be worth re-employing.

The recession, therefore, not only brought this latent conflict into the open, but also tended to put pressure on both sides to formalise loose informal arrangements or 'understandings'. The Company had to acknowledge openly that it was prepared to recognise the closed shop principle. B.I.S.A.K.T.A. had to accept the legitimacy of the 'black list'. The black list thus served the function of saving face for management by prescribing an area in which freedom still existed for them in the recruitment of labour. The case serves as an instructive example of the kind of adjustment that is necessary to accommodate conflicting principles within the existing framework of negotiation.

4. The System at Work: B.I.S.A.K.T.A. and the Use of Settlement Procedures

In this section I will make some observations on the use made by B.I.S.A.K.T.A. (or sometimes management against B.I.S.A.K.T.A.) of procedures for the settlement of disputes, which went outside the plant. The period covered is 1945–61. In Table XVIIA, we have summarised the use made of statutory and ad hoc procedures on the North East Coast during this period. The figures given refer to the place where the matter was settled. The ad hoc committees appeared to operate on matters relating to the disciplining of individual work-people, where a speedy settlement is called for, although neutral committees can and do deal with similar cases. The issue under the heading Industrial Court we have included for the sake of completeness. It was in fact an issue which arose, not from an individual plant, but was a claim for time and a half instead of time and a quarter for mid-week overtime, which was brought forward by a district committee of B.I.S.A.K.T.A. The claim was rejected by the industrial court. The employers defended the case on the grounds of 'custom and practice' and 'the state of trade' which, they said, did not justify the increase.

It will be noted that up to and including 1953 three neutral committees was the sum total of procedural activity outside the plant (1948, 1950 and 1953). By contrast, thirteen of the twenty-

TABLE XVIIA

B.I.S.A.K.T.A. AND THE SETTLEMENT OF DISPUTES

The Use made of Statutory and Ad Hoc Procedures on the North East Coast 1945–61.

Year	Ad Hoc Committees	Neutral Committees	Arbitration	Industrial Court	Total
1945	—	—	—	—	0
1946	—	—	—	—	0
1947	—	—	—	—	0
1948	—	1	—	—	1
1949	—	—	—	—	0
1950	—	1	—	—	1
1951	—	—	—	—	0
1952	—	—	—	—	0
1953	—	1	—	—	1
1954	—	4	—	—	4
1955	—	1	—	—	1
1956	—	1	—	—	1
1957	—	—	—	—	0
1958	—	—	1	—	1
1959	—	2	—	—	2
1960	2	4	—	—	6
1961	1	2	2	1	6
Total	3	17	3	1	24

four settlements took place in 1958 and the following three years. These included all the Arbitration cases, the ad hoc committees and the Industrial Court settlement, together with eight of the seventeen matters, which were settled by neutral committees. Indeed, the 1960–61 period accounts for exactly half of the issues during the whole period covered.

As Table XV makes clear, this is not to be accounted for by an increase in the numbers of production workers during the period, for in fact the reverse was the case. Indeed, this fact lay behind the union belief that the greater use of formal bargaining procedures in the post 1958 period was a sign that management was using the recession to tighten control over matters of discipline. The use of procedures, which involve going outside the plant for settlement of disputes, is a useful indicator of the severity of management-union conflict. Although I am inclined to accept the union interpretation, it should be pointed out that the system itself did not appear to be seriously threatened at this stage, since the absolute number of issues going through in this way is not great. Further, it should be noted that there were considerable differences as between firms, in the use made of such procedures. In particular, one firm, and that not the largest, was responsible for one ad hoc committee, nine neutral committees and two arbitration issues, in other words, half of the total issues. In this respect, therefore, there was not uniform pressure on the system from all the firms in the district.

In Table XVIIB, I have classified the issues that were settled outside the individual plant, in relation to the main content of the question. It will be seen that they relate predominantly to wages

TABLE XVIIB

B.I.S.A.K.T.A. AND THE SETTLEMENT OF DISPUTES

A classification of the issues leading to the use of Statutory and Ad Hoc Procedures on the North East Coast, 1945–61.

Type of Issue	Ad Hoc Committees	Neutral Committees	Arbitration	Industrial Court	Total
Wages	—	16	2	1	19
Hours	—	1	—	—	1
Demarcation	—	—	—	—	0
Redundancy	—	—	—	—	0
Manning	—	—	—	—	0
Industrial Discipline	3	—	1	—	4
Other work Arrangements	—	—	—	—	0
T.U. issues	—	—	—	—	0
Total	3	17	3	1	24

issues – nineteen out of the twenty-four. Four were concerned with matters of industrial discipline and the remaining question was over hours of work. On investigation of the groups involved in these disputes two points of interest stand out. The first is that the mills rather than the melting shop side of the steel works tend to be involved. Seven claims arose from the former and three from the latter (not all claims of course are necessarily related to a specific section of the plant). The issues arising from the mills in the main referred to differences between management and the union over rates for particular groups of jobs; sometimes during the transition from provisional to final rates (this was usually the case) and occasionally to revise rates for particular jobs in the light of further experience. Thus in one case it was found that working conditions were worse than expected and a compensating bonus was claimed; in another case an increase in rates was claimed in the light of new requirements for the changing of rolls.

The second point of interest is that nine of the disputes involved clerical, technical or supervisory staff (two of the ad hoc committees, six of the neutral committees, and one of the arbitration cases). The ad hoc committee cases were appeals against suspension in one instance and dismissal in another. The other matters, however, were collective issues in the sense that the union was attempting to establish more favourable conditions of employment. In one case this was a successful claim that all clerks, chemists, stocktakers and foremen in a particular firm should receive three weeks' annual holiday instead of the then two. Other claims that figured prominently were for the introduction of wage-age scales for clerical workers. This is a strategy commonly employed by unions that deal exclusively for clerical and supervisory grades (such as A.S.S.E.T., D.A.T.A. and the C.A.W.U.). The emergence of these questions underlines the attempt of the union, which has traditionally concerned itself with manual workers, to represent adequately these groups. But, by the same token, management is confronted with claims from groups, which they tend to regard as part of management or, at least, extensions of management. Thus it is sometimes suggested by management in the industry that supervisors ought not to have a dual loyalty, that is management responsibilities and union membership. It has not been easy in consequence to form supervisors' branches in firms. Supervisors have sometimes been encouraged instead to join the Staff Association, set up by the Company for them. It tends to be a social club, but can sometimes negotiate as a company union, with the employer. For the union there is the problem of establishing foreman's branches in the first place. Given managerial opposition to the unionisation of foremen, it needs a strongly developed union consciousness on the part of a few supervisors to get the branch off the ground. There is next the question of how far up the staff ladder a man can progress before having to withdraw his union membership. This came out crucially in one neutral committee, when the employers agreed to discuss a wages issue affecting Casting and Loading Bay Supervisors, but refused to recognise that the procedure as laid down covered Assistant Shift Managers and refused, therefore, to discuss the question as it affected them. It is not without significance that the union preferred to call the Assistant Shift Managers, Sample Passers (in the context of the melting shop) which is the more traditional terminology for the post. The ambivalence of supervisors to trade union membership can well be understood (and this was reported by a trade union official concerned with, what for him was a crucial problem). Not only is their strong managerial discouragement, even to the extent in one instance known to us of refusing to promote a man to a post of Shift Manager, despite his proved ability, because he let it be known that he would not give up his union membership, but there is the question derived from this as to whether the union can, so to speak, deliver the goods for these men.

It is therefore, not only the kinds of issue, which, as we have seen, mainly relate to wages and industrial discipline matters, but also the groups involved in the dispute that help us to see the points of friction in the system and their significance more clearly. In the case of the manual workers we see that wage disputes are quite often associated with major technical changes – but the conflicts which emerge are those which are accepted by both sides as being legitimately regulated by the system. The white collar disputes, on the other hand, help to pin-point the boundaries of the system. It is the process of and conflict over legitimation itself that is being examined. It serves as a timely reminder that 'the system' cannot in empirical terms be regarded as a static entity. Boundaries are continually being drawn, blurred, and re-drawn only to be blurred again.

5. *The System and Overt Conflict: the Post-war Strike Pattern*

In an earlier part of this chapter, I drew attention to the fact that, with the growth of regulated procedures for the settlement of disputes, the strike came to be regarded as a sign of failure by both sides when it was used. For this reason, an examination of the part played by strikes in the North East steel industry, would appear to be particularly appropriate. In doing this, one is not necessarily subscribing to the view that all such strikes in fact undermine the industrial relations system. Some strikes, for example, may draw attention to specific weaknesses or deficiencies in the system, which may then be remedied if so desired.

The strike data, that I will now comment on, are derived from an analysis of newspaper sources, which has been checked against Ministry of Labour regional aggregates. Recorded strikes, as I have termed them, may be official or unofficial, but they exclude disputes which lasted for less than a day or involved fewer than ten workers (except where the loss of working days exceeded 100).

In Table XVIIIA, I have classified all the recorded strikes in relation to the year in which they took place and the reasons given for striking. During this period the total number on the payroll varied between 40,000 and 45,000. It will be seen that the total number of recorded strikes was very small, averaging less than two a year. Indeed, with the exception of 1954, there were never more than three strikes in one year and in three of those years (1950, 1957 and 1958) there were no strikes at all.

Of the strikes that did take place, almost half were directly related to wages questions. These were of two main kinds. First, there were two claims for 'condition' money. The conditions in the one case were held to be excessively dirty and in the other case excessively hot. Secondly, and more commonly, disputes arose over the actual wages structure. Arguments over the method of payment and the differentials between occupations were prominent here.

The number of strikes in the category Trade Union Issues is somewhat misleading, since five of these were sympathy strikes, which took place within the same firm within the space of a few days. They were all in support of a group of template makers who were already out on strike on a wage issue. It is important also to note this since it is directly responsible for the higher strike total of 1954. Since these small strikes clustered around the one issue, it is fair to point out that there is nothing particularly abnormal about the 1954 strike pattern. One should also notice the absence of demarcation strikes throughout this whole period.

Table XVIIIB indicates the length of stoppage in relation to

TABLE XVIIIA

Recorded Strikes in the North East Iron and Steel Industry 1949–61

Year	Wages	Hours	Demarcation	Redundancy	Manning	Industrial Discipline	Other Work Arrangements	Trade Union Issues	Total
1949	1	—	—	—	1	—	—	1	3
1950	—	—	—	—	—	—	—	—	0
1951	—	—	—	—	1	—	—	—	1
1952	—	—	—	—	—	—	1	—	1
1953	1	—	—	—	—	—	—	—	1
1954	2	—	—	—	—	—	—	5	7
1955	2	—	—	—	—	—	—	—	2
1956	3	—	—	—	—	—	—	—	3
1957	—	—	—	—	—	—	—	—	0
1958	—	—	—	—	—	—	—	—	0
1959	—	1	—	—	—	—	—	—	1
1960	1	—	—	—	1	—	—	—	2
1961	—	—	—	—	—	1	—	—	1
Total	10	1	0	0	3	1	1	6	22

TABLE XVIIIB

Length of Stoppages in Recorded Iron and Steel Strikes on the
North East Coast 1949–61

Type of Issue	Length of Stoppage			Total
	1–3 days	4–7 days	Over 7 days	
Wages	3	2	5	10
Hours	1	—	—	1
Demarcation	—	—	—	0
Redundancy	—	—	—	0
Manning	2	1	—	3
Industrial Discipline	1	—	—	1
Other Work Arrangements	1	—	—	1
Trade Union Issues	5	1	—	6
Total	13	4	5	22

the type of issue. Length of stoppage is, of course, a useful index of the severity of a strike. Nearly three-fifths of the strikes lasted for three days or less and over three-quarters were finished within a week. The strikes lasting over a week were all wage disputes. One of the longest strikes was of a fortnight's duration in 1953. It was the first strike in the plant for thirty-three years. Four hundred members of the Allied Crafts came out on strike alleging that union officials had signed an agreement to reduce tonnage bonus rates without getting the men's consent. The union officials felt that management had a case because the introduction of new equipment had substantially improved output. They felt, and told their members, that the settlement which they had negotiated with management was more satisfactory than would have been obtained by taking the matter to Arbitration. Management based their case on a 1936 agreement with the unions, which allowed for a revision of rates following a change of practice. They pointed out that output had nearly doubled since 1936. The basis of the conflict between the parties appeared to be one of time perspective. The workers maintained that their current earnings would be cut by 15/– to 18/– a week. Management and union officials argued that this would only be a temporary loss and that earnings would continue to improve with increased production.

The fact, however, that there was any reduction of earnings during a period of rising output and prosperity for the firm suggests a certain tactical mishandling on the part of management and union officials, whatever the overall correctness of their agreement. Not surprisingly it led to protests among the rank and file that they had been betrayed by their own officials. However, despite the vehemence of their protest, they did not achieve their objective of redressing the settlement.

The longest of the strikes lasted for just under a month in 1954. It arose because management in one firm refused to concede a claim from a group of template makers for a percentage tonnage bonus to be incorporated into their wages. Template workers have traditionally been paid on a time rate basis. Their work is regarded as highly skilled and this has been reflected in a higher base rate than has obtained in most crafts. But the take-home pay of many other craftsmen was nevertheless higher in many instances. This was because their work was regarded as more directly related to production, thus qualifying them for a bonus on tonnage output. Interestingly enough this was the issue over which other craftsmen in the same union (the Boilermakers) staged a series of sympathy strikes. They had nothing personal to

TABLE XVIIIC

NUMBERS DIRECTLY INVOLVED IN RECORDED IRON AND STEEL STRIKES
ON THE NORTH EAST COAST 1949–61

Type of Issue	Numbers Directly Involved				Total
	1–100	101–200	201–300	300 +	
Wages	6	2	—	2	10
Hours	—	—	—	1	1
Demarcation	—	—	—	—	0
Redundancy	—	—	—	—	0
Manning	2	—	1	—	3
Industrial Discipline	1	—	—	—	1
Other work Arrangements	—	1	—	—	1
Trade Union Issues	6	—	—	—	6
Total	15	3	1	3	22

O   199

gain from such action. It appeared to stem from certain moral feelings about what is or is not 'fair'.

Another indicator of the severity of strike activity relates to the numbers directly involved. This is shown in Table XVIIIC. Here we see that in two-thirds of the recorded strikes 100 or less men were directly involved. In only 14% of the strikes were more than 300 men directly involved. These included the Allied Crafts strike, to which I have already referred, which arose from the change in the basis of the tonnage bonus. There was also an official Allied Crafts strike in 1956 in support of a wage claim for all craftsmen in the industry. This strike involved the 7,000 craftsmen then employed in the North East sector of the industry. The only other strike in this category occurred in 1959 when a B.I.S.A.K.T.A. branch closed a plant down by bringing out some 800 members. The branch claimed that management had caused short time to be worked in a way which broke a guaranteed minimum week agreement. The case is of some interest and we will outline it briefly.

When a straightening machine in a particular mill broke down, on a Thursday, management sent telegrams to the nine men due to come in on the next shift, who were affected by this breakdown, telling them not to report back until the following Monday. The branch officials claimed that a written domestic agreement included prior consultation with the branch before such action could properly be taken. This condition, they asserted, had not been fulflled. They argued that the men should have been transferred to other work, particularly as it was near Christmas. They felt that it was especially unfair that the men's earnings should have been adversely affected at such a time. Although the branch officials acted unconstitutionally against the rules of a union which has a reputation for keeping its representatives in line, there is no evidence that these officials were disciplined by their national executive in any way. The branch officials themselves maintained that this action did lead to some improvement subsequently in the management-union consultation procedure.

In Table XVIIID, I have shown the extent to which particular unions were involved in strike activity during the period 1949–61. Plainly, the craft unions were the main instigators and participants in strike action. The relatively large number attributed to the Boilermakers as compared to other unions is of interest but ought

Unions Involved in Recorded Iron and Steel Strikes on the North East Coast 1949–61

Type of Issue	UNION													
	B.I.S.A.K.T.A.	B.M.S.	A.E.U.	E.T.U.	A.U.B.T.W.	A.S.W.	U.P.A.	A.U.F.W.	P.T.U.	Black-smiths	Roll Turners	Allied Crafts	T.G.W.U.	N.UG.M.W.
Wages	—	4	2	2	2	1	2	1	1	1	1	1	2	—
Hours	1	—	—	—	—	—	—	—	—	—	—	—	—	—
Demarcation	—	—	—	—	—	—	—	—	—	—	—	—	—	—
Redundancy	—	—	—	—	—	—	—	—	—	—	—	—	—	—
Manning	1	1	—	—	—	—	—	—	—	—	—	—	—	1
Industrial Discipline	—	—	—	1	—	—	—	—	—	—	—	—	—	—
Other Work Arrangements	—	1	—	—	—	—	—	—	—	—	—	—	—	—
Trade Union Issues	—	6	—	—	—	—	—	—	—	—	—	—	—	—
Total	2	12	2	3	2	1	2	1	1	1	1	1	2	1

not, perhaps to be exaggerated. It will be recalled that the five sympathy strikes were called by members of this union. While they were separate strikes and to some extent involved different personnel, they were all over the same issue. Again, in two other cases the Boilermakers acted in conjunction with other unions.

The greater militancy of the craft unions so far as strike activity is concerned, is reflected also in the fact that they alone were involved in strikes that lasted over a week. One case here relates to a strike which was not exclusively confined to the steel industry. It arose when the Patternmakers came out in all Pattern-making establishments in the North East, in 1960, on the grounds that the employers had refused to negotiate with them over a wage claim.

Only two strikes involved B.I.S.A.K.T.A. members during the whole period. One of these we have discussed already. The other dispute occurred in 1960. Fifty machine operators, who were working under an incentive payment scheme, objected to being taken off the job on which the incentive applied and told to off-load material which was coming into the shop.

There were then during this period very few recorded strikes in the North East steel industry. The typical strike was of short duration. It was usually called by a single union and directly involved less than 100 men. It usually occurred in a particular plant. All the strikes which did begin in individual firms began as 'unofficial' and started before negotiating procedures had been exhausted. But most of them also might be characterised as 'perishable' disputes, in which a premium is placed on speed of action in response to what is felt to be unconstitutional or unfair managerial behaviour. They might be regarded in a sense as the backwash arising from the belief in the sanctity of custom and practice as the regulating principle of industrial relations. For example, the only strike which involved a general union, the N.U.G.M.W., was in 1951 when 275 labourers, platers' helpers and loaders walked out of a plant. This was because a plater's helper had been transferred to a job as slinger's helper, when the plater he had been helping was unoccupied. The union convener objected to the management's decision because, he said, there were other platers who were short of help at the time and that, in any case, the job of slingers' helper belonged to another union (presumably the C.E.U.).

There is no evidence of concerted strike action being taken by all unions in a plant at any one time. There is a curious irony in the fact that the nearest likelihood of that occurred in 1955 when a joint strike was threatened at South Durham in an attempt to get the Cargo Fleet plant Works Manager reinstated, as reported in the *Northern Echo* during January and February. A difference of opinion had arisen between the Managing Director and the Works Manager as to whether or not one could get more output with existing plant and layout. The men described the Works Manager as 'the most popular boss they ever had' and said that he had their respect and confidence. Justifying their strike threat they observed: 'The trades union movement has such a broad democratic basis in opposing what we regard as injustice, that this extends to what happens within the management . . . and we do feel an injustice has been done'.

Conclusion

What I have tried to show in this chapter is, first, the conjunction of circumstances which promoted and sustained a prolonged period of industrial peace in the British iron and steel industry, and, in particular, its North East sector. Secondly, I have looked at a number of salient features of the structure and functioning of the industrial relations system of the North East steel industry during the post-war period.

In terms of strike statistics it is quite evident that in the North East, the industry's reputation for industrial peace is still justified. The vicissitudes of private and public ownership, Conservative and Labour governments are not in any obvious way related to the level of strike activity. Equally, we noted that the largest union in the industry, B.I.S.A.K.T.A., did not commonly take disputes which arose in the plant for external plant settlement. Nevertheless, in the post-1958 period some slack in the system was, so to speak, taken up, insofar as increasing (though scarcely excessive) use was made of extra-plant dispute procedures. What I would suggest is that the sources of this strain on the system are to be located in the organisational and technological changes which were implemented in a climate of recession. A common union interpretation was that the recession altered the balance of power in management's favour. In consequence there were, for example, managerial attempts to tighten control over matters of discipline:

> In full employment, management tends to allow things in an attempt to get 19 shifts, for which it needs a special application to the union every week. They then, after 1958, tried to put their house in order a little too late, which led to arbitrary behaviour. For example, on absenteeism, which was pretty high in full employment, they have tightened up. The men feel strongly about this . . . Also, in this area the mill stops working at the changeover of shift times for 20-40 minutes. The national agreement says that there should be no stoppage . . . since 1958 they have tried to implement the agreement.

This cashing-in on their power resources might be said to constitute a management offensive. It represents a shift from a leniency to a stringency pattern of labour relations. But it was also maintained by the union that, by following procedure closely (and refusing to settle matters formally or informally at plant level) management could use such institutional arrangements as a defensive measure against union aggression during periods of recession. Thus it was said: 'Problems tend to drag on and take a long time before being settled . . . when we had the boot on our foot we could move more quickly. Management now are deliberately stalling on certain issues and our lads have guessed this.'

Here is an example of the kind of stalling tactics that could be applied. A particular plant, because of the tight market, was looking for all possible sales openings. They took on a substantial number of orders for semi-finished material in the form of billets for export. The craftsmen's tonnage bonus, however, was only paid on finished material. They claimed that, because of the alteration in the pattern of selling, semi-finished material should also be included – 'it had passed through the rolls and in their opinion was finished material so far as the Company was concerned'. The matter could not be settled by the shop stewards and the relevant District Officials were called in. The Company then suggested that the matter be held over until some new mills were completed, when the whole question of the craftsmen's bonus would be reviewed. This was not well received by the unions. The Company then called for an adjournment on the grounds that, having inspected the wording of the relevant district agreement, they were not at all clear whether they would

be correct in including semi-finished material for bonus, even
with a reduction of the bonus rate. This kind of behaviour may
not unfairly be described as the managerial equivalent of working-
to-rule.

However, the movement towards a more stringent pattern of
industrial relations has not been as great as it could have been.
In particular one suspects that managerial prerogatives on manning have, on the whole, been exercised judiciously. In the first
place manning arrangements in relation to new plant and equipment have not, during the period surveyed, departed quantita-
tively from traditional manning patterns in any radical way.
Secondly, and very important, the running-in period of new plant
has been a time when the original manning decisions taken by
management could be challenged by the unions in the light of
experience. Hence final agreements about rates and manning have
been collectively decided upon in the context of plant bargaining.

Since much adverse comment exists about the state of British
industrial relations, often in a very parochial perspective, it is
perhaps of interest to hear the view of the American scholar,
Abraham Siegel, on the British steel industry:

> In the light of the 1959 American experience with the work rules
> issue, the practices of the British bargaining machinery, for example,
> with respect to the relegation of issues to the proper working level
> of familiarity in the bargaining hierarchy, are certainly worth more
> than a casual glance.[1]

---

[1] Siegel, op. cit., p. 317.

CHAPTER SIX

Redundancy Conflict in an
Isolated Steel Community

THE conflict referred to in the title of this chapter arose
when different answers were given to the question 'who
should be dismissed?', following a recession in trade at the
Consett Iron Company in 1961.[1] I attempt to demonstrate that by
a social-structural analysis one can obtain a clearer understanding
of the nature of such conflict. While any particular case will have
idiosyncratic features that make it unique, the mode of analysis
may be applied to other situations which have a family resemblance.

The paper is divided into two main sections:

I. A discussion of the extent to which a generalised belief system
exists in the country at large concerning the principles which should
govern dismissals arising from redundancy. I shall indicate some
potential sources of conflict arising from the application of any
such principles.

II. A presentation of the Consett case in the light of the above discussion. Essentially I shall ask: how the various interest groups
defined the situation confronting them. Towards what goal or goals
was their action directed? What criteria did they appeal to, what
means did they advocate and what resources did they mobilise
in the pursuit of their goals?

1. *Selection for Dismissals: The Generalised Belief System*

Among the more important studies of redundancy problems and
procedures one may cite the following:

[1] My thanks are due to the Consett Iron Company for permission to carry
out the research and for their generous help and co-operation.

Redundancy Conflict in an Isolated Steel Community

(i) Acton Society Trust, *Redundancy: A Survey of Problems and Practices* (1958). This work was carried out on a national basis and reported on policies pursued by the nationalised sector of industry and 200 firms in the private sector.

(ii) Ministry of Labour, 'Redundancy in Great Britain', *Ministry of Labour Gazette,* February 1963. This was another national survey and brought up to date an earlier Ministry of Labour publication, 'Security and Change'. It reports on the policies of 371 private firms, industry-wide arrangements existing in the private sector, provisions in the nationalised industries and in National and Local Government Service.

(iii) Hilda R. Kahn, *Repercussions of Redundancy* (1964).[1] This was a 1 in 10 sample inquiry into the experiences and attitudes of workers who were made redundant in Birmingham in 1956. Redundancy in this area arose mainly as a result of a temporary recession in the car industry.

(iv) Dorothy Wedderburn, *Redundancy and the Railwaymen* (1965).[2] This is a study of the impact of the railway contraction plan, announced in 1962, upon two railway workshops: Gorton, Manchester and Faverdale, Darlington. Redundancy in this context was a direct result of structural changes taking place in the industry.

(v) Dorothy Wedderburn, *White Collar Redundancy: a Case Study* (1964).[3] This was an account of a redundancy episode occurring in a particular firm, English Electric. The redundancy arose following the sudden cancellation, by the Government of a defence contract for the Blue Water Guided Missile. It affected workers in two of the firm's plants: Stevenage and Luton.

In the two studies conducted by Wedderburn, the official redundancy policies are described and the attitudes of the men affected to these policies ascertained through interviews.

Apart from situations in which a firm closes down and all employees are made redundant, the question 'who should go first?' inevitably arises. On the evidence of the representative studies referred to above, one may suggest that at a very general

[1] Hilda R. Kahn, *Repercussions of Redundancy* (Allen and Unwin, 1964).

[2] University of Cambridge, Department of Applied Economics, Occasional Papers, 4. Cambridge University Press.

[3] University of Cambridge, Department of Applied Economics, Occasional Papers, I. (Cambridge University Press).

level there is an evaluative consensus relating to the kind of considerations that, it is felt, should apply. These beliefs may be expressed as follows:

1. The number of employees to be dismissed should be kept to a minimum.
2. Length of service should be taken into consideration so that, broadly, the rule 'last in first out' should operate.
3. But the rule may be modified on certain grounds:
    (a) Some groups or individuals may be held to have less claim to a job regardless of their seniority (e.g. married women, men over 65).
    (b) Some groups or individuals may be held to have more claim to a job, regardless of their seniority (i) on the grounds of efficiency (ii) on the grounds of special need (e.g. handicapped workers. young men finishing apprenticeship).

In a particular redundancy situation, it is clear that the potential sources of conflict over who should be dimissed are numerous. Among the more important are:

1. Arguments about the appropriateness of implementing re-dundancy procedures, as a means of dealing with the problems of the firm or industry. It may be suggested that alternative measures such as cutting out overtime, introducing short-time working, re-deploying labour within the undertaking, and allowing for 'natural wastage' of labour, are adequate. Where the threat to labour comes from technological change, resistance to redundancy may arise on the grounds that the shrinkage in the size of the labour force (where its inevitability is acknowledged) could be done more gradually, without resort to dismissal. Where the threat comes from changes in market demand, the same arguments may be used. But in this case there may also be differences of opinion concerning the nature of the recession. Is it likely to be of short or long duration? In the case of short term recessions, restrictions on overtime, short-time working and the re-deploy-ment of labour in the firm have much to be said for them as alternative solutions to redundancy. In any case, beliefs about the kind of redundancy being experienced are, one may predict, likely to affect the character of the solutions which are regarded as 'fair'.

2. Arguments about whether or not dismissals have been kept to a minimum. The points raised in the first example may be applied here also except that there is a limited acceptance of the inevitability of redundancy, in this situation.

3. The legitimacy of the generalised belief system may be questioned. For example, it may be held that the last in first out rule should not be modified on any grounds. Or, instead of the 'last in first out' rule being the primary consideration and then being modified on the grounds of efficiency, the efficiency rule may be regarded as the primary rule. It may be treated as an exclusive rule, or admit of modification with reference to the seniority principle, or, for that matter, other considerations. The Ministry of Labour survey makes clear that in fact very few firms specify efficiency as the sole criterion, but in the case of the Civil Service within each 'redundancy unit' the 'inefficient' are the first to go and only after that does the 'last in first out' principle apply.

4. There may be disagreement on the weight to be attached to different elements in the generalised belief system. These disagreements will take the form of asking how far the rule of 'last in first out' should be modified by other considerations; or, what weight should be attached to one set of considerations, say, efficiency compared with another set of considerations, say, preferential treatment for hardship cases. The Ministry of Labour survey found that 40% of the firms operated policies based on a combination of factors relating to length of service and efficiency. Another 40% operate discriminatory policies against certain categories of workers first and then go on to apply some form of seniority plus efficiency policy.

5. Semantic conflicts may emerge over the operational definition of terms and categories. Thus the point of reference for the application of the 'last in first out' principle may be a section, a department, a plant, a firm and so on, with very different implications for those involved. Again, there may be differences of opinion as to who should be discriminated against before the 'last in first out' rule is applied. In Kahn's survey, 62% of her respondents regarded 'last in first out' as the fairest policy in time of redundancy but of these

> 86% were nevertheless of the opinion that married women should be asked to go first, 63% that men over 65 should and 42% that coloured and foreign workers should. Fully 26% of the 220 men

held that all three should be dispensed with in such a contingency before last in first out was to operate, while nearly 43% believed at least 2 of the 3 should.[1]

The Acton Society survey reported that discrimination against women, part-time, or night shift workers and workers of pensionable age was common; but discrimination against aliens as such was unusual.

'Efficiency' too, is susceptible to great differences of interpretation. In the first place a particular occupational group or work group may be exempted from dismissal on the grounds that their function is essential. In the second place efficiency considerations may have a more individualistic basis: the separation of the efficient sheep from the inefficient goats within a work group or occupational group. The actual measurement of efficiency varies a good deal. The Acton Society Trust report noted that some firms

> invoke records of ability pay and merit awards to lend objectivity to their assessment . . . others have no such inhibitions and state roundly that they will take into account 'adaptability', 'workroom conduct' and 'good general relations' and that the management's decision will be final.[2]

6. Finally, we may notice the possibility of procedural conflicts. There may be arguments, for example, about the appropriate parts to be played respectively by management and unions in the concrete determination of redundancy procedures. Again, there may be disagreement over the way the redundancy situation is handled, rather than with the principles underlying dismissals. Thus Wedderburn observes in *White Collar Redundancy* that, 'Whatever steps the Company had taken to explain how redundant workers were to be selected, the great majority (three-quarters) of the men we interviewed insisted that they did not know what was happening'.[3]

In general, therefore, one may suggest that conflict may be generated (a) in relation to the form of the proposals for dis-

---

[1] Kahn, op. cit., pp. 224–5.

[2] Acton Society Trust Report, op. cit., p. 33. In quoting this comment one is not, of course, subscribing to the view that any of these factors effectively measure efficiency.

[3] Wedderburn, op. cit., p. 15.

missal policy (i.e. generalised conflicts about norm legitimacy), (b) in relation to the content of the proposals relating to dismissal policy (i.e. particularised conflicts about norm legitimacy) and (c) in relation to the handling of the proposals for dismissals (i.e. conflicts about normative regulation).

I have now discussed some of the major forms of potential conflict arising from redundancy dismissal policy. We may turn now to the Consett case and attempt to locate and account for the redundancy conflict that emerged there.

2. *The Consett Case*[1]

The circumstances in which redundancy at Consett came to be regarded as necessary can be briefly outlined. In 1961, the steel industry was faced with a recession in trade, which had been induced by the credit squeeze the Conservative government was then operating. As the shipbuilding industry and the motor car industry, to name two major customers, began to cut down on their supplies, the steel industry began to suffer. At Consett, the general situation confronting the industry was aggravated by the fact that a transition was being made from an old plate mill to a new one. Thus, at the same time as labour productivity was increasing, sales opportunities were falling. Instead of being able to run the two mills simultaneously for as long as originally intended, the closure of the old mill was accelerated by adverse market conditions. In the summer of 1961, the management informed union representatives at a joint meeting of all unions, the Joint Consultative Committee, that a large scale redundancy was imminent. In the event, some 422 men were initially declared redundant out of a total work force of just under 7,000 – that is, about 6%. Ultimately, this figure rose to just over 600 – between 8 and 9% of the original work force, before the recession began to lift in the spring of 1962.

The official proposals from the Company relating to who should be made redundant, reflected the generalised belief system, mentioned earlier. In substantive terms this involved:

[1] The field work is based on an analysis of relevant documentary material provided by the Company. Many of those involved, including 'key influentials' were also interviewed. Interviews were carried out by A. J. Odber, G. Roberts and the writer.

(a) Ensuring that foreign workers, women doing men's work, and men over the age of 65 went first.
(b) Applying the rule of last in first out on a plant basis.
(c) Excluding craftsmen and 'specialists' whose jobs could not be taken over by anyone else at short notice, from the redundancy arrangements, on the grounds of efficiency.
(e) Excluding men under the age of 21, on the grounds of special needs for them to stay in employment.

Before going on to indicate the sources of conflict and consensus with these proposals, let us clarify why the Company reached the position of regarding its dismissal policy as 'the most equitable method'.

In the first place, the policy was an expression of the special sense of responsibility and obligation which the Company felt towards Consett and the surrounding neighbourhood. Because the Company was the dominant employer in the area it was evident that the Company's fortunes were indissolubly linked with those of the community. In the days of the early iron masters this relationship had taken the form of a benevolent paternalism – the provision of Company houses, a public park and general oversight of the town's welfare. A good example of the kind of relationship engendered is to be found in a letter written by the Chairman of the Consett and District United Friendly Societies in 1877 to William Jenkins, J.P., the General Manager of the Consett Iron Works:

> We . . . beg to return to you our sincere thanks for the many favours we have received at your hand, more especially with our annual procession and gala. We feel assured that it is to a sincere desire on your part to forward the welfare of our members and their families that we owe the generous aid you have given us, and also the kindly manner in which you have personally come forward to assist us. It is a matter for congratulation with us that, while we are using our best endeavours to spread the principles of our Societies, and thereby improving the moral and physical condition of the people, we should have the countenance and support of a gentleman possessing the influence which your position amongst us naturally gives you. . . .[1]

This letter conveys the spirit of a feudal relationship carried

[1] *The History and Biography of West Durham* (1881), pp. 38–9.

over into an industrial context. This kind of relationship has, over the years, been profoundly modified, although at least one manager in the Company was prepared to argue that the 'psychological remnants of feudalism' was still in evidence. Be that as it may, the sense of dependence on the Company, which the economic decline of the West Durham Coalfield served to emphasise, was still felt and voiced. In September 1960, for example, the then Chairman of the Consett Urban District Council could write in the Company's House Journal:

> I feel I am voicing the public thought when I say how much we appreciate having the Consett Iron Company as the centre of our activities . . . and how much the inhabitants, workers, and traders, not forgetting the Council, are dependent on the progress and expansion which have made Consett known all over the world. . . . The Management and the Directors are to be congratulated and praised for their decisions (during the very difficult times) to resist the temptation to move the works to the coast, and for the decision to modernise and extend at Consett.

The period alluded to in the last sentence was the 1930s· Immediately before the Second World War, the Company had set up a strip mill in Jarrow and the rumour was strong that this was the first step of a gradual transfer of the whole Company. It was in the recognition of this special relationship with the surrounding community that the Company chose, as the central plank in its redundancy arrangements, the principle of 'last in first out' on a plant basis. Since the most recent arrivals were, in the main, not Consett men, it was argued that this method was least harmful to the community itself. Further, by operating the rule on a plant wide basis, it meant that middle-aged men would be less likely to suffer redundancy than younger men and, in particular, that fathers would not be out of work while their sons were still employed.

The rules for dismissal relating to the ascribed status, the seniority or the needs of the participants serve, it may be suggested, to reflect and reinforce both the in-group/out-group dichotomy between community and non-community members, and the internal social differentiations existing within the community.

We may notice, secondly, that, in the interests of efficiency, the Company had to concern itself, not only with the size of its labour force, but also with the quality of it. Craftsmen and 'specialists', either because of the conventions of existing union rules, and/or for clear functional reasons, could be regarded as having skills that were non-transferable, at least in any immediate sense. The problem the Company faced in relation to these groups was one of relative shortage of supply in the array of skills that they represented.

When, after a long period of prosperity, a recession hits an industry, it is usually possible to defer for a limited period any thought of laying off maintenance craftsmen. Such workers can be deployed in the thorough overhaul of machinery and equipment. This is particularly true in a continuous shift industry. As these tasks are completed, however, the decision then has to be taken as to whether to make some of these men redundant or whether to under-employ the existing manpower. In the Consett case, bearing in mind the relative geographical isolation of the town, to make craftsmen redundant might be to lose many of them altogether. Given that their skills were a prerequisite of efficient plant utilisation, a shortage of such personnel could impair the efficiency of the Company when trade returned to normal.

This dual concern on the part of Company policy-makers to accommodate itself to the value system of the local community, on the one hand, and attempt to maintain the plant as a viable economic unit on the other hand, led to the selection of criteria for redundancy which were at least partially conflicting. But it was the elaboration of a particular form of compound justice. Further, in arriving at what they regarded as the appropriate 'mix', the Company claimed that it was following an established precedent: its policy was not only in line with pre-war redundancy procedures, but also with the practice which was followed in 1958 – their only experience of post-war redundancy. On that occasion, the Company maintained, the unions agreed and the policy was put into effect 'in a completely harmonious manner'.

We may now go on to consider the extent to which, and the ways in which particular groups deviated from the official Company policy. Although a great deal of the debate crystallised round the question: should the 'last in first out' principle be applied on a plant or a departmental basis? this does not in itself bring out the complexity of the issues. In the Summary Chart of the Sources of Redundancy Conflict at Consett,[1] I have listed the major groups involved, their evaluation of the character of the recession, their goal orientation in relation to redundancy policy and the instrumental behaviour they adopted in an attempt to achieve their goals. It now remains to work through this and to describe and to analyse the conflict in terms of the social processes involved.

On the grounds that their function is essential, the craftsmen were exempted from the redundancy procedure. Therefore, objections from the craft unions were not to be expected and, with the exception of the E.T.U., they were not forthcoming. The E.T.U., however, included electricians' mates within its membership. The union argued, on their behalf, that the electrical department, including mates, should be regarded as a separate maintenance department and that any necessary redundancy of craftsmen's mates should be treated solely with reference to departmental needs. The E.T.U. position may be viewed in the light of the fact that B.I.S.A.K.T.A. had competing claims for the allegiance of craftsmen's mates. The Company scheme of the plant-wide seniority rule involved the transfer of men between departments. This meant that B.I.S.A.K.T.A. men would inevitably infiltrate into the Electrical Department. The E.T.U. had not always organised craftsmen's mates, hence the fear that the Company scheme would lead to a reversal of the union's fortunes in this respect. Indeed, in subsequent discussion with the Company, there were differences of opinion concerning how many electricians' mates were in the E.T.U. and how many in B.I.S.A.K.T.A. The E.T.U. claimed that all the men were in their union, but the existence of a debate on a factual question perhaps indicates the relative insecurity of the E.T.U. in relation to the organisation of this group. To oppose the scheme would be to indicate to the mates that the union had their interests at heart. By denoting electricians mates as a class distinct from other labourers, who should not go into the general category of interchangeable labour, the number of E.T.U. men made redundant would be minimised. At the same time, if successful, the opposition would be of strategic value to the E.T.U. in that, effectively, a single union department would have been established. In that the Electrical Department did have a well established, auto-

---

[1] See below, pp. 226–8.

nomous and acceptable consultative system, the union's attempt to draw the boundary line there was understandable. The difficulty was, however, that if the electricians' mates were to be treated as a special category, then what about the fitters' mates? The B.I.S.A.K.T.A. branch to which fitters' mates belonged also wanted redundancy to operate on a departmental basis. The Joint B.I.S.A.K.T.A. Branches Committee in the plant did not support this view, however, for reasons which we discuss below. This gave added strength to the Company's position when it came to negotiating with the E.T.U. area official. Further, the Company was able to point out that the union was a signatory to a 1942 domestic agreement, which gave the firm the right to deploy its labourers and dispense with them as it saw fit.

It is significant that, even under stress, the E.T.U. official was prepared to accept as binding an agreement into which his union had voluntarily entered, and overt conflict was in this case avoided. This is not to say that in the light of the current experience, the union might not subsequently seek to revoke or change the agreement by constitutional means. Indeed, the union official indicated that the whole question would be re-opened when normal working conditions were resumed at the works.

It is also worth noting that there has been a tendency in the steel industry on the part of management to try and get away from the one for one craftsman/mate ratio. It is possible, though by no means clear, that the E.T.U. was worried that the recession might result in changes of this kind. Clearly, to have all the mates in their union, should such an issue manifest itself, would add to their bargaining strength. And organisational changes of this sort could be more readily disguised if redundancy operated on a plant-wide basis.

Although the E.T.U.'s objections led to a skirmish with the Company, it was the dissent of the National Union of Blast-furnacemen which had the widest repercussions. The N.U.B., like the E.T.U., was concerned to maintain union control of jobs in particular departments. It resisted, therefore, the suggestion that redundancy procedures should operate on a plant-wide basis, since this would involve the transfer of B.I.S.A.K.T.A. members into the Blast Furnaces and Coke Works Departments. This they regarded as infiltration. In any case, there was a further advantage to be gained from departmentally based redundancy schemes. It is the finishing processes that suffer first in the event of a redundancy and, bearing this in mind, the N.U.B. members would be the last to suffer from the effects of recession. But the union felt that there were impartial grounds on which its positon could be justified. When, therefore, N.U.B. members were dismissed under the official redundancy arrangements, the union took the case through the negotiating procedure, appealing on behalf of its members on the grounds of wrongful dismissal.

In its appeal, which went outside the Company to an ad hoc Joint Committee and then to National Arbitration, the N.U.B. demonstrated that, in the steel industry at large, it was common practice to operate redundancy procedures on a departmenta basis. Recent examples were brought forward from South Durham and Dorman Long as evidence. These firms were in the same region, the North East Coast, and this perhaps gave added strength to the union's case, for the Company was not in a position to suggest that there were regional agreements that differed from national practice. In making this point, it is clear that the N.U.B. was not accepting as valid the distinctive community frame of reference on which the Company placed so much emphasis. Instead it implied that a standardised redundancy procedure applicable throughout the industry was a preferable and more just solution. Insofar as it could portray the Company as being out of step with other firms in the industry (with the implication that its geographical position did not entitle it to special consideration) it could hope to gain the sympathy of the arbitrator. The Company challenged the validity of the union's contention. It maintained that in all the cases cited there was an important difference. The redundancies did not occur in integrated steel works such as Consett but on sites where there was only one type of plant and hence, it was argued, the question under discussion at Consett did not arise. This is a fine point in that the plants in question were parts of wider combines, but it represents a difference of opinion with the union over the substantive content of the industrial rule of law on this point.

The N.U.B. went on to challenge the consistency of a Company policy which operated a system of promotion by seniority on a departmental basis for production workers, while, at the same time, adhering to a system of redundancy and demotion on a plant-wide basis. The contradiction lay in the fact that plant-wide redundancy resulted in inter-departmental transfers, but the men who were so transferred were replacing men to whom, in departmental terms, they were inevitably junior. Thus the custom and practice of the seniority system was held to invalidate the redundancy procedure.

Finally, the N.U.B. questioned the procedural method by which the redundancy was handled. They did not accept the right of the Joint Consultative Committee to make decisions about redundancy, which could be regarded as in any way binding on individual unions. In this they were constitutionally correct. The 1946 Agreement between the Iron and Steel Trades Employers' Association and the N.U.B.:

> Provides the following machinery for dealing with questions affecting blast furnaces, which is characteristic of procedures both written and unwritten in the industry:
> 1. Questions of a general character are to be dealt with at meetings between representatives of the Association and of the Union.
> 2. Differences at individual works are to be dealt with in the first place between the works management and the workmen concerned. The workmen have the right to call in the works' delegate and/or the district official of the union and the management likewise have the right to call in a district association or a district sectional official . . .[1]

The high degree of consensus on the Joint Consultative Committee, to which the Company could rightly point, was therefore set aside by the N.U.B. as irrelevant since, in procedural terms it was not a decision taking body.

On the basis of these contentions the N.U.B. claimed that, although it was in a minority camp vis-à-vis other unions, it was still justified in appealing against wrongful dismissal on behalf of its members. The Arbitrator upheld the union's claim. In his summing up he observed:

> There is no material difference between the parties on matters of fact so far as the present dispute is concerned. Further, both agree that seniority in the sense of length of service should be the decisive factor in determining which men should be declared redundant. The difference lies in how seniority should be defined. It is clear

[1] Ministry of Labour, *Handbook of Industrial Relations* (H.M.S.O., 1961), p. 43.

that as far as promotion is concerned, under the agreed rules, it is service in a section which determines seniority and therefore those joining a section take precedence after those already working in that section, whatever their seniority elsewhere might have been. The Association maintains that seniority rules make no reference to redundancy, the matter now in dispute is outside their scope and can be interpreted on a different principle. I find this difficult to accept – the seniority rules must be interpreted at need in the light of custom and practice.

In considering the bearing of the 1958 redundancy arrangements on the 1961 situation, he stated that there appeared to be some conflict of evidence as regards union reactions to them but 'in any case one such precedent cannot be held to stand against majority custom and practice'. He ruled accordingly that 'when redundancy necessitates dismissals the seniority rules relating to promotion shall apply'.

The reactions of other unions and management to the N.U.B.'s position and to the decision of the Arbitrator are of great interest. The Company had not only claimed that its policy was based on equity but explicitly pointed out that this involved 'fulfilling its primary responsibility to the Consett community rather than an outlying area'. At the Arbitration proceedings there were signed statements on behalf of the N.U.G.M.W., T.G.W.U., Allied Crafts, and B.I.S.A.K.T.A. Joint Branches Committee, which endorsed the Company's policy as being satisfactory and appropriate. The B.I.S.A.K.T.A. statement was particularly interesting in that it outlined the belief system on which its support was based. One can in fact distinguish a number of inter-related elements:

(a) There is a distinction drawn between the role of the Joint Consultative Committee and union-management negotiation:

> The Company and the trade unions both recognised that the Consultative Committee is not the negotiating body but it is the medium by which the firm notifies the trade union representatives of major policies, then leaving it to the union to go back to their members after the official statement to see what would be their line of approach; then for the unions to contact the firm through their negotiating machinery whether they agree or not to the suggestions outlined by the firm.

For B.I.S.A.K.T.A. a collective decision was taken in favour of the Company's policy, but this decision was not reached without inter-branch conflict. Each B.I.S.A.K.T.A. branch has a jealously guarded autonomy in negotiating with the firm. The role of the B.I.S.A.K.T.A. Joint Branches Committee is, therefore, a very delicate one. Its formal scope is laid down in Rule 16 of the B.I.S.A.K.T.A. Rule Book:

> For the purpose of co-ordination and consultation on matters of common and general interest to the members, the Executive Council shall authorise where it considers necessary, the establishment of Joint Committees at works where there are a number of branches of the organisation or in an area within the division. It shall draw up standing orders under which such committees shall function so as to ensure that they do not in any way encroach upon the autonomy of the branches nor interfere with the functioning of negotiating machinery existing in the various sections of the industry.

The practical problem is: when does legitimate co-ordination become illegitimate coercion? Two of the branches wanted the seniority rule to be applied on a departmental basis. The case of the fitters' mates we have already discussed. In the same branch were the general labourers. These mainly were composed of recent entrants. They belonged to a pool of labour before going on to particular promotion lines, and as such were allocated to various departments. As a group they were very much at risk when it came to redundancy, but more of their members were likely to be sheltered if dismissal was departmentally based. The other dissenting branch was a small stocktakers' branch. They not only favoured the departmental ruling but also felt that they should be classified as specialists and thus kept in employment. The sensitivity of the branches to their independent status was reflected in the fact that charges of unwarranted interference of branch officials in the affairs of other branches were sent to the Executive Council of the union. Neither the validity of these charges nor the outcome is known, but they are obvious symptoms of inter-branch conflict.

The presentation of a united front, as symbolised in the joint statement to the Arbitrator is most likely to be attributed to the political expertise of two union 'elder statesmen' who, besides holding senior branch positions, were lay members of the union's National Executive Council. Their leadership, in Weberian terms, was based on a mixture of traditional and legal components. They had been union officials for many years and were commonly re-elected without opposition, but they were of course elected on the basis of the union constitution. It was not impossible for them so to structure the situation that a majority vote on the B.I.S.A.K.T.A. Joint Committee would constitute a democratic decision of B.I.S.A.K.T.A. The Joint Committee could then act as a means of social control bringing deviant branches into line with 'official' union policy. To put it another way, the Joint Branches Committee effectively prescribed what was the legitimate response to the redundancy situation and this circumscribed the decision-making role of individual branches.

(b) The joint statement to the Arbitrator re-affirmed the Company's recognition of its special relationship with the Consett community. Given the hope that this was a temporary recession, it was argued that 'last in first out' on a Company basis was a fair and equitable basis and the best method suitable to that particular time. It was stated that the men of Consett 'have got their commitments and ties in the town . . . and have been very good workers'. The cross-cutting ties of the Company and community were emphasised when the writer went on to observe:

> As a public representative with a wide experience on trade union matters and negotiations I know that the general principle of the method by which the redundancy was carried out had the full support of the townspeople . . . if we had carried it out on a departmental basis it would have had very serious consequences on the people as a whole.

(c) The importance of inter-union co-operation during this period was spelt out:

> We stressed very strongly that we did not want to use this for individual trade union advantage because it was dangerous for a community like ours where recession at all times brings hardship to create any friction between respective unions.

Inter-departmental transfers were, therefore, recognised as temporary and individuals were not asked to transfer to another union where this would normally be expected. If, after these temporary measures, an individual chose to stay in his new department, then it would be necessary for him to change his union membership, where his new job was normally under the control of another union.

This statement by the B.I.S.A.K.T.A. Joint Branches Committee serves to indicate the reasons why the majority of the men accepted the Company's official definition of the situation – the evaluation of the character of the recession, the ends to be considered, and the appropriate behaviour to achieve those ends. 'Rocking the boat' in the light of this commitment to consensus becomes the cardinal sin. The word sin might almost be taken in its literal meaning here for, as one B.I.S.A.K.T.A. official observed:

> First in last out on a plant basis was a good trade union and Christian approach – you should always think of the good of the people as a whole, not in sectional interests.

The strong feelings which the N.U.B.'s victory at Arbitration engendered in the defeated majority can well be imagined. It was described, for example, by a B.I.S.A.K.T.A. official as 'a dirty trick' and by a member of senior management as 'a glaring miscarriage of justice'. In terms of community interest, the N.U.B. take on the character of a renegade group:

> The renegade not only puts into question the values and interests of the group, but also threatens its very unity. Renegadism signifies and symbolises a desertion of those standards of the group considered vital to its well-being, if not to its actual existence . . . Renegadism threatens to break down the boundary lines of the established group. Therefore the group must fight the renegade with all its might since he threatens symbolically, if not in fact, its existence as an ongoing concern.[1]

This comment of Coser's applies to the individual within the group, but it has its parallel here to the group within the community. Thus one suspects that the very act of taking the case to Arbitration tended to lead to a closing of the ranks between management and the remaining unions. It is by analogy an illustration of Coser's contention that:

> The perception of this inside 'danger' on the part of the remaining group members makes for their 'pulling together' for an increase in

[1] L. Coser, *The Functions of Social Conflict* (Routledge and Kegan Paul, 1956), p. 69.

their awareness of the issues at stake, and for an increase in participation; in short, the danger signal brings about the mobilisation of all group defences. Just because the struggle concentrates the group's energies for purposes of self-defence, it ties the members more closely to each other and promotes group integration.[1]

The Arbitration award to the N.U.B. meant that, in order to accommodate the legitimated minority view and the strongly held majority union view any future redundancies would have to be worked out partly on a plant-wide basis and partly on a departmental basis. This gave added administrative difficulty and, indeed, a small redundancy which was attempted on this mixed basis proved very troublesome to handle. This tended to lead to a situation in which work sharing was preferred to redundancy.[2]

I have left until last those whom we have characterised as management dissentients. These men were not an organised group as such, but it was noticeable that at middle management level there was a tendency to support the view that departmentally based redundancy was preferable to considerations of plant-wide redundancy. The rationale behind this view may be briefly enumerated:

1. Redundancy on a plant-wide basis with the concomitant inter-departmental transfers of work-people involves an initial re-training programme. In practice this training was frequently given to them by the men whom they were going to replace. This could not be an easy relationship to sustain. Sometimes the trainer would leave before the new occupant of the job was fully trained.

2. Newness in a job characteristically gives rise to poorer workmanship. This was reflected in an increased wastage on scrap. The firm was, in consequence, losing in competitive strength at a time when it was most needed.

3. It was felt that the official Company policy gave rise to an inordinate loss of younger men. It was pointed out, for example, that it was the younger men who went out in the redundancy of 1958. Now, 22 months later, many of them were out of work again. Because 1958 was the first post-war redundancy to hit the

[1] Ibid., p. 71.
[2] Even on this, the N.U.B. found themselves out of step with the majority. After a period of work sharing they had a secret ballot on whether to continue or whether to have redundancy in the department by seniority. They chose the latter course.

firm it was, perhaps, not too difficult to adopt the 'it can happen once but it won't happen again' attitude. But a repeat episode in 1961 was bound to create much more uncertainty and to bring thoughts of migration to the fore. In that young men tend to be more foot-loose, it could reasonably be argued that the Company's policy, so far as it emphasised seniority of service as a criterion of discrimination (particularly in its plant-based form) was liable to accelerate a movement away from the area. It was in fact estimated by the Personnel Department of the Company that of the 600 men who lost their jobs, some 50% were lost to the firm – though possibly not all of them permanently. But certainly the loss of confidence on the part of the younger generation in the area as a source of job opportunities and economic security, insofar as it encouraged migration, would lead to an ageing work population and a declining community.

4. There was, finally, the secondary re-training problem which, it was pointed out, would emerge as the recession began to lift. As that happened, men who had been transferred were given the choice of staying in their present job or reverting to their old one. Those who chose to stay in their present job, might well cause the men whom they replaced, and who were now returning, to take a different kind of job, for which they would need some training. Conversely, those who chose to return to their old jobs would theoretically be replaced by the returning original incumbents of the job. But not all of the men who were made redundant did return and the men who actually took the jobs might need special training.

It is likely that the tendency of middle management to think in this way was a function of the immediacy of responsibility for output which was theirs. The Company policy-makers, for their part, were aware that the plant-wide method of redundancy involved them in more administrative cost and inconvenience, but they argued that this was a positive indication of their good faith towards the Consett community. The essence of the alternative view put forward here was that such good faith was best expressed by an over-riding concern with competitive efficiency. As one proponent of this view put it:

> The plant is detached from the rest of the steel industry and therefore there is a need to be very competitive. The area as a whole depends on the plant. There is a humanitarian or community aspect

in our stress on efficiency. We do this in the men's interest as well as our own.

In other words the conviction was expressed that while in the short run the official policy on redundancy might promote a feeling of well-being in the community, in the long run the proposed solution might defeat the ends it purported to serve, namely, the survival and welfare of the community.

Conclusion

I have sought in this account to locate the sources and levels of inter-group conflict, which arose in relation to the Company's official redundancy dismissal policy. In order to do this effectively the problem was first placed in the context of the generalised belief system concerning redundancy procedures for dismissal, as revealed in surveys undertaken on the subject in this country. The particular case studied here showed no basic disagreement with the legitimacy of the generalised belief system and in that sense at least it may be said to be a 'representative' case study. At the same time, to do justice to the social processes involved in the particular case, it has been necessary to seek to understand the ways in which the various groups perceived their interests and defined the situation in which they found themselves.

As one proceeds to analyse the issue in this way, it becomes evident that one may talk meaningfully about the existence of competing rationalities: since strong logical arguments are advanced on the basis of different value assumptions. The implication is that one cannot speak of 'pure rationality'. Each system of rationality is bounded by evaluative considerations of what is the desirable end(s) to achieve and by normative considerations of what are the appropriate means to utilise in attaining such an end(s). Both these sets of considerations are themselves based on calculations which are typically imperfect of the costs and consequences of particular actions.

The sociologist, by using the method advocated by Max Weber, of 'subjective understanding' may seek in a systematic way to make explicit the value assumptions, which underlie the behaviour of the interested parties. This approach takes conflicts of interest as a normal feature of social relations. But, at the same time, it would be a mistake to conclude that value assumptions are necessarily 'closed' categories (or 'sentiments', as the Hawthorne investigators and others have called them). They are at least in some measure amenable to attention by the impact of empirical evidence. For example, one would expect that the evaluation of the character of the recession is something which can be affected by the introduction of new information. Or again, through inter-group discussion, agreement may be reached about the priority of goals, or accommodation may be reached over the extent to which conflicting goals may be attained. One is not of course suggesting that this is automatically the case over all issues. But, insofar as it is so, the positive implication for management is that by contributing to a greater cognitive awareness of a particular situation, sociological analysis may aid managerial skills in minimising conflicts of interest.[1]

SUMMARY CHART OF THE SOURCES OF REDUNDANCY CONFLICT
AT CONSETT

Group	Evaluation of the character of the recession	Perception of ends to which behaviour should be directed	Reference point for 'Last in first out'	Instrumental Behaviour to Achieve Ends		
				Other differences with company's definition of terms and categories	Questioning Company's procedure for handling redundance	Mobilising Resources
Company policy-maker	Short term trade recession	Pursuit of interests limited by prevailing norms defining community interest	Plant	—	—	(a) Use of Joint Consultation (b) Use of domestic agreements (c) Gaining T.U. support in arbitration case against N.U.B.

[1] It remains the case however, that since perception is selective, there are built in constraints which will affect the degree of acceptance of a cognitive statement issued by a member of an 'opposing' group, even when evidence is brought forward, to substantiate it.

SUMMARY CHART OF THE SOURCES OF REDUNDANCY CONFLICT
AT CONSETT—*cont.*

Group	Evaluation of the character of the recession	Perception of ends to which behaviour should be directed	Reference point for 'Last in first out'	Instrumental Behaviour to Achieve Ends		
				Other differences with company's definition of terms and categories	Questioning Company's procedure for handling redundance	Mobilising Resources
Allied Crafts (excluding E.T.U.)	Agreement with Company policy-makers			No	No	Support for management in Arbitration case against N.U.B.
BISAKTA majority view	Agreement with Company policy-makers			No	No	(a) Joint Branches Committee used to develop and maintain inter-branch policy. (b) Support for management in Arbitration case against N.U.B.
E.T.U.	Primarily short term recession but organisational changes may lead to permanent reduction in labour force	Individual Trade Union interests predominate	Department Trade Union interests predominate	Electricians' mates should qualify as 'specialists'	Uncertain about validity of Joint Consultation	Trade Union official brought in for domestic discussions with management. Attempts to assert union control over specified jobs

227

SUMMARY CHART OF THE SOURCES OF REDUNDANCY CONFLICT
AT CONSETT—*cont.*

Group	Evaluation of the character of the recession	Perception of ends to which behaviour should be directed	Reference point for 'Last in first out'	Instrumental Behaviour to Achieve Ends		
				Other differences with company's definition of terms and categories	Questioning Company's procedure for handling redundance	Mobilising Resources
BISAKTA minority view	Short term trade recession	Individual T.U. Branch interests predominate	Department	Fitters' mates and Stocktakers should qualify as 'specialists'	No	Assertion of branch autonomy. Appeals to Union's National Executive
N.U.B.	Fear of longer term recessions. Possibly fear of technological redundancy	Individual Trade Union interests	Department	No	Refusal to accept validity of Joint Consultation as basis for decision-taking	(a) Attempts to assert union control over specified jobs. (b) Use of industrial disputes procedures through to Arbitration
Management	Fear that temporary recession could lead to more permanent market problems if corrective action not taken	Economic rationality should predominate 'Real' Community interest dependent on Company efficiency	Department	No	No	Expression of personal views – no known mobilisation in group terms

The Sociology of Work

Trends and Counter-trends[1]

THE study of the social relations and organisations which stem from men's work activities is not a new sphere for the sociologist. Among the more influential earlier writers were Marx, Engels, Max Weber and Durkheim. Their reflections on the nature of work in modern industrial societies can, on the whole, be said to have created a tradition of sociological pessimism. I would like to indicate some of the sources of this pessimism and then to describe some of the ways in which this tradition has been modified in more recent sociological writing.

In the Marx-Engels canon it is typically argued that the very process of the division of labour diminishes man's freedom. 'For as soon as the division of labour begins', it is claimed, 'each man has a particular, exclusive sphere of activity which is forced upon him and from which he cannot escape. He is a hunter, a fisherman, a shepherd, a critical critic and must remain so if he does not want to lose his means of livelihood.'[2] It is true that an idyllic picture is painted of life in a communist society, in which the division of labour would no longer exist. It would be possible to 'hunt in the morning, fish in the afternoon, rear cattle in the evening, criticise after dinner, in accordance with my inclination, without ever becoming hunter, fisherman, shepherd or critic.'[3] This utopian vision contrasts vividly with the Marxist analysis

---

[1] This Appendix is based upon, but not identical with, a broadcast talk given in January 1966, in the B.B.C. study series, 'The Sphere of the Sociologist'.

[2] T. B. Bottomore and M. Rubel (eds.) Karl Marx. *Selected Writings in Sociology and Social Philosophy* (Penguin, 1963), p. 110.

[3] Ibid, p. 111.

of the impact of industrialism on the division of labour. But it helps to explain the assessment of the trend.

'The stunting of man's faculties,' claims Engels, 'grows in the same measure as the division of labour which attains its highest development in manufacturing. Manufacturing splits up each trade into its separate fractional operations, allots each of them to an individual labourer as his life calling and then claims him for life to a particular detail function and a particular tool. And not only labourers, but also the classes directly or indirectly exploiting the labourers are made subject through the division of labour to the tool of their function.'[1]

Durkheim, in his celebrated book on the division of labour, unlike Marx and Engels, stresses in many places the social benefits which a properly co-ordinated and agreed upon division of tasks can confer upon a society. Yet he also recognises that industrial societies may be prone to certain 'abnormal' forms of the division of labour, which may be de-humanising in their effects on the individual:

'The division of labour,' he observes, 'has often been accused of degrading the individual by making him a machine. And truly, if he does not know whither the operations he performs are tending, if he relates them to no end, he can only continue to work through routine. Every day he repeats the same movements with monotonous regularity but without being interested in them and without understanding them . . . He is no longer anything but an inert piece of machinery, only an external force set going which always moves in the same direction and the same way. Surely, no matter how one may represent the moral ideal one cannot remain indifferent to such a debasement of human nature.'[2]

A machine-based technology is seen then as actually or potentially creating an industrial work force performing unskilled tasks which have little intrinsic meaning. Yet these routine repetitive tasks are such that they control the worker rather than the other way round. The position of the industrial worker, in short, is one of alienation.

In Max Weber's analysis of bureaucracy the theme of the de-humanisation of work in industrial society is developed

[1] F. Engels, Herr Eugen Duhring's *Revolution in Science* (Anti-Duhring) (Moscow: Foreign Languages Publishing House, 1947), pp. 435-6.

[2] E. Durkheim, *The Division of Labour in Society* (Glencoe Free Press, 1964), p. 371.

230

further. Bureaucratic organisations were seen by him as raising to the optimum point the technical advantages of precision, speed, unambiguity, knowledge of the files and cost reduction. In his judgment, 'the fully developed bureaucratic mechanism compares with other organisations exactly as does the machine with the non-mechanical modes of production'.[1] The bureaucratic official is seen as having a very limited, carefully defined and closely supervised sphere of competence. He is portrayed as a member of an organisation in which commands flow downwards in an orderly fashion. Above all, he is subject to impersonal rules not of his own making. 'The more the bureaucracy is de-humanised,' comments Weber, 'the more completely it succeeds in eliminating from official business love, hatred and all purely personal, irrational and emotional elements which escape calculation. This is the specific nature of bureaucracy and is appraised as its specific virtue.'[2]

The minute sub-division of tasks, from which meaning has been drained and freedom removed, tend to be regarded as a natural, if not an inevitable, consequence of both a machine-based technology and the process of bureaucratisation. It is a preoccupation with the alienating character of work in such contexts which gives rise to the tradition of sociological pessimism.

When we turn to more recent sociological writing, it is evident that the tradition has left its mark and yet, at the same time, some important qualifications are made. Modern empirical research certainly points, for example, to the important influence of technology upon both worker and managerial behaviour, but it draws attention to the differing technological environments which co-exist in modern industrial societies. The well-known studies at the Hawthorne plant of the Western Electric Company, Chicago, had demonstrated that work groups who were engaged on identical tasks tended to exercise more control over the level of earnings and output than groups whose members were engaged on different tasks. Leonard Sayles in his book *The Behaviour of Industrial Work Groups* has taken the matter further. His essential thesis is that the technology of the work situation can separate or promote friendship cliques, can simplify or complicate work

[1] H. H. Gerth and C. Wright Mills (eds.) *From Max Weber: Essays in Sociology* (Routledge and Kegan Paul, 1948), p. 214.
[2] Ibid, p. 216.

team relations and can accordingly influence the degree to which the worker can become part of an effective pressure group and thus exercise some control over the conditions of his work situation. Some groups lack sufficient internal cohesion to implement their demands or even formulate them to management; other élite groups performing essential tasks rarely have to fight for their rights since they are usually conceded by management; but in still other situations groups are sufficiently mobilised to fight for their rights but these are not automatically granted by management. Such an approach has interesting implications when considering the industrial relations climate of a plant. Sayles identifies and illustrates the kind of work situation in which overt conflict is likely to occur:

> Serious problems are likely to occur in that middle ground between jobs which are obviously machine- or management-paced and jobs over which the employee retains a large degree of controls, as is true of craft occupations. A good example in the middle range is the trim line in plants manufacturing automobile bodies. Management has developed extensive time studies to support the speed at which the line moves – all without worker control. But employees in the department have never given up insisting that time studies are not accurate, that the recalitrance of trim materials (cloth) and the 'judgmental' qualities of their jobs make many of these studies inaccurate. The continuous struggle caused by the differences between the rates demanded by employees is one of the outstanding sources of wildcat strikes in the automobile industry.[1]

Much assembly line work, however, is such that the worker has little control over the pace, rhythm, quality or method of work. Most contemporary observers would certainly agree that these are the marks of alienation. Highly rationalised production control provides a text book example of the scientific management concern to transfer intelligence from the shop floor. Yet the militance of car workers, in spite of, or through their unions is a by-word, which suggests that such workers do not passively accept their alienated condition. Similarly Warner and Low's well documented account of the strike at Newburyport in the New England shoe industry, is seen as a response to the supplanting of craft techniques of manufacture by mass production techniques. As control over job content, techniques and standards was taken

[1] L. Sayles, *The Behavior of Industrial Work Groups* (Wiley, 1958), p. 65.

from the worker, he reacted by linking up with a national union organisation whose collective resources and bargaining expertise ensured that he was not left powerless.

But in any case, as Robert Blauner has pointed out in his significant book *Alienation and Freedom,* technological progress is not always associated with an increasingly minute sub-division of labour, as the earlier sociologists tended to assume. In continuous process industries, such as chemicals, the opportunities for a worker to play a vital part in operating and maintaining expensive plant are stressed. The result, in his opinion, is 'meaningful work in a more cohesive, integrated industrial climate . . . new dignity from responsibility and a sense of individual function.'[1]

More generally, the possibility that work may be humanised as automated forms of production are applied to large scale industry, where technically and economically feasible, has been discussed by a number of writers, notably the French sociologist Georges Friedmann. He sees them as eliminating the need for semi-skilled machine operators, generating a demand for a new artisan class and new skills involving the creation and regulation of delicate and precise equipment and, in so doing, restoring an intellectual quality to work. Automation, in his judgment, constitutes a new stage in the dialectics of mechanisation and, at the same time grounds for hope rather than pessimism for those working with such productive systems.

When one turns to the treatment of bureaucracy in industrial society one finds again that the tradition of sociological pessimism has left its mark. It is indeed embellished in the late C. Wright Mills' study of the American Middle Classes, *White Collar.* The office worker is seen as subject to standardised and mechanised office routines. He is not a person by simply 'an item in an enormous file'. The centrality of the selling function is viewed with grave misgivings by Mills. The salesmen are depicted as alienated from themselves, since their very personalities, their smiles and their kindly gestures, are exploited in the selling situation for their commercial relevance. Even the old professions of law, medicine and teaching are regarded as falling bastions of freedom. Since they now operate typically in bureaucratic contexts the result in Mills' view is to reduce the status of the pro-

[1] R. Blauner, *Alienation and Freedom* (Wiley, 1964).

fessional to that of a technician who purveys packaged advice of one sort or another. Needless to say, Mills is not impressed with studies which purport to show that many white collar workers are satisfied with their jobs. Such sentiments simply reflect the morale of cheerful robots. 'Whatever satisfaction alienated men gain from work occurs within the framework of alienation'. Mills' emphasis on the negative aspects of white collar work is too selective and impressionistic to be really convincing. Certainly the uniformly oppressive nature of bureaucracy is contested by other writers. Alvin Gouldner, for example, argues that for too long the study of bureaucracy has been associated with what he calls a mood of metaphysical pathos. In his study of an American gypsum plant he shows that not all bureaucratic rules are imposed from above unilaterally. Some rules may be the product of discussion and be regarded as beneficial to the parties concerned rather than crippling. In this respect it makes sense to talk about representative bureaucracy.

But whether rules are representatively based or not, they may often be manipulated by people who are allegedly controlled by them. Rules governing appointments, promotion and even the job classifications on which salary scales are based, may in fact be subject to bargaining and personal influence. Melville Dalton's colourful study *Men Who Manage*, is in large measure a description of the ways in which rules are used as bargaining counters. 'To those with power and using power,' he writes, 'rules and procedures were not sacred guides but working tools to be revised, ignored or dropped as required in striking successive balances between company goals on the one side and their personal ends *and* the claims of their supporters on the other . . .' Those who barely filled their offices were all rule devotees. 'They resisted change and were quick to fear any clique activity and to label it as "dirty".' Those who worked through cliques tended for their part to view it as 'a way of dealing with situations that were too urgent and dynamic for formal handling'.[1]

What current research into bureaucratic organisations has tended to emphasise, is that while a precisely delineated division of labour based on hierarchical authority may be efficient for conditions in which past decisions and patterns of behaviour are a reliable guide for the future, in conditions of rapid social and

[1] M. Dalton, *Men Who Manage* (Wiley, 1959), pp. 30-1.

economic change other arrangements may be more appropriate. The electronics industry, for example, needs managers who have to search for innovations which will give them an edge in a highly competitive market, and, at the same time adapt to and live with the innovations of their competitors. Roles may be blurred, communications may be problem-centred based on technical knowledge and expertise rather than formal authority. The demand for flexibility of behaviour in such a context makes the alleged conformity of the organisation man pathological and ritualistic. It is for these and other reasons that Michael Crozier puts forward, albeit with qualifications, the view that 'contrary to the fear of so many humanists and revolutionary prophets of doom, we can expect more promises of liberalisation than standardisation'.[1]

Contemporary sociological writing has, then, continued to handle these great themes of the influence of technology and bureaucracy on man in industrial society. But insofar as it stresses the diversity of work experiences which may co-exist within these frameworks there is less readiness to speak in global terms about the lot of industrial man and the plight of the bureaucrat. Alienation may be a risk but it is not always a reality. And not all the signposts point in the direction of increasing alienation. To this extent modern sociology speaks the language of guarded optimism. No doubt Marx and Wright Mills are muttering in the wings that it is also the language of false consciousness!

---

[1] M. Crozier, *The Bureaucratic Phenomenon* (Tavistock, 1964), p. 298.

An Example of a Demarcation Procedural and Apportionment Agreement

DEMARCATION PROCEDURE

ENGINEERS' AND PLUMBERS' WORK

Applicable to Shipyards, Engine Works and Shiprepairing Yards on the Tyne

IT IS MUTUALLY AGREED that the following procedure shall be substituted for and supersede that laid down in Clause 8 of the Notes appended to the List of Apportionment of Engineers' and Plumbers' Work, dated 14 September 1914, viz.:

1. In the event of a demarcation question between Fitters and Plumbers arising in an associated Shipyard, Engine Works, or Shiprepairing Yard on the Tyne, there shall be no stoppage of work either of a partial or general character, but such question shall be considered and dealt with in accordance with the provisions of this Agreement, and in no case shall men be paid off through a demarcation difference.

2. When a question arises an endeavour shall be made in the first instance by the men concerned to arrive at a settlement, failing which a meeting of the Management and the Yard or Works' Representatives of both trades shall take place.

   In the event of no settlement being arrived at a further meeting shall be arranged at the firm's offices, at which the delegates of each of the parties shall be present, and failing settlement, the previous practice of the firm shall continue pending a decision of a Joint Committee as provided herein. Should there be a difference of opinion as to the previous practice, or where no previous practice exists, the management, after hearing all parties, shall be at liberty to give a temporary decision as to how the work shall be done meantime, but this not to prejudice the ultimate settlement of the question.

3. A Committee shall be formed for the purpose of settling disputes as to the demarcation of work arising between Fitters and Plumbers in Shipyards, Engineering Works and Shiprepairing Yards on the Tyne. The Committee shall consist of three Fitters, three Plumbers, and three Employers (one Shipbuilder, one Engineer, and one Shiprepairer). The members forming the Committee shall be elected by their respective constituents. The Secretary of the Employers' Local Associations shall act as Secretary of the Committee.

4. All disputes as to the demarcation of work that have not been settled in the Yard or Works in which they have arisen, shall be submitted to the Committee by the Firm giving notice in writing to the Secretary, who shall convene a meeting of the Committee, in accordance with paragraph 10.

   In the event of any member of the Committee being unable to attend any meeting, the party whom such member represents may supply a substitute to attend the meeting.

5. Representatives of the parties concerned shall state their case to the Committee, and all parties shall have power to call witnesses.

6. Six shall form a quorum at any meeting of the Committee. In all cases the voting power of the three parties represented on the Committee shall be equal, i.e. should one of the representatives of any of the three parties be absent, a like number of the representatives of the other two parties shall abstain from voting. Should a tie in voting on any question that may be submitted to the Committee arise, through the absence of any members, the decision on such question shall be adjourned to a full meeting of the Committee.

7. In coming to decisions the Committee shall adhere to the principles contained in the 1914 List of Apportionment of Fitters' and Plumbers' Work, and in the event of any particular question in dispute not being covered by the List, past practice of the particular Yard or Works where the dispute has arisen shall be taken into account.

8. The Committee's decisions shall (unless, owing to special circumstances the Committee otherwise decide) be confined to the Yard or Works in which the question arose, and continue for 12 months, and for such further time as they are not called in question by

being brought before the Committee for reconsideration, and shall be accepted by the parties as final and binding.

9. The expenses of the Committee to be ascertained annually, shall be borne between the parties represented thereon to the extent of one-third each.

10. Meetings of the Committee shall be held in January, May and September respectively, where necessary, and all questions referred to the Committee at least 10 days before any fixed date for a meeting shall be placed on the Agenda of the meeting for that date.

11. At the January meeting the Committee shall elect one of their number to act as Chairman, who shall continue in office until the following January meeting, or until his successor is elected. At such meeting the Committee shall also transact any other business.

12. A report of each meeting shall be circulated to the members of the Committee.

13. Committee decisions shall be printed from time to time as an appendix to the List of Apportionment of Work, dated 14 September 1914.

14. This agreement shall come into force as from 1st November 1928.

Signed for and on behalf of
The Amalgamated Engineering Union –

> T. R. DOBINSON
> THOS. GARDNER
> J. C. LITTLE, O.D.D.
> J. BOWMAN, District Secretary

Signed for and on behalf of
The United Operative Plumbers' Association –

> W. G. DENHAM
> J. WIPER
> Wm. SIMPSON
> J. W. STEPHENSON, District Secretary

Signed for and on behalf of the Employers' Associations, as follows:

The Tyne Shipbuilders' Association –

> D. R. MACDONALD

The North-East Coast Engineering Employers' Association (Tyne District)

> T. B. McBRIDE

The North East Coast Shiprepairers' Association –

J. W. TOCHER
JAMES CAMERON,

Bolbec Hall,
Westgate Road,
Newcastle-on-Tyne,
15 October 1928.

Secretary, Employers' Association

LIST OF APPORTIONMENT OF ENGINEERS' AND PLUMBERS' WORK

Applicable to Shipyards, Engineering Works, and Shiprepairing Yards on the Tyne

ITEM ONE

Water Ballast Tank and Bilge Suction and Delivery Pipes, including Valve Boxes, and all connections; also Pipes and Connections from Ballast Tanks and Bilges not provided with Suctions, to spaces so provided.

NOTE.—Cast Iron Pipes, with Spigot and Faucet Joints mixed with flanges, Engineers and Plumbers to work conjointly.

ENGINEERS	PLUMBERS
Valve Boxes complete.	Cast Iron Flanged Pipes complete on repair work, except in Boiler Rooms, Engine Rooms and Tunnels – outside of Double Bottom.
Cast Iron Flanged Pipes complete on new work; and on repair work in Boiler Rooms, Engine Rooms and Tunnels – outside of Double Bottom.	
Wrought Iron or Steel Pipes, with flanges machined or faced, to fix, joint and strap.	Wrought Iron or Steel Pipes, with rough or unfaced flanges and screwed ferrule joints, to fix, joint and strap.
	Make template, bend and fit all wrought iron or steel pipes.
Copper Pipes complete, including jointing to pipes of any other material except lead.	Lead Pipes complete, including jointing to pipes of any other material.

239

ITEM TWO

Downton and Hand Deck Pumps and Connections.

ENGINEERS

Fit and fix to steel decks Downton and Hand Deck Pumps, with their mechanical gearing, also valves and deck change plates in connection therewith, including pump extension chambers, other than lead, wrought iron, or steel.
Copper Pipes complete.
Cast Iron Pipes complete.

Foot Valves, Deck, Bulkhead, and Ship Side fittings connecting to the foregoing pipes.

PLUMBERS

Fit and fix pump extension chambers, if of lead, wrought iron, or steel.

Lead Pipes complete.
Wrought Iron or Steel Pipes complete, including bending.
Foot Valves, Deck, Bulkhead, and Ship Side fittings connecting to the foregoing pipes.

ITEM THREE

Gravitation Drains and Flooding Arrangements on War Vessels.

ENGINEERS

Magazine direct Flooding Pipes and Valves.
Copper Pipes complete.
Cast Iron Pipes complete.
Drain Pipes from Barbettes and Torpedo Tubes, also from Torpedo Rooms when they join either of the former as a combined drain to the Ship's Bottom, to fix, joint and strap.
Fit and fix valves attached to ship's deck or structure, including gearing complete.
Fit and joint cast deck pieces.

PLUMBERS

Lead Pipes complete.
Drain Pipes from intermediate decks and flats to ship's Bottom, including valves not attached to Ship's deck or structure, also drains from Torpedo Rooms when led independently to the Ship's Bottom, to fix, joint and strap.

Fit and joint Wrought Iron deck pieces.

All Pipes and Valves which are Suctions from bilges or other compartments are provided for under Item 1.

Appendix B

ITEM FOUR

Scupper Valves and Pipes.

ENGINEERS

Fit and fit Scupper Valves attached to side and bottom of War Vessels, and where they are required to be chipped and filed to place on Merchant Vessels.

PLUMBERS

Fit and fix Scupper Valves to side and bottom of Merchant Vessels excepting where they are required to be chipped and filed to place.

Scupper Pipes complete.

ITEM FIVE

Sounding Pipes, Air, Overflow, and Independent Filling Pipes for Water Tanks.

PLUMBERS

Sounding Pipes, Air, Overflow, and independent Filling Pipes for Fresh and Salt Water Tanks, Ballast Tanks, and Fore and After Peaks complete.

ITEM SIX

Water Service Pipes for Engines and Shafting, also Steam and Drain Pipes from Whistles, Gauges and Safety Valves.

ENGINEERS

Copper and Brass Pipes complete.

Wrought Iron or Steel Pipes on engines to fix, joint and strap.

PLUMBERS

Lead Pipes complete.

Wrought Iron or Steel Pipes to fix, joint and strap all pipes except those on engines.

Appendix B

ITEM SEVEN

Fresh and Salt Water Services and Discharges or Drains for all Domestic Purposes.

ENGINEERS

Fit and fix Cocks and Valves attached to side and bottom of War Vessels; and where they are required to be chipped and filed to place on Merchant Vessels.

Fix, joint and strap Sea Suction and Sanitary Pump Delivery Pipes in Engine and Boiler Rooms, and delivery pipe up to Sanitary Tank when of copper and flanged.

Fit and fix Steam and Motor Pumps and Ejectors.

PLUMBERS

Fit and fix Cocks and Valves attached to side and bottom on Merchant Vessels, excepting where they are required to be chipped and filed to place.

Suction, Discharge and Supply Pipes, Tanks and Connections for Fresh and Salt Water, including those to and from Steam and Hand Pumps complete.

Fit and fix Hand Pumps.

ITEM EIGHT

Fresh Water Condensers, Condenser Tanks and Connections.

ENGINEERS

Fix Condensers in position, and all valves attached thereto.

Steam Pipes and Fittings complete.

Circulating Water Pipes, when of copper or cast iron, complete.

PLUMBERS

Fresh Water Pipes and Fittings complete.

Circulating Water Pipes, when of wrought iron or steel, complete, including bending.

ITEM NINE

Wash Deck and Water Fire Extinguishing Pipes and Connections.

ENGINEERS

Copper Pipes complete.

Wrought Iron or Steel Pipes on War Vessels, to fix, joint and strap.

PLUMBERS

Lead Pipes complete.

Wrought Iron or Steel Pipes complete on Merchant Vessels.

ITEM TEN

Steam Fire Extinguishing.

ENGINEERS
Work complete on War Vessels.
Copper Pipes complete on Merchant Vessels.

PLUMBERS
Work complete on Merchant Vessels, excepting Copper Pipes.

ITEM ELEVEN

Pipes to Shipbuilders' Auxiliary Machinery.

ENGINEERS
Steam, Exhaust, and Drain Pipes, when of Copper or Cast Iron, complete.
Steam Pipes, when of Steel, to fix, joint and strap.

PLUMBERS
Steam, Exhaust, and Drain Pipes, when of Wrought Iron, complete.
Exhaust and Drain Pipes, when of Steel, to fix, joint and strap.

ITEM TWELVE

Steam Heating Installations for all Domestic Purposes.

ENGINEERS
Work complete on War Vessels.

PLUMBERS
Work complete on Merchant Vessels.

ITEM THIRTEEN

Magazine Cooling, Ventilating Pipes, Ventilating Automatic Valves and Connections.

ENGINEERS
Fit and fix Automatic Valves and Valves of the Sluice Type.

PLUMBERS
Fit and fix Magazine Cooling Pipes, also Ventilating Pipes and Louvres.

ITEM FOURTEEN

Telegraph, Thermometer and Voice Pipes.

ENGINEERS

Fit, fix, joint and strap Wrought Iron or Steel Flange Pipes, and Inspection Boxes for Telegraphs.

Prepare Wrought Iron or Steel Pipes for Telegraphs when tubes are split in halves and secured by tap bolts.

PLUMBERS

Fit, fix, joint and strap Wrought Iron or Steel Ferruled Pipes and Inspection Boxes for Telegraphs.

Prepare Wrought Iron or Steel Pipes for Telegraphs, except when tubes are split in halves and secured by tap bolts.

Thermometer and Voice Pipes complete.

ITEM FIFTEEN

Pipes and Connections for Bulk Oil Cargoes, and Oil Fuel for the Engines and Boilers.

ENGINEERS

Cargo Filling, Suction and Discharge Pipes complete, including Cofferdam and Pump Room Suction Connections.

Valves, Deck Pieces and Branch Pipes complete from Steam and Exhaust Pipes on Deck to Heating and Steaming-out Pipes inside Oil Cargo and Fuel Compartments.

Fuel Discharge Pipes to Engines and Boilers, to fix, joint and strap.

Fuel Filling and Suction Pipes complete on War Vessels.

Fuel Heating Pipes complete on War Vessels.

Copper Pipes complete.

PLUMBERS

Running up with lead of Thimbles, or Expansion Joints.

Fuel Filling and Suction Pipes complete on Merchant Vessels except when of copper.

Heating and Steaming-out Pipes inside Oil Cargo and Fuel Compartments complete on Merchant Vessels except when of copper.

Gas Escape Pipes complete, except when of copper.

Deck Steam and Exhaust Pipes follow the line of demarcation as in Item 11.

This item to apply to installations for Molasses or other liquid cargoes carried in bulk.

Appendix B

Cocks, Valves and Fittings in Continuation of Pipes including those attached to Ship's Structure, unless where otherwise apportioned.

ENGINEERS

Cocks, Valves and Fittings in continuation of Pipes fixed by Engineers.

Gearing and Rods to Cocks and Valves, including Universal and other Joints, Stuffing Boxes and Bushes.

Fit and fix Wrought Iron or Steel Pipes for protection of valve rods when tubes are split in halves and secured by tap bolts.

PLUMBERS

Cocks, Valves and Fittings in continuation of Pipes fixed by Plumbers.

Fit and fix Wrought Iron or Steel Pipes for protection of valve rods, except when tubes are split in halves and secured by tap bolts.

ITEM SEVENTEEN

Independent Cocks and Valves attached to Ship's Structure unless where otherwise apportioned.

ENGINEERS

All valves.

Cocks on War Vessels.

Gearing and Rods to Cocks and Valves, including Universal and other Joints, Stuffing Boxes and Bushes.

PLUMBERS

Cocks on Merchant Vessels.

Fit and Fix Wrought Iron or Steel Pipes for protection of Valve Rods.

ITEM EIGHTEEN

Cross Connections between Pipes, Cocks or Valves.

ENGINEERS

On work done by Engineers.

PLUMBERS

On work done by Plumbers.

ITEM NINETEEN

Works Plant.

ENGINEERS

Steam and Exhaust Pipes complete.

Steam Heating Pipes of Copper, with flanged joints complete.

Hydraulic Pressure and Return Water Pipes complete.

Compressed Air Pipes, when of Cast Iron, complete with valves and fittings. All pipes and connections between Compressors and 1st Reservoirs.

PLUMBERS

Steam Heating Pipes of Copper, with screwed joints complete.

Steam Heating Pipes of Wrought Iron or Steel complete.

Gas Pipes complete.

Water Pipes complete for all purposes except hydraulic.

Lead Pipes complete.

Running up with lead of spigot and faucet joints.

Compressed Air Pipes, when of Wrought Iron or Steel, complete, including cocks, valves, fittings, hoses and their connections.

ITEM TWENTY

Sundries.

ENGINEERS

Fixing, jointing and strapping the following:

Internal Pipes for Boilers.

Boiler Feeds and Suctions.

Main and Auxiliary Steam Pipes.

Waste Steam Pipes.

Ash Cooling Pipes, except when of lead.

Oil Cooling and Oil Service Pipes.

Water Cooling Pipes on Internal Combustion Engines.

Hydraulic Pipes on board ship.

PLUMBERS

Chemical Fire Extinguishing and Disinfecting Pipes, Valves and Fittings complete.

Filling Pipes to Oil Store Tanks complete.

Ash Cooling Pipes when of lead complete.

Brine Pipes complete.

Metal Lining of Store Rooms, etc.

Pipes and fittings for compressed air when used for power purposes on board ship to follow the apportionment laid down for Steam Pipes.

NOTES

1. Where the word 'complete' is used, it includes marking all holes making template, fitting and fixing, jointing and strapping.

2. Screwing and fitting of flanges to be done at the option of Employers.

3. Making templates for, and bending of Wrought Iron and Welded Steel Pipes to be done by Plumbers.

4. When a joint has to be made between pipes or fittings fixed by Engineers and pipes or fittings fixed by Plumbers, it shall, failing agreement between the two trades, be done as directed by the Employer.

5. In the foregoing List the purpose for which any installation or fitting is primarily required is to decide its title; subsidiary or emergency connections and uses are not to affect the apportionment.

6. This apportionment List is for the purpose of regulating work between Engineers and Plumbers only, and does not award it to either of the foregoing to the exclusion of other trades.

7. This List shall come into operation on 19 October 1914, for all jobs not actually started, but work on all jobs in progress shall be finished by the respective Trades under existing conditions.

*8. The undersigned as the Revision Committee, shall decide any question that may arise as to the interpretation or application of any of the items in the foregoing List:

Signed for and on behalf of

The Amalgamated Society of Engineers –

> JAMES RATCLIFFE, District Delegate
> T. R. ROBINSON
> THOS. BOWMAKER, District Secretary

Signed for and on behalf of

The Steam Engine Makers' Society –

> WM. F. DAWTRY, General Secretary

* This provision is superseded by the Demarcation Procedure Agreement, dated 15 October 1928, copy inserted at the beginning of this Section (see opening paragraph).

Appendix B

Signed for and on behalf of

The United Operative Plumbers' Association –
> LACHLAN MACDONALD,
> > Assistant General Secretary
> ROBERT SCORER
> WILLIAM SIMPSON
> SEPTIMUS SIGSWORTH,
> > District Secretary

Signed for and on behalf of the Employers' Associations as follows:

The Tyne Shipbuilders' Association –
> D. R. MACDONALD,
> > Chairman of the Committee

The Tyne Engineers' Association –
> R. WALLIS

The North-East Coast Shiprepairers' Association –
> H. R. CAMERON
> JAMES CAMERON,
> > Secretary, Employers' Association

Bolbec Hall,
Westgate Road,
Newcastle-on-Tyne,
11 September 1914.

APPENDIX C

Status in Steel

A Group Discussion

THE following extracts are from a tape-recorded group discussion between four blue collar workers in a Steel company, members of a W.E.A. class and two research workers. Names are not revealed and the company not identified in this edited version. The discussion centres on various kinds of status distinction evident in the Steel industry and the group members' perception of the significance of the distinctions and the factors affecting them. The earlier part of the discussion, not reported here, dealt with status distinctions between clerical and manual workers. We take up the discussion as a research worker is turning the group's attention to a new set of status considerations: those linked with the seniority system on the production side of the plant:

Research Worker: Well, I think we will just move off this note for a bit and move to a different aspect of status and this is concerned with the question of the age of different workers. Now this, I think, is particularly relevant to the production side of things where you have got the seniority system. Now what sort of status would you say that the older worker has in either a Rolling Mill or a Steel Plant, in relation to his age? Does it make much difference?

Electrician: Do you mean on production?

Research Worker: I'm thinking of production now in particular.

Crane Driver: Well, I don't think it raises any. In fact there is one chap a roller, who has asked to come off rolling and to go onto labouring.

Research Worker: When did this happen?

Crane Driver: A fortnight since. And I have tried to weigh that up and I can't because actually he has done that himself.

Research Worker: He has asked to come off?

249

Crane Driver: To come off.

Research Worker: But you don't know why?

Crane Driver: Well, I would say maybe he thinks the job is too much for him, but in status – it does not mean a thing.

Electrician: I think seniority is the best word to use, purely seniority. But that's a job, if you were on the production side, you hope to get someday, but you realise that there are so many in line for it that it would take another atom bomb to clear a few out.

You know I don't think we look at it from the status point of view as I say. I would say that we do on the maintenance side with regard to people upgraded to foreman. There's a certain status. You hear a chap say, as a chap said in our place: 'I'm on the other side of the fence now'. But, as I said, he might say that, but we don't take it as it would mean in the old days. I mean we tend to make a joke of it now, where at one time it probably meant something. But it only meant something because you were ignorant of the true facts, where today you know that even though he is a foreman, he is not going to get any more money. The only thing he is going to have is, if he is off sick, his wages are going to come in. But we know that will be ironed out in a few years time when we achieve the same thing.

Crane Driver: Another thing, comparing the old and the new. A roller in the old mills enjoyed the status in so much as the rolling gear was a separate unit – and he decided when to put stuff on or not to, in his own particular time. The new mill is part of an assembly line where he finds he is only one of a team. He has to go as fast as the assembly line is moved, so, actually speaking, for all he is still a roller, he is a smaller cog, and I don't think even the emphasis is on his turning the professional job out. The machine is actually set . . . Down at the old mill it used to be a continuous back and forwards, you know, until you got it exact, sort of style, but not so now. The plate comes along the line and it goes automatically through and nine times out of ten its correct, its level.

Research Worker: He doesn't decide how many times it has to pass through now?

Crane Driver: He might have two passes, but very rare. But as I say, his status is going so much that he can't stop that line nowadays, as he would do in the old days. He hasn't the authority. He would have the authority in so much as a plate was bad, of course. He could stop it and roll it back. But it doesn't amount to any great thing.

Electrician: It hasn't the meaning it had in the old days.

Welder A: The big thing I would like to mention is that I know two or three that's had the opportunity to make progress in the steel industry, as we have been discussing, but they preferred to remain put and stay as they are.

Research Worker: As opposed to becoming a roller you mean, or what?

Welder A: Yes, or even progressing further up the tree.

Research Worker: Up into the staff?

Welder A: They preferred to stay where they are. They were quite happy in the jobs they were doing. They had a certain amount of responsibility – they were quite happy with that amount and they were not prepared to take any more, even for considerably higher wages. And I know one chap in particular, that, as far as he is concerned, he doesn't look up to any man higher up in the tree than he is. And I think he is as well off – I mean this has a big bearing on it hasn't it? – how you are situated at home. Now he is fairly well off, he always smokes the best cigarettes and one thing and another, you know. He probably smokes better cigarettes than the roller does. He's gone on like this for years. He owns his own motor car and he can chop it and change it whenever he feels like it, and of course, as far as he is concerned, status doesn't come into it with him. He's doing the job he chooses.

Research Worker: Does this mean in fact that he is on a line, a seniority line, and he chooses not to go up the line? Is this right?

Welder A: That's true, yes.

Research Worker: How often does this happen then?

Crane Driver: It happens fairly frequently.

Research Worker: Does it?

Crane Driver: Yes. I will tell you why in a lot of cases. I will take my own for instance. We have sixteen cranes, overhead cranes, in M. and between the bottom crane, the lowest crane, and the top crane, there is a very narrow margin in the wage. Now somewhere in between that line you find some chaps will say: 'Oh dear, this job's easier than what the higher job is.' And there's maybe only 2/– difference, so he says: 'Oh, I'll stay put'. And the man behind him moves up. But he is moving up to nowhere – maybe moving up to harder work, but without recompense. Of course, these things are in the new mill. We are discussing wages now that are not actually fixed. They are supposed to get only a 'temporary' wage – but it's two years of course.

Electrician: But there is a movement that way, that there are not the big gaps between any jobs now, as there used to be.

Research Worker: You mean in wages?

Electrician: But unfortunately in wages the move is not upward. It is downward, sometimes, even to the likes of us. We are approaching the stage now where you might as well say we are semi-skilled. The steel industry is not a happy industry as compared to others. I mean when I look at our union magazine and I see people getting 7/6d an hour on day work and I'm only getting 6/- for shift work – I begin to think, well, things are not as good as they should be. But status – I don't think we even look at it as status . . .

Welder B: Would you not say that status is more a matter of mind than it is of actual wages or something that is tangible?

Research Worker: I would have thought, you see, that in the old days, because the roller was obviously in control of things, much more than he is now, that people would look up to him and say that obviously he is a fine fellow. He is doing a really good job and he is being paid a lot of money compared to us. Now isn't what you are saying really that you don't think in terms of status now, because he's really no different from everybody else to a large extent? Can this be the case?

Crane Driver: Well . . . you mentioned a roller – that's a different thing altogether. When I mentioned rollers before, these rollers on an assembly line, called rollers and so forth are pretty high paid jobs. But the top rollers at the beginning of your mill, well I'm afraid that them chaps do still think along those lines of what you are quoting. But I mean nobody takes any notice of it of course, but they still come to work dressed as good as what you are now Jack. And they don't seem to like to mingle with the chaps.

Electrician: Well, they can't, they are sort of . . .

Crane Driver: That's true.

Welder A: But I still say that it is the individual. Whilst the roller thinks he owns a high position the people don't look up to him at present day as what they did pre-war. That feeling's not there with all the undermen, so to speak.

Crane Driver: Well, I think if we were talking to a roller and talking between ourselves, I mean there's a big gap you see. We know with working on the shop floor, and they must know it, that these chaps are the chaps that force the pace, whether we like it or not. But they may not admit that to you.

Electrician: Oh, they do.

Crane Driver: You might say: 'Well, what's he playing at, he's belting stuff through there regardless'. You are on short time, but he is still on £5 or £5 10s. a shift. Even if he only worked four shifts, he has still got £20 and you are on four shifts along with him – you are down to £8. He doesn't consider in the likes that: 'Oh well, I'll ease up here.' No doubt maybe he has no alternative, but I don't even think they consider that. They are the chaps that make the pace.

Welder A: That's what I was going to come in with – they have got no alternative. Everything is pre-planned now and they have to work to a programme. So, whilst the chap along the line says: 'What's he playing at? He's still belting it through,' and, you know, 'We've got our shift's work done', sort of style, in the planning office, which is doing all the pre-planning, they are not worried about whether you may be shifted out or not. They want a certain amount of work production. So whereas before the rollers had more or less control of the mill, that's practically taken off altogether now.

Crane Driver: Well, he must have lost status, in so much as his job is concerned. As David says, he is working to a set rule from the planning office, and so forth. In the old mill again, I think the roller was a man something like the old steel smelter was. He knew what was best when he rolled a plate. Under the new process, a lot of that is taken away from him . . .

Welder A: Another instance was in the olden times, if a slab came up for re-roll and the roller looked at it and thought it was not hot enough, he just automatically kicked it off the rolls and sent it back and waited for the next one. And if that was not hot enough he sent that back, and then he went and complained to the heater and made them put more gas in the furnace. Now when that slab comes up I've seen them break rolls valued at £800–£900.

Research Worker: Why's this?

Welder A: The slab goes through – but it's not hot enough. But it's sent off – it's supposed to be right: 'They make the decisions. We couldn't care less.'

Chorus: Yes, that's right.

Crane Driver: This is perfectly true. At present we have a spindle cradle in the mill that's broken in two or three places.

Electrician: Now you see we (i.e. electricians) are sitting in a room where we can't see the rolls – just the motors going round. But we can tell by the number of alarms we get up, and by the charts, that he's having an awful job to get that roll. You can hear the speed of the set going down.

Welder A: But he cannot make the decision and say: 'I'm sending that down.'

Research Worker: No. Who does make the decision now?

Welder A: The planning officer – sitting over in an office.

Crane Driver: I wouldn't say to that extent, David. I mean, at the same time, for all we are running him down, sort of style, he is in charge of them rolls. And if a slab comes along there and it is not correct, I would say that it's more than his life's worth to attempt to roll it. What they do is – the gears there just automatically lift it clear. It's just the same thing as a cobble. When the plate goes wrong, it's just lifted clear. It is not – you just try and roll it, sort of style. I mean you just could not do that. It's not just the plates that you are doing no good – you are breaking the gear. Well, that just wouldn't do at all.

Welder A: I mean in the past they have broken numerous rolls and they have also broken the main shears.

Chorus: Aye. Yes, yes.

Research Worker: Is this because the roller is not trained sufficiently well to go on the new job?

Welder A: No. I think all this work has been taken away from him.

Crane Driver: Somebody is pushing him.

Research Worker: Could that be the important thing? Especially with the new mill starting, perhaps he feels that he's really got to get a shift on, otherwise he will be out of that box and they will be trying someone else. And so he wants to really try and get the tonnage up, so that the output during the time that he is running it, is as good as it is during the time the other blokes are running it?

Crane Driver: You hit the nail on the head there.

Electrician: You see, when you come to status, it doesn't always mean from the outside looking in. It's within as well, *among* the rollermen. Whatever friction you get at the lowest level, it is always far more sensitive when you get to the top level, until you get the sort of gloating that goes on at someone else's mistake.

And you get that among a lot of foremen on the craftsmen side: a sort of smug satisfaction that some other foreman 'dropped a clanger', you see. Now this is not the tendency at the bottom level to do that. You would rather shield a chap than sort of give it an airing. But as it moves up, there seems to be more eyes watching on it, you see, and more people are interested in the mistake.

Crane Driver: In the new mill at present it seems to me as if they have reached, I wouldn't say their target, but they have reached what they can do. It took off with 90 slabs on A shift and B came out with 92. And the next shift came out, C shift it was, 95 and it went on and on and on and on, each one. I mean if anyone has a mind to go and look at the records you will find that it is true. It has crept up shift by shift, until it has reached a state now where I suppose they say: 'Well, he's got two different from me. It doesn't matter, I couldn't do it.'

Electrician: It would just have to be like the long distance runner. The wind would just have to be right and everything just right, just to get that little bit, that fraction.

Crane Driver: There comes a happy feeling when A shift has a 200 and B shift 199 – 'Well, he is only one in front, so it doesn't really matter.' It's reached that.

Electrician: But it has reached a maximum, then the firm start talking about a bonus for you – which is going to be a pittance over the maximum amount.

Welder A: I would like to say in comparison you could think of this – status has been taken away from the roller in the same way as it has from the first hand smelter. He (the smelter) hasn't got control of that furnace now. He knows what the carbon should be, but he hasn't got control. He doesn't say: 'We tap now – the carbon's ready.' And there are numerous cases happening now where there aren't actually losses of full furnaces of special carbon, because they can turn it down into mild steel. It is not wasted, but there are numerous times that there is special steel put into that furnace and special ingredients to bring the carbon up to a certain height. They reach that and, at the moment of tapping everything isn't just right – or they haven't had word from the office in time – but for all that the smelter could tap. He's not allowed to – and they may have lost several hundred pounds, and all the special ingredients – and it's reduced to mild steel. It's just the same as the roller – he's had his status taken away from him – he doesn't have the same status now as he had pre-war.

Research Worker: Well, what we seem to have established pretty well is that the smelter and the head roller seem to have lost out a bit in terms of the number of decisions they actually take and the amount of responsibility that they have. Now another thing that has occurred to me here: is the chief roller, for example, still an older man, or might he be a younger man? And the same question might apply to the smelters as well.

Crane Driver: I don't know about the smelters, but what has happened down in the old and new (mills) again – two rollers came up and they are now on burning.

Welder B: They were two rollers from the old mill moved back.

Research Worker: They didn't start rolling at all at the new mill?

Crane Driver: No. They didn't get that opportunity.

Welder B: No. You see at the new mill, the firm reserve the right to make the appointments. There is no seniority.

Research Worker: Yes. You think that's right do you?

Welder B: No. That's normal.

Crane Driver: We actually fought against it, but it somehow or other just petered out, like. And I think it is generally accepted now, I think even by the two chaps concerned. They felt that they couldn't have coped.

Electrician: That was the point I wanted to come to, like. The older rollers, when they do come into the new mill, I don't say the oldest of them, but the older of them, probably get a try at the new gear. But not being sufficiently young in outlook, they operate in a sort of grudging manner – probably psychological reasons come into it. But then, at that particular time, you have the manager breathing down your neck and it doesn't take much to start an argument. And the next thing is that the roller packs up. Well they (management) are quite happy about that. You see, they haven't made him pack up. And you usually find that that happens.

Research Worker: Is this the case here?

Crane Driver: It's happened. Now it's happened on the automatic shears. They did give two chaps that I know a test on them and, believe me, they went through hell, like, trying to keep up with the new ideas, you see. Well, since then, these two have actually reached the age of retirement. But instead of, in the old mill there was a set line of seniority, that was altered. And now there is actually young chaps on these jobs. Probably a seniority line will be established now with the young chaps at the head. That's giving the younger ones that much time, so that they can adjust themselves to it. But the older ones just couldn't keep up with them.

Research Worker: It was too fast for them?

Crane Driver: It was too fast, yes.

Research Worker: What about when the oxygen lances were introduced into the smelting shop. Now this must have posed a number of problems to the actual . . . Well, I suppose you would know about that (Welder A) because you were on the welding side?

Welder A: There's no pre-training.

Research Worker: There's no pre-training at all?

Welder A: Trial by error.

Research Worker: As far as the smelters are concerned this is?

Welder A: Yes.

Research Worker: What did the senior smelters think about this. Were they reluctant to receive these oxygen lances?

Welder A: They were very reluctant to try anything that's new. Actually, put yourself in their place. You are asked to operate them and you don't actually know what's happening. And you are in the dark, and you are pressing buttons and one thing and another, and you don't know . . .

Electrician: And at the back of your mind you don't want to make a mistake, if you can help it. And it makes you very wary you see. You hold the can if anything should go wrong. You've made the mistake. But you couldn't say: 'Well, I haven't been trained on it.'

Research Worker: So it was actually the first hands who were responsible for this?

Welder B: There is always the point as well that introducing new methods of speeding up production and getting more tonnage out is inclined to bring down the wage.

Electrician: All this is in the back of your mind while you are being . . .

Welder B: I think that the majority of good trade unionists are inclined to hang back a little bit, you know, always have a little bit at the back of the boot.

Research Worker: But with smelters, they would be on the smelters' scale. So if more tonnage came out this would cause no trouble?

Electrician: But at the back of their minds they are thinking . . .

Welder A: How long does this go on? You see, if they found they were getting 25 thousand tons out instead of the previous 16 thousand tons, well, the manager, or someone like, will not allow that. This has happened before, when an old mill closed down and a new one opened . . . The Company officials weren't happy with the amount of tonnage bonus. You see, we reached a stage where we received a £2 a week bonus, as against the previous 15/– or 17/–. So they said: 'We (management) cannot have this.' So they brought all the unions in and we had a revision of bonus and they brought us back down to 21/– with a maximum of 25/–, which hung around 25/– for a long, long time, until, eventually, it went up to somewhere in the region of 32/– to 35/–.

Research Worker: This was a local agreement was it?

Welder A: Yes. You get this type of thing reoccurring though, when they are introducing anything as far as boosting production. This is always at the back of the mind of the operator. 'How much am I going to lose?' at the outset.

Electrician: And it's not wrong to think that way as far as he is concerned.

Welder A: Maybe not. But getting back to the point we were discussing about the training, they definitely haven't had half an hour's training . . .

Welder B: Would this not be a question – whether it is possible to train anybody in a thing like that? I mean, it was purely experimental.

Welder A: Well, they have been used in other firms. We weren't the first.

Research Worker: I am interested to find out what role the senior men and people like the head roller and the first hand smelter actually play in the branch. Do they play an important role in the branch? If you have meetings, for instance, what sort of role do these blokes play? I mean, as likely as not, they would not be actually holding a union position, but because they are very experienced and because they are senior men, does this give them any edge in the argument?

Crane Driver: It has done, Graham, it has in the past. I've noticed the top roller who used to be down there was Brown and he was secretary of that particular union branch. But in the course of events he has just dropped out and now you find, at least I have found, that they don't bother going to meetings at all. We used to look up to them and I think that the secretary or the chairman was always the roller or somebody pretty well up towards that. But not so now. They don't seem to bother.

Electrician: Yes. Here is where status comes in again. A change has definitely taken place.

Crane Driver: I don't think they are really interested now. I think one time they did look along the lines and say: 'Yes, I am the roller. I am the secretary too.' By being the roller his name was on the sheet. You automatically said: 'He's the roller. He is the man.' But they had more responsibility towards the men than they have now.

Electrician: Well, it's gone. It's gone by the way.

APPENDIX D

The Shop Steward's Role

A Comment on the North East of England[1]

B. C. ROBERTS, in his well-known study, *Trade Union Government and Administration*, has written:

> On the efficiency and judgment of the stewards depends to a great extent the general temper of industrial relations and the smooth functioning of factory procedure for the ventilation of grievances and the settlement of disputes.

Few people, I imagine, would wish to question this assessment, and, perhaps because of this, when industrial relations 'problems' arise, it is commonly the shop steward who serves as scapegoat. Consider some of the oft-repeated charges: he ignores procedures, breaks agreements, makes exorbitant wage demands, usurps the authority of the foreman, encourages unofficial strikes, combines unconstitutionally with other shop stewards, obstructs management and inhibits technical change. But is it all really as simple as this? I should like, in this short article, to touch on some of the issues involved here. Unless otherwise stated, I shall be drawing on some industrial relations research undertaken in the North East of England, in which I participated. This included interviews and discussions with shop stewards and management mainly in the Iron and Steel, Engineering and Shipbuilding industries.

The basic trouble with the allegations made against shop stewards is that they beg too many questions and rarely do justice to the complexity of the subject. The field of industrial relations is characterised by what academic writers tend to call 'antagonistic co-operation' — a phrase which implies that identity of

[1] This Appendix is reprinted from *Voice of North East Industry* (September, 1966) where it appeared under the title, 'The Vital Role of the North East Shop Steward'.

interests on some things and conflicts of interest on others necessarily co-exist between management and labour. The strategic long term concerns of the players on the industrial relations stage are no doubt to identify and sustain the areas of common agreement and to regulate the areas of disagreement. Traditionally Joint Consultation has symbolised the attempt to do the first and collective bargaining the attempt to do the second. But it is because there are genuine conflicts of interest (which no amount of exhortation from the Government or any-one else can remove) that it has been properly said: 'The study of industrial relations as a day to day problem is an examination of the tactics used by both sides to improve their situation.' (Ross Stagner.) Such tactics may or may not be at the expense of the other side.

Certainly the shop steward, to be successful, must be a master tactician. This does not always imply militancy. Thus one A.E.U. steward commented: 'In the early days, when I used to be a bit hot-headed, I used to stamp and rave about the place. But over the years you get more diplomatic and get to know the people you are dealing with.' It does not imply either that every grievance that a worker may raise is automatically taken through procedure. The steward (and this was noted in all the firms visited) typically sifts the grievances brought to him. Another A.E.U. steward commented on this graphically:

> Nine out of ten grievances aren't as good as a man thinks and you'll maybe talk him out of it. If you listen to them you've got no idea what some of the fellows come with. Some fellows are fantastic. One man a fortnight ago was two thou' down on a cut, so it was scrapped. He wanted me to go round and argue that it wasn't his fault. It was the drawing or the machine or anything. I checked it, found that everything was O.K. and refused to go.

By sifting grievances, stewards find themselves acting as Personnel Managers or Supervisors, but to describe it as usurping authority is surely very misleading.

In all the firms visited, there was agreement between management and shop stewards about the desirability of settling differences domestically. Both sides felt that things tended to get too 'legalistic' and to get lost in procedure once they went outside the plant. The role of the union district official is accordingly minimised at plant level. He is 'on call' but both sides prefer not to call him. Thus an N.U.G.M.W. steward commented:

> The official will come down to the works any time if there is a problem that can't be resolved. A week yesterday he came down and informed the crane men and slingers of a new agreement reached with management on wages. This was the first time since 1947 that a local official has been called in and I feel that this is a pretty good record. The shop stewards try to avoid bringing in the local officials as far as possible. In this particular case we felt that in some respects we had failed but at least we did get an offer from the firm which we had of course rejected in this case.

The tendency of district officials only to visit firms when there was trouble did not mean that their contact with shop stewards was necessarily limited. The major unions arrange to see their stewards on a quarterly or monthly basis to discuss rates and working conditions in an industry or trade for a particular district and stewards themselves usually expressed satisfaction with the way they could get into contact easily with district officials. And this meant that stewards were able to combine a detailed knowledge of their own plant with a wider knowledge of district trends and issues. Further co-ordination amongst stewards of different unions, both within and between plants, was in evidence in the Shipbuilding and Engineering industries through the existence of C.S.E.U. meetings for stewards at plant or yard and district levels. These, of course, are a legitimate part of the industrial relations scene and they do seem to be quite well developed in the North East.

The common desire to settle matters domestically is testimony to the reality of workplace bargaining. Firms are not always organised to cope with this reality and this sometimes makes it difficult to observe the niceties of procedural agreements. In the Steel industry, for example, workers' representatives noted that, within a firm, negotiating procedure had become too formalised and centralised. It was argued, for example, that the departmental manager cannot make an effective decision: 'He has no real power. Plans are made at meetings and he is regulated by these.' There was strong feeling that 'the system makes a monkey out of people. You don't like over-stepping people but some lower down either won't or can't take responsibility.' A departmental manager himself commented: 'The system is suspect and time-wasting. I would like more responsibility. The men themselves are confused by the present system. They open a discussion by saying, "We know you can't settle this by yourself but constitutional procedure demands that we see you".'

The formalisation of negotiating procedures in a plant presumably in the interests of efficiency and wage control, may have unexpected consequences. It may lead to unwanted formality on the union side. A B.I.S.A.K.T.A. Works Representative noted: 'There is an old practice in Steel of ringing up or just walking in. Here they are trying to make us follow written procedure. I said: "I'll play it your way. You write to us as well." When they wanted to change to 21 shifts they just rang us up and asked for a decision. I said: "You must wait until I've seen my membership".' Again it may give to the stewards the impression that they are being given the 'run round'. Procrastination may be an uncomfortable way for management of buying time. It can certainly lead to unconstitutional action of one sort or another. And ironically enough, a matter which has been unsettled for months, for reasons unknown, is settled as soon as a stoppage takes place. These may relate to money matters, but quite often relate to working conditions – for example the lack of adequate ventilation or heating in the workplace. Dr. Garfield Clack, who has studied small strikes – 'downers' as they are sometimes called – in the Engineering industry, has suggested that they are sufficiently widespread and frequent to represent a way of life and that they are 'as much a lubricant as an abrasive in the operation of shop floor relations'. Sometimes, a short stoppage (which rarely reaches, or perhaps qualifies for the Ministry of Labour's statistics) is not a result of long delays over the settlement of issues, but over a matter of principle, when the issue itself is perishable – where for example the violation of a manning agreement, or alleged victimisation by management is in question.

The position of the shop steward in relation to the short stoppage is by no means clear cut. On issues of principle he, as the elected leader of the men, might well encourage a stoppage. Sometimes, he is sympathetic, if not the instigator of the men's actions. An A.E.U. steward in a shipyard commented on one incident when 'the men were worked up emotionally and they walked out. I advised the men that they were not being consti-

Appendix D

tutional but my heart was definitely with them.' At other times he is opposed to their action. A Boilermakers' steward reflected: 'You don't call the strike. I talked to a mass meeting about changing pay day from Tuesday to Saturday. I said we must stand by the agreement, etc. I spoke for about half an hour and thought I'd done a real good job. But after a hot head got up and called for a strike, up went the hands.' But in any case, it is usually the steward who has to clarify the issues involved in order to discuss them with management. And it is he who often acts as the agent of social control, persuading the men not to leave the yard or plant or getting them to start work again on the assurance that management have agreed to negotiate the matter immediately.

It is in the workplace that many of the substantive rules of industrial relations are formulated, challenged and modified, and rights are established, only to be redrawn at some later date. A great deal of emphasis recently has been placed on the importance of managerial initiative in the development of soundly based industrial relations policies. It is clear that such initiative can only be exercised by coming to terms with the reality of the shop steward's power. This is not simply the external power of the full employment economy, but internal power based on the fact that he represents the interests of particular work groups – their standards of fairness and justice, beliefs about methods of work, earnings levels and so on. His influence as 'gatekeeper' to the work groups, who are the de facto source of his authority, is a crucial element in developing a constructive approach to necessary technical and organisational changes. To engage in active consultation will certainly bring out conflicts of interest (which if not openly encountered in this way, might prove to be more damaging for both sides subsequently) but it is also likely to minimise needless points of friction. In this respect, one suspects that the North East, in common with all other regions in the country, still has a long way to go.

Select Bibliography

ALLEN, V. L. *Power in Trade Unions*. Longmans, 1954.

ALLEN, V. L. *Trade Union Leadership*. Longmans, 1957.

AMALGAMATED ENGINEERING UNION. Written evidence to the Royal Commission on Trade Unions and Employers' Associations. 1966.

BALDAMUS, W. *Efficiency and Effort*. Tavistock Publications, 1961.

BLACKBURN, R. and COCKBURN, A. (eds.). *The Incompatibles: Trade Union Militancy and the Consensus*. Penguin, 1967.

BLAUNER, R. *Alienation and Freedom*. Wiley, 1964.

BOULDING, K. *Conflict and Defense*. Harper, 1963.

BROWN, R. K. 'Participation, Conflict and Change in Industry'. *S.R.*, Vol. 13, No. 3, 1965.

CAMERON, G. C. Post-war strikes in the North-East Shipbuilding and Ship-repairing Industry. *B.J.I.R.*, Vol. II, No. 1, 1964.

CLACK, GARFIELD. *Industrial Relations in a British Car Factory*. Cambridge University, 1967.

CLACK, GARFIELD. 'How Unofficial Strikes help Industry'. *Business*, July, 1965.

CLEGG, H. A. *The General Union*. Blackwell, 1954.

CLEGG, H. A. and ADAMS, REX. *The Employers' Challenge*. Blackwell, 1957.

CLEGG, H. A., FOX, ALEN and THOMPSON, A. F. *A History of British Trade Unions since 1889*, Vol. 1. Oxford, 1964.

CONFEDERATION OF BRITISH INDUSTRY. *Evidence to the Royal Commission on Trade Unions and Employers' Associations*, 1965.

COOPER, JACK. *Industrial Relations: Sweden shows the way*. Fabian Research Pamphlet, May 1963.

COSER, LEWIS. 'On Terminating Conflict', *Conflict Resolution*, Vol. 5, December 1961.

COSER, LEWIS. *The Functions of Social Conflict*. Routledge and Kegan Paul, 1956.

CROZIER, M. *The Bureaucratic Phenomenon*. Tavistock Publications, 1963.

DAHRENDORF, R. *Class and Class Conflict in an Industrial Society*. Routledge and Kegan Paul, 1959.

DUBIN, R. 'A Theory of Conflict and Power in Union-Management Relations'. *Industry and Labour Relations Review*, Vol. 13, July 1960.

DUNCAN, P. 'Conflict and Co-operation among Trawlermen'. *B.J.I.R.*, Vol. 1, No. 3, 1963.

Select Bibliography

DUNLOP, J. T. *Industrial Relations Systems*. Holt, 1958.

DURKHEIM, EMILE. *The Division of Labour in Society*. Glencoe Free Press, 1964.

ELDRIDGE, JOHN E. T. 'Plant Bargaining in Steel: North East Coast Case Studies'. *S.R.*, Vol. 13, No. 2, July 1965.

EVANS, E. W. and GALAMBOS, P. Work Stoppages in the U.K., 1957–64. *Oxford Bulletin*, February 1966.

FLANDERS, A. *The Fawley Productivity Agreements*. Faber and Faber, 1964.

FLANDERS, A. *Industrial Relations: What is Wrong with the System?* Faber and Faber, 1965.

FLANDERS, A and CLEGG, H. A. *The System of Industrial Relations in Great Britain*. Blackwell, 1963.

FORCHEIMER, K. 'Some International Aspects of the Strike Movement', *Oxford Bulletin*, Vol. 10, No. 1, January 1948.

FOX, A. *Industrial Sociology and Industrial Relations*. H.M.S.O., 1966.

FOX, A. 'Managerial Ideology and Labour Relations'. *B.J.I.R.*, November 1966.

FRIEDMAN, G. *Industrial Society*. Glencoe Free Press, 1955.

FRIEDMAN, G. *The Anatomy of Work*. Heinemann, 1961.

GENERAL AND MUNICIPAL WORKERS UNION. *Evidence submitted to the Royal Commission on Trade Unions and Employers' Associations*. 1966.

GOLDTHORPE, JOHN H. 'Attitudes and Behaviour of Car Assembly Workers: a deviant case and a theoretical critique'. *B.J.S.*, Vol. XVII, No. 3, September 1966.

GOULDNER, ALVIN W. *Wildcat Strike*. Routledge and Kegan Paul, 1955.

KERR, C. *Labor and Management in Industrial Society*. Harper, 1964.

KUHN, JAMES W. *Bargaining in Grievance Settlement*. Columbia, 1961.

KNOWLES, K. G. J. C. *Strikes: a study in Industrial Conflict*. Blackwell, 1952.

KNOWLES, K. G. J. C. *Strike-proneness and its Determinants*. Second World Congress of Sociology, Liege, 1953.

KNOWLES, K. G. J. C. 'Strikes and their Changing Economic Content'. *Oxford Bulletin*, Vol. 9, September 1947.

KORNHAUSER, A. et al. (eds.). *Industrial Conflict*. McGraw Hill, 1954.

LAMMARS, C. J. *Strikes and Mutinies*. Inst. of Sociology of the University of Leyden, 1966.

LERNER, S. W. *Breakaway Unions and the Small Trade Union*. Allen and Unwin, 1961.

LERNER, S. W. and BESCOBY, J. 'Shop Stewards Combine Committee in the British Engineering Industry'. *B.J.I.R.*, Vol. IV, No. 2, 1966.

LERNER, S. W. and MARQUAND, J. 'Workshop Bargaining, Wage Drift and Productivity in the British Engineering Industry'. *Manchester School*, January 1962.

LOCKWOOD, DAVID. 'Arbitration and Industrial Conflict'. *B.J.S.*, Vol. 6, 1955.

LUPTON, T. 'Industrial Behaviour and Personnel Management'. *Inst. of Personnel Management*, 1964.

MARSH, A. I. *Industrial Relations in Engineering.* Pergamon, 1965.

MARSH, A. I. 'Managers and Shop Stewards'. *Inst. of Personnel Management*, 1963.

MARSH, A. I. *Dispute Procedures in British Industry*, Part I. H.M.S.O., 1966.

MCCARTHY, W. and CLIFFORD, B. 'The Work of Industrial Courts of Inquiry'. *B.J.I.R.*, 1966.

MCCARTHY, W. E. J. 'The Reasons Given for Striking'. *Oxford Bulletin*, Vol. 21, 1959.

MCCARTHY, W. E. J. *The Closed Shop in Britain.* Blackwell, 1964.

MCCARTHY, W. E. J. *The Role of Shop Stewards in British Industrial Relations.* H.M.S.O., 1966.

MCCORMICK, B. J. 'Trade Union Reaction to Technological Change in the Construction Industry'. *Yorkshire Bulletin*, Vol. 16, No. 1, May 1964.

MINISTRY OF LABOUR. *Handbook of Industrial Relations.* H.M.S.O., 1961.

MINISTRY OF LABOUR. *Final Report of the Committee of Inquiry under the Rt. Hon. Lord Devlin into certain matters concerning the Port Transport Industry.* Cmnd. 2734, H.M.S.O., 1965.

MINISTRY OF LABOUR. *First Report of the Court of Inquiry into certain matters concerning the Shipping Industry.* Cmnd. 3025. H.M.S.O., 1966.

MINISTRY OF LABOUR. *Motor Industry Joint Labour Council Report by Mr A. J. Scamp, J.P., on the activities of the Council.* H.M.S.O., 1966.

MINISTRY OF LABOUR. *Report of a Court of Inquiry into the causes and circumstances of a dispute between the Ford Motor Company Limited, Dagenham and members of the Trade Unions represented on the Trade Union side of the Ford National Joint Negotiating Committee.* H.M.S.O., 1963.

MINISTRY OF LABOUR. *Report of a Court of Inquiry into the problems caused by the introduction of web-offset machines in the printing industry, and the problems arising from the introduction of other modern printing techniques and the arrangements which should be adopted within the industry for dealing with them.* Cmnd. 3184, H.M.S.O., 1967.

MINISTRY OF LABOUR. *Written Evidence of the Ministry of Labour to the Royal Commission on Trade Unions and Employers' Associations.* H.M.S.O., 1965.

Select Bibliography

PATERSON, T. T. *Glasgow Limited*. Cambridge, 1960.

PATERSON, T. T. and WILLETT, F. J. 'Unofficial Strike'. *S.R.*, Vol. 43, No. 4, 1957.

P.E.P. *Trade Unions in a Changing Society*. June 1963.

PHELPS-BROWN, E. H. *The Growth of British Industrial Relations*. Macmillan, 1959.

POPE, LISTON. *Millhands and Preachers*. Yale, 1942.

ROBERTS, B. C. (ed.). *Industrial Relations: Contemporary Problems and Perspectives*. Methuen, 1962.

ROBERTS, B. C. *Trade Union Government and Administration*. Bell, 1956.

ROSS, A. M. and HARTMAN, PAUL T. *Changing Patterns of Industrial Conflict*. Wiley, 1960.

ROSS, N. J. *Workshop Bargaining: A New Approach*. Fabian, 1966.

ROSS, N. J. *The Democratic Firm*. Fabian, 1964.

ROYAL COMMISSION ON TRADE UNIONS AND EMPLOYERS' ASSOCIATIONS. *Research Paper 4:* (1) Productivity Bargaining
(2) Restrictive Labour Practices
H.M.S.O., 1967.

SAYLES, L. R. *Behavior of Industrial Work Groups*. Wiley, 1958.

SCHELLING, THOMAS C. *The Strategy of Conflict*. O.U.P., 1963.

SHARP, I. G. *Industrial Conciliation and Automation in Great Britain*. Allen and Unwin, 1950.

SMELSER, N. J. *The Sociology of Economic Life*. Prentice Hall, 1963.

SYKES, A. 'Unity and Restrictive Practices in the British Printing Industry'. *S.R.*, Vol. 8, 1960.

TRANSPORT AND GENERAL WORKERS UNION. *Evidence submitted to the Royal Commission on Trade Unions and Employers' Associations*. 1966.

T.U.C. *Evidence submitted to the Royal Commission on Trade Unions and Employers' Associations*. 1966.

TURNER, H. A. *The Trend of Strikes*. Leeds University Press, 1963.

TURNER, H. A. *Trade Union, Growth, Structure and Policy*. Allen and Unwin, 1962.

TURNER, H. A. et al. *Labour Relations in the Motor Industry*. Allen and Unwin, 1967.

TURNER, H. A. and BESCOBY, J. 'Strikes, Redundancy and the Demand Cycle in the Motor Car Industry'. *Oxford Bulletin*, May 1961.

UNIVERSITY OF LIVERPOOL, Dept. of Social Science. *The Dock Worker*. Liverpool, 1956.

U.S. DEPT. OF LABOUR. *Collective Bargaining in the Basic Steel Industry*. 1961.

WARNER, W. L. and LOW, J. O. *The Social System of a Modern Factory*. Yale University Press, 1947.

WEBB, S. and B. *Industrial Democracy*. Longmans, 1920.

WEBER, ARNOLD R. (ed.). *The Structure of Collective Bargaining*. Glencoe Free Press, 1961.

WEDDERBURN, DOROTHY. *Redundancy and the Railwaymen*. University of Cambridge, Dept. of Applied Economics. Occasional Papers, 4. Cambridge University Press.

WEDDERBURN, DOROTHY. *White Collar Redundancy: a Case Study* (1964). Cambridge University. Applied Economics Occasional Paper, 1. Cambridge University Press.

WEDDERBURN, K. W. *The Worker and the Law*. Penguin, 1965.

ZWEIG, F. *Productivity and Trade Unions*. Blackwell, 1951.

Index of Names

Subject Index

The International Library of
Sociology
and Social Reconstruction

Edited by W. J. H. SPROTT
Founded by KARL MANNHEIM

ROUTLEDGE & KEGAN PAUL
BROADWAY HOUSE, CARTER LANE, LONDON, E.C.4

CONTENTS

PRINTED IN GREAT BRITAIN BY HEADLEY BROTHERS LTD
109 KINGSWAY LONDON WC2 AND ASHFORD KENT

GENERAL SOCIOLOGY

Brown, Robert. Explanation in Social Science. *208 pp. 1963. (2nd Impression 1964.) 25s.*

Gibson, Quentin. The Logic of Social Enquiry. *240 pp. 1960. (2nd Impression 1963.) 24s.*

Homans, George C. Sentiments and Activities: Essays in Social Science. *336 pp. 1962. 32s.*

Isajiw, Wsevelod W. Causation and Functionalism in Sociology. *About 192 pp. 1968. 25s.*

Johnson, Harry M. Sociology: a Systematic Introduction. *Foreword by Robert K. Merton. 710 pp. 1961. (4th Impression 1964.) 42s.*

Mannheim, Karl. Essays on Sociology and Social Psychology. *Edited by Paul Keckskemeti. With Editorial Note by Adolph Lowe. 344 pp. 1953. (2nd Impression 1966.) 32s.*

Systematic Sociology: An Introduction to the Study of Society. *Edited by J. S. Erös and Professor W. A. C. Stewart. 220 pp. 1957. (3rd Impression 1967.) 24s.*

Martindale, Don. The Nature and Types of Sociological Theory. *292 pp. 1961. (3rd Impression 1967.) 35s.*

Maus, Heinz. A Short History of Sociology. *234 pp. 1962. (2nd Impression 1965.) 28s.*

Myrdal, Gunnar. Value in Social Theory: A Collection of Essays on Methodology. *Edited by Paul Streeten. 332 pp. 1958. (2nd Impression 1962.) 32s.*

Ogburn, William F., and **Nimkoff, Meyer F.** A Handbook of Sociology. *Preface by Karl Mannheim. 656 pp. 46 figures. 35 tables. 5th edition (revised) 1964. 40s.*

Parsons, Talcott, and **Smelser, Neil J.** Economy and Society: A Study in the Integration of Economic and Social Theory. *362 pp. 1956. (4th Impression 1967.) 35s.*

Rex, John. Key Problems of Sociological Theory. *220 pp. 1961. (4th Impression 1968.) 25s.*

Stark, Werner. The Fundamental Forms of Social Thought. *280 pp. 1962. 32s.*

FOREIGN CLASSICS OF SOCIOLOGY

Durkheim, Emile. Suicide. A Study in Sociology. *Edited and with an Introduction by George Simpson. 404 pp. 1952. (4th Impression 1968.) 35s.*

Socialism and Saint-Simon. *Edited with an Introduction by Alvin W. Gouldner. Translated by Charlotte Sattler from the edition originally edited with an Introduction by Marcel Mauss. 286 pp. 1959. 28s.*

Professional Ethics and Civic Morals. *Translated by Cornelia Brookfield. 288 pp. 1957. 30s.*

Gerth, H. H., and **Mills, C. Wright.** From Max Weber: Essays in Sociology. *502 pp. 1948. (6th Impression 1967.) 35s.*

Tönnies, Ferdinand. Community and Association. *(Gemeinschaft und Gesellschaft.) Translated and Supplemented by Charles P. Loomis. Foreword by Pitirim A. Sorokin. 334 pp. 1955. 28s.*

3

SOCIAL STRUCTURE

Andreski, Stanislaw. Military Organization and Society. *Foreword by Professor A. R. Radcliffe-Brown. 226 pp. 1 folder. 1954. Revised Edition 1968. 35s.*

Cole, G. D. H. Studies in Class Structure. *220 pp. 1955. (3rd Impression 1964.) 21s.*

Coontz, Sydney H. Population Theories and the Economic Interpretation. *202 pp. 1957. (2nd Impression 1961.) 25s.*

Coser, Lewis. The Functions of Social Conflict. *204 pp. 1956. (3rd Impression 1968.) 25s.*

Dickie-Clark, H. F. Marginal Situation: A Sociological Study of a Coloured Group. *240 pp. 11 tables. 1966. 40s.*

Glass, D. V. (Ed.). Social Mobility in Britain. *Contributions by J. Berent, T. Bottomore, R. C. Chambers, J. Floud, D. V. Glass, J. R. Hall, H. T. Himmelweit, R. K. Kelsall, F. M. Martin, C. A. Moser, R. Mukherjee, and W. Ziegel. 420 pp. 1954. (4th Impression 1967.) 45s.*

Kelsall, R. K. Higher Civil Servants in Britain: From 1870 to the Present Day. *268 pp. 31 tables. 1955. (2nd Impression 1966.) 25s.*

König, René. The Community. *224 pp. 1968. 25s.*

Lawton, Dennis. Social Class, Language and Education. *192 pp. 1968. 21s.*

Marsh, David C. The Changing Social Structure in England and Wales, 1871-1961. *1958. 272 pp. 2nd edition (revised) 1966. (2nd Impression 1967.) 35s.*

Mouzelis, Nicos. Organization and Bureaucracy. An Analysis of Modern Theories. *240 pp. 1967. 28s.*

Ossowski, Stanislaw. Class Structure in the Social Consciousness. *210 pp. 1963. (2nd Impression 1967.) 25s.*

SOCIOLOGY AND POLITICS

Barbu, Zevedei. Democracy and Dictatorship: Their Psychology and Patterns of Life. *300 pp. 1956. 28s.*

Crick, Bernard. The American Science of Politics: Its Origins and Conditions. *284 pp. 1959. 32s.*

Hertz, Frederick. Nationality in History and Politics: A Psychology and Sociology of National Sentiment and Nationalism. *432 pp. 1944. (5th Impression 1966.) 42s.*

Kornhauser, William. The Politics of Mass Society. *272 pp. 20 tables. 1960. (2nd Impression 1965.) 28s.*

Laidler, Harry W. History of Socialism. Social-Economic Movements: An Historical and Comparative Survey of Socialism, Communism, Co-operation, Utopianism; and other Systems of Reform and Reconstruction. *New edition in preparation.*

Lasswell, Harold D. Analysis of Political Behaviour. An Empirical Approach. *324 pp. 1947. (4th Impression 1966.) 35s.*

Mannheim, Karl. Freedom, Power and Democratic Planning. *Edited by Hans Gerth and Ernest K. Bramstedt. 424 pp. 1951. (2nd Impression 1965.) 35s.*

Mansur, Fatma. Process of Independence. *Foreword by A. H. Hanson. 208 pp. 1962. 25s.*

Martin, David A. Pacificism: an Historical and Sociological Study. *262 pp. 1965. 30s.*

Myrdal, Gunnar. The Political Element in the Development of Economic Theory. *Translated from the German by Paul Streeten. 282 pp. 1953. (4th Impression 1965.) 25s.*

Polanyi, Michael. F.R.S. The Logic of Liberty: Reflections and Rejoinders. *228 pp. 1951. 18s.*

Verney, Douglas V. The Analysis of Political Systems. *264 pp. 1959. (3rd Impression 1966.) 28s.*

Wootton, Graham. The Politics of Influence: British Ex-Servicemen, Cabinet Decisions and Cultural Changes, 1917 to 1957. *316 pp. 1963. 30s.*
Workers, Unions and the State. *188 pp. 1966. (2nd Impression 1967.) 25s.*

FOREIGN AFFAIRS: THEIR SOCIAL, POLITICAL AND ECONOMIC FOUNDATIONS

Baer, Gabriel. Population and Society in the Arab East. *Translated by Hanna Szöke. 288 pp. 10 maps. 1964. 40s.*

Bonné, Alfred. State and Economics in the Middle East: A Society in Transition. *482 pp. 2nd (revised) edition 1955. (2nd Impression 1960.) 40s.*
Studies in Economic Development: with special reference to Conditions in the Under-developed Areas of Western Asia and India. *322 pp. 84 tables. 2nd edition 1960. 32s.*

Mayer, J. P. Political Thought in France from the Revolution to the Fifth Republic. *164 pp. 3rd edition (revised) 1961. 16s.*

Trouton, Ruth. Peasant Renaissance in Yugoslavia 1900-1950: A Study of the Development of Yugoslav Peasant Society as affected by Education. *370 pp. 1 map. 1952. 28s.*

CRIMINOLOGY

Ancel, Marc. Social Defence: A Modern Approach to Criminal Problems. *Foreword by Leon Radzinowicz. 240 pp. 1965. 32s.*

Cloward, Richard A., and **Ohlin, Lloyd E.** Delinquency and Opportunity: A Theory of Delinquent Gangs. *248 pp. 1961. 25s.*

Downes, David M. The Delinquent Solution. A Study in Subcultural Theory. *296 pp. 1966. 42s.*

Dunlop, A. B., and **McCabe, S.** Young Men in Detention Centres. *192 pp. 1965. 28s.*

Friedländer, Kate. The Psycho-Analytical Approach to Juvenile Delinquency: Theory, Case Studies, Treatment. *320 pp. 1947. (6th Impression 1967.) 40s.*

Glueck, Sheldon and **Eleanor.** Family Environment and Delinquency. *With the statistical assistance of Rose W. Kneznek. 340 pp. 1962. (2nd Impression 1966.) 40s.*

Mannheim, Hermann. Comparative Criminology: a Text Book. *Two volumes. 442 pp. and 380 pp. 1965. (2nd Impression with corrections 1966.) 42s. a volume.*

Morris, Terence. The Criminal Area: A Study in Social Ecology. *Foreword by Hermann Mannheim. 232 pp. 25 tables. 4 maps. 1957. (2nd Impression 1966.) 28s.*

Morris, Terence and **Pauline,** assisted by **Barbara Barer.** Pentonville: A Sociological Study of an English Prison. *416 pp. 16 plates. 1963. 50s.*

Spencer, John C. Crime and the Services. *Foreword by Hermann Mannheim. 336 pp. 1954. 28s.*

Trasler, Gordon. The Explanation of Criminality. *144 pp. 1962. (2nd Impression 1967.) 20s.*

SOCIAL PSYCHOLOGY

Barbu, Zevedei. Problems of Historical Psychology. *248 pp. 1960. 25s.*

Blackburn, Julian. Psychology and the Social Pattern. *184 pp. 1945. (7th Impression 1964.) 16s.*

Fleming, C. M. Adolescence: Its Social Psychology: With an Introduction to recent findings from the fields of Anthropology, Physiology, Medicine, Psychometrics and Sociometry. *288 pp. 2nd edition (revised) 1963. (3rd Impression 1967.) 25s. Paper 12s. 6d.*
The Social Psychology of Education: An Introduction and Guide to Its Study. *136 pp. 2nd edition (revised) 1959. (4th Impression 1967.) 14s. Paper 7s. 6d.*

Halmos, Paul. Towards a Measure of Man: The Frontiers of Normal Adjustment. *276 pp. 1957. 28s.*

Homans, George C. The Human Group. *Foreword by Bernard DeVoto. Introduction by Robert K. Merton. 526 pp. 1951. (7th Impression 1968.) 35s.*
Social Behaviour: its Elementary Forms. *416 pp. 1961. (2nd Impression 1966.) 32s.*

Klein, Josephine. The Study of Groups. *226 pp. 31 figures. 5 tables. 1956. (5th Impression 1967.) 21s. Paper, 9s. 6d.*

Linton, Ralph. The Cultural Background of Personality. *132 pp. 1947. (7th Impression 1968.) 16s.*

Mayo, Elton. The Social Problems of an Industrial Civilization. With an appendix on the Political Problem. *180 pp. 1949. (5th Impression 1966.) 25s.*

Ottaway, A. K. C. Learning Through Group Experience. *176 pp. 1966. 25s.*

Ridder, J. C. de. The Personality of the Urban African in South Africa. A Thematic Apperception Test Study. *196 pp. 12 plates. 1961. 25s.*

Rose, Arnold M. (Ed.). Human Behaviour and Social Processes: an Interactionist Approach. *Contributions by Arnold M. Rose, Ralph H. Turner, Anselm Strauss, Everett C. Hughes, E. Franklin Frazier, Howard S. Becker, et al. 696 pp. 1962. 70s.*

Smelser, Neil J. Theory of Collective Behaviour. *448 pp. 1962. (2nd Impression 1967.) 45s.*

Stephenson, Geoffrey M. The Development of Conscience. *128 pp. 1966. 25s.*

Young, Kimball. Handbook of Social Psychology. *658 pp. 16 figures. 10 tables. 2nd edition (revised) 1957. (3rd Impression 1963.) 40s.*

SOCIOLOGY OF THE FAMILY

Banks, J. A. Prosperity and Parenthood: A study of Family Planning among The Victorian Middle Classes. *262 pp. 1954. (2nd Impression 1965.) 28s.*

Burton, Lindy. Vulnerable Children. *about 272 pp. 1968. 35s.*

Gavron, Hannah. The Captive Wife: Conflicts of Housebound Mothers. *190 pp. 1966. (2nd Impression 1966.) 25s.*

Klein, Josephine. Samples from English Cultures. *1965. (2nd Impression 1967.)*
1. Three Preliminary Studies and Aspects of Adult Life in England. *447 pp. 50s.*
2. Child-Rearing Practices and Index. *247 pp. 35s.*

Klein, Viola. Britain's Married Women Workers. *180 pp. 1965. 28s.*

McWhinnie, Alexina M. Adopted Children. How They Grow Up. *304 pp. 1967. (2nd Impression 1968.) 42s.*

Myrdal, Alva and **Klein, Viola.** Women's Two Roles: Home and Work. *238 pp. 27 tables. 1956. Revised Edition 1967. 30s. Paper 15s.*

Parsons, Talcott and **Bales, Robert F.** Family: Socialization and Interaction Process. *In collaboration with James Olds, Morris Zelditch and Philip E. Slater. 456 pp. 50 figures and tables. 1956. (2nd Impression 1964.) 35s.*

THE SOCIAL SERVICES

Ashdown, Margaret and **Brown, S. Clement.** Social Service and Mental Health: An Essay on Psychiatric Social Workers. *280 pp. 1953. 21s.*

Goetschius, George W. Working with Community Groups. *About 256 pp. 1968. about 35s.*

Goetschius, George W. and **Tash, Joan.** Working with Unattached Youth. *416 pp. 1967. 40s.*

Hall, M. Penelope. The Social Services of Modern England. *416 pp. 6th edition (revised) 1963. (2nd Impression with a new Preface 1966.) 30s.*

Hall, M. P., and **Howes, I. V.** The Church in Social Work. A Study of Moral Welfare Work undertaken by the Church of England. *320 pp. 1965. 35s.*

Heywood, Jean S. Children in Care: the Development of the Service for the Deprived Child. *264 pp. 2nd edition (revised) 1965. (2nd Impression 1966.) 32s.*

An Introduction to Teaching Casework Skills. *190 pp. 1964. 28s.*

Jones, Kathleen. Lunacy, Law and Conscience, 1744-1845: the Social History of the Care of the Insane. *268 pp. 1955. 25s.*

Mental Health and Social Policy, 1845-1959. *264 pp. 1960. (2nd Impression 1967.) 28s.*

Jones, Kathleen and **Sidebotham, Roy.** Mental Hospitals at Work. *220 pp. 1962. 30s.*

Kastell, Jean. Casework in Child Care. *Foreword by M. Brooke Willis. 320 pp. 1962. 35s.*

Nokes, P. L. The Professional Task in Welfare Practice. *152 pp. 1967. 28s.*

Rooff, Madeline. Voluntary Societies and Social Policy. *350 pp. 15 tables. 1957. 35s.*

Shenfield, B. E. Social Policies for Old Age: A Review of Social Provision for Old Age in Great Britain. *260 pp. 39 tables. 1957. 25s.*

Timms, Noel. Psychiatric Social Work in Great Britain (1939-1962). *280 pp. 1964. 32s.*

Social Casework: Principles and Practice. *256 pp. 1964. (2nd Impression 1966.) 25s. Paper 15s.*

Trasler, Gordon. In Place of Parents: A Study in Foster Care. *272 pp. 1960. (2nd Impression 1966.) 30s.*

Young, A. F., and **Ashton, E. T.** British Social Work in the Nineteenth Century. *288 pp. 1956. (2nd Impression 1963.) 28s.*

Young, A. F. Social Services in British Industry. *about 350 pp. 1968. about 45s.*

SOCIOLOGY OF EDUCATION

Banks, Olive. Parity and Prestige in English Secondary Education: a Study in Educational Sociology. *272 pp. 1955. (2nd Impression 1963.) 32s.*

Bentwich, Joseph. Education in Israel. *224 pp. 8 pp. plates. 1965. 24s.*

Blyth, W. A. L. English Primary Education. A Sociological Description. *1965. Revised edition 1967.*
1. Schools. *232 pp. 30s.*
2. Background. *168 pp. 25s.*

Collier, K. G. The Social Purposes of Education: Personal and Social Values in Education. *268 pp. 1959. (3rd Impression 1965.) 21s.*

Dale, R. R., and **Griffith, S.** Down Stream: Failure in the Grammar School. *108 pp. 1965. 20s.*

Dore, R. P. Education in Tokugawa Japan. *356 pp. 9 pp. plates. 1965. 35s.*

Edmonds, E. L. The School Inspector. *Foreword by Sir William Alexander. 214 pp. 1962. 28s.*

Evans, K. M. Sociometry and Education. *158 pp. 1962. (2nd Impression 1966.) 18s.*

Foster, P. J. Education and Social Change in Ghana. *336 pp. 3 maps. 1965. (2nd Impression 1967.) 36s.*

Fraser, W. R. Education and Society in Modern France. *150 pp. 1963. 20s.*

Hans, Nicholas. New Trends in Education in the Eighteenth Century. *278 pp. 19 tables. 1951. (2nd Impression 1966.) 30s.*
Comparative Education: A Study of Educational Factors and Traditions. *360 pp. 3rd (revised) edition 1958. (4th Impression 1967.) 25s. Paper 12s. 6d.*

Hargreaves, David. Social Relations in a Secondary School. *240 pp. 1967. 32s.*

Holmes, Brian. Problems in Education. A Comparative Approach. *336 pp. 1965. (2nd Impression 1967.) 32s.*

Mannheim, Karl and **Stewart, W. A. C.** An Introduction to the Sociology of Education. *206 pp. 1962. (2nd Impression 1965.) 21s.*

Musgrove, F. Youth and the Social Order. *176 pp. 1964. 21s.*

Ortega y Gasset, José. Mission of the University. *Translated with an Introduction by Howard Lee Nostrand. 86 pp. 1946. (3rd Impression 1963.) 15s.*

Ottaway, A. K. C. Education and Society: An Introduction to the Sociology of Education. *With an Introduction by W. O. Lester Smith. 212 pp. Second edition (revised). 1962. (5th Impression 1968.) 18s. Paper 10s. 6d.*

Peers, Robert. Adult Education: A Comparative Study. *398 pp. 2nd edition 1959. (2nd Impression 1966.) 42s.*

Pritchard, D. G. Education and the Handicapped: 1760 to 1960. *258 pp. 1963. (2nd Impression 1966.) 35s.*

Simon, Brian and **Joan** (Eds.). Educational Psychology in the U.S.S.R. *Introduction by Brian and Joan Simon. Translation by Joan Simon. Papers by D. N. Bogoiavlenski and N. A. Menchinskaia, D. B. Elkonin, E. A. Fleshner, Z. I. Kalmykova, G. S. Kostiuk, V. A. Krutetski, A. N. Leontiev, A. R. Luria, E. A. Milerian, R. G. Natadze, B. M. Teplov, L. S. Vygotski, L. V. Zankov. 296 pp. 1963. 40s.*

SOCIOLOGY OF CULTURE

Eppel, E. M., and **M.** Adolescents and Morality: A Study of some Moral Values and Dilemmas of Working Adolescents in the Context of a changing Climate of Opinion. *Foreword by W. J. H. Sprott. 268 pp. 39 tables. 1966. 30s.*

Fromm, Erich. The Fear of Freedom. *286 pp. 1942. (8th Impression 1960.) 25s. Paper 10s.*
The Sane Society. *400 pp. 1956. (3rd Impression 1963.) 28s. Paper 12s. 6d.*

Mannheim, Karl. Diagnosis of Our Time: Wartime Essays of a Sociologist. *208 pp. 1943. (8th Impression 1966.) 21s.*
Essays on the Sociology of Culture. *Edited by Ernst Mannheim in co-operation with Paul Kecskemeti. Editorial Note by Adolph Lowe. 280 pp. 1956. (3rd Impression 1967.) 28s.*

Weber, Alfred. Farewell to European History: or The Conquest of Nihilism. *Translated from the German by R. F. C. Hull. 224 pp. 1947. 18s.*

9

SOCIOLOGY OF RELIGION

Argyle, Michael. Religious Behaviour. *224 pp. 8 figures. 41 tables. 1958. (3rd Impression 1965.) 25s.*

Knight, Frank H., and **Merriam, Thornton W.** The Economic Order and Religion. *242 pp. 1947. 18s.*

Stark, Werner. The Sociology of Religion. A Study of Christendom.
Volume I. Established Religion. *248 pp. 1966. 35s.*
Volume II. Sectarian Religion. *368 pp. 1967. 40s.*
Volume III. The Universal Church. *464 pp. 1967. 45s.*

Watt, W. Montgomery. Islam and the Integration of Society. *320 pp. 1961. (3rd Impression 1966.) 35s.*

SOCIOLOGY OF ART AND LITERATURE

Beljame, Alexandre. Men of Letters and the English Public in the Eighteenth Century: 1660-1744, Dryden, Addison, Pope. *Edited with an Introduction and Notes by Bonamy Dobrée. Translated by E. O. Lorimer. 532 pp. 1948. 32s.*

Misch, Georg. A History of Autobiography in Antiquity. *Translated by E. W. Dickes. 2 Volumes. Vol. 1, 364 pp., Vol. 2, 372 pp. 1950. 45s. the set.*

Schücking, L. L. The Sociology of Literary Taste. *112 pp. 2nd (revised) edition 1966. 18s.*

Silbermann, Alphons. The Sociology of Music. *Translated from the German by Corbet Stewart. 222 pp. 1963. 28s.*

SOCIOLOGY OF KNOWLEDGE

Mannheim, Karl. Essays on the Sociology of Knowledge. *Edited by Paul Kecskemeti. Editorial note by Adolph Lowe. 352 pp. 1952. (3rd Impression 1964.) 35s.*

Stark, W. America: Ideal and Reality. The United States of 1776 in Contemporary Philosophy. *136 pp. 1947. 12s.*
The Sociology of Knowledge: An Essay in Aid of a Deeper Understanding of the History of Ideas. *384 pp. 1958. (3rd Impression 1967.) 36s.*
Montesquieu: Pioneer of the Sociology of Knowledge. *244 pp. 1960. 25s.*

URBAN SOCIOLOGY

Anderson, Nels. The Urban Community: A World Perspective. *532 pp. 1960. 35s.*

Ashworth, William. The Genesis of Modern British Town Planning: A Study in Economic and Social History of the Nineteenth and Twentieth Centuries. *288 pp. 1954. (3rd Impression 1968.) 32s.*

Bracey, Howard. Neighbours: On New Estates and Subdivisions in England and U.S.A. *220 pp. 1964. 28s.*

Cullingworth, J. B. Housing Needs and Planning Policy: A Restatement of the Problems of Housing Need and "Overspill" in England and Wales. *232 pp. 44 tables. 8 maps. 1960. (2nd Impression 1966.) 28s.*

Dickinson, Robert E. City and Region: A Geographical Interpretation. *608 pp. 125 figures. 1964. (5th Impression 1967.) 60s.*
    The West European City: A Geographical Interpretation. *600 pp. 129 maps. 29 plates. 2nd edition 1962. (3rd Impression 1968.) 55s.*
    The City Region in Western Europe. *320 pp. Maps. 1967. 30s. Paper 14s.*

Jennings, Hilda. Societies in the Making: a Study of Development and Redevelopment within a County Borough. *Foreword by D. A. Clark. 286 pp. 1962. (2nd Impression 1967.) 32s.*

Kerr, Madeline. The People of Ship Street. *240 pp. 1958. 23s.*

Mann, P. H. An Approach to Urban Sociology. *240 pp. 1965. (2nd Impression 1968.) 30s.*

Morris, R. N., and **Mogey, J.** The Sociology of Housing. Studies at Berinsfield. *232 pp. 4 pp. plates. 1965. 42s.*

Rosser, C., and **Harris, C.** The Family and Social Change. A Study of Family and Kinship in a South Wales Town. *352 pp. 8 maps. 1965. (2nd Impression 1968.) 45s.*

RURAL SOCIOLOGY

Haswell, M. R. The Economics of Development in Village India. *120 pp. 1967. 21s.*

Littlejohn, James. Westrigg: the Sociology of a Cheviot Parish. *172 pp. 5 figures. 1963. 25s.*

Williams, W. M. The Country Craftsman: A Study of Some Rural Crafts and the Rural Industries Organization in England. *248 pp. 9 figures. 1958. 25s. (Dartington Hall Studies in Rural Sociology.)*
    The Sociology of an English Village: Gosforth. *272 pp. 12 figures. 13 tables. 1956. (3rd Impression 1964.) 25s.*

SOCIOLOGY OF MIGRATION

Eisenstadt, S. N. The Absorption of Immigrants: a Comparative Study based mainly on the Jewish Community in Palestine and the State of Israel. *288 pp. 1954. 28s.*

Humphreys, Alexander J. New Dubliners: Urbanization and the Irish Family. *Foreword by George C. Homans. 304 pp. 1966. 40s.*

11

SOCIOLOGY OF INDUSTRY AND DISTRIBUTION

Anderson, Nels. Work and Leisure. *280 pp. 1961. 28s.*

Blau, Peter M., and **Scott, W. Richard.** Formal Organizations: a Comparative approach. *Introduction and Additional Bibliography by J. H. Smith. 326 pp. 1963. (2nd Impression 1964.) 28s. Paper 15s.*

Eldridge, J. E. T. Industrial Disputes. Essays in the Sociology of Industrial Relations. *about 272 pp. 1968. 40s.*

Hollowell, Peter G. The Lorry Driver. *272 pp. 1968. 42s.*

Jefferys, Margot, with the assistance of Winifred Moss. Mobility in the Labour Market: Employment Changes in Battersea and Dagenham. *Preface by Barbara Wootton. 186 pp. 51 tables. 1954. 15s.*

Levy, A. B. Private Corporations and Their Control. *Two Volumes. Vol. 1, 464 pp., Vol. 2, 432 pp. 1950. 80s. the set.*

Liepmann, Kate. Apprenticeship: An Enquiry into its Adequacy under Modern Conditions. *Foreword by H. D. Dickinson. 232 pp. 6 tables. 1960. (2nd Impression 1960.) 23s.*

Millerson, Geoffrey. The Qualifying Associations: a Study in Professionalization. *320 pp. 1964. 42s.*

Smelser, Neil J. Social Change in the Industrial Revolution: An Application of Theory to the Lancashire Cotton Industry, 1770-1840. *468 pp. 12 figures. 14 tables. 1959. (2nd Impression 1960.) 42s.*

Williams, Gertrude. Recruitment to Skilled Trades. *240 pp. 1957. 23s.*

Young, A. F. Industrial Injuries Insurance: an Examination of British Policy. *192 pp. 1964. 30s.*

ANTHROPOLOGY

Ammar, Hamed. Growing up in an Egyptian Village: Silwa, Province of Aswan. *336 pp. 1954. (2nd Impression 1966.) 35s.*

Crook, David and **Isabel.** Revolution in a Chinese Village: Ten Mile Inn. *230 pp. 8 plates. 1 map. 1959. 21s.*
The First Years of Yangyi Commune. *302 pp. 12 plates. 1966. 42s.*

Dickie-Clark, H. F. The Marginal Situation. A Sociological Study of a Coloured Group. *236 pp. 1966. 40s.*

Dube, S. C. Indian Village. *Foreword by Morris Edward Opler. 276 pp. 4 plates. 1955. (5th Impression 1965.) 25s.*
India's Changing Villages: Human Factors in Community Development. *260 pp. 8 plates. 1 map. 1958. (3rd Impression 1963.) 25s.*

Firth, Raymond. Malay Fishermen. Their Peasant Economy. *420 pp. 17 pp. plates. 2nd edition revised and enlarged 1966. (2nd Impression 1968.) 55s.*

Gulliver, P. H. The Family Herds. A Study of two Pastoral Tribes in East Africa, The Jie and Turkana. *304 pp. 4 plates. 19 figures. 1955. (2nd Impression with new preface and bibliography 1966.) 35s.*
Social Control in an African Society: a Study of the Arusha, Agricultural Masai of Northern Tanganyika. *320 pp. 8 plates. 10 figures. 1963. 35s.*

Hogbin, Ian. Transformation Scene. The Changing Culture of a New Guinea Village. *340 pp. 22 plates. 2 maps. 1951. 30s.*

Ishwaran, K. Shivapur. A South Indian Village. *about 216 pp. 1968. 35s.* Tradition and Economy in Village India: An Interactionist Approach. *Foreword by Conrad Arensburg. 176 pp. 1966. 25s.*

Jarvie, Ian C. The Revolution in Anthropology. *268 pp. 1964. (2nd Impression 1967.) 40s.*

Jarvie, Ian C. and **Agassi, Joseph.** Hong Kong. A Society in Transition. *about 388 pp. 1968. 56s.*

Little, Kenneth L. Mende of Sierra Leone. *308 pp. and folder. 1951. Revised edition 1967. 63s.*

Lowie, Professor Robert H. Social Organization. *494 pp. 1950. (4th Impression 1966.) 42s.*

Maunier, René. The Sociology of Colonies: An Introduction to the Study of Race Contact. *Edited and translated by E. O. Lorimer. 2 Volumes. Vol. 1, 430 pp. Vol. 2, 356 pp. 1949. 70s. the set.*

Mayer, Adrian C. Caste and Kinship in Central India: A Village and its Region. *328 pp. 16 plates. 15 figures. 16 tables. 1960. (2nd Impression 1965.) 35s.*
Peasants in the Pacific: A Study of Fiji Indian Rural Society. *232 pp. 16 plates. 10 figures. 14 tables. 1961. 35s.*

Smith, Raymond T. The Negro Family in British Guiana: Family Structure and Social Status in the Villages. *With a Foreword by Meyer Fortes. 314 pp. 8 plates. 1 figure. 4 maps. 1956. (2nd Impression 1965.) 35s.*

DOCUMENTARY

Meek, Dorothea L. (Ed.). Soviet Youth: Some Achievements and Problems. *Excerpts from the Soviet Press, translated by the editor. 280 pp. 1957. 28s.*

Schlesinger, Rudolf (Ed.). Changing Attitudes in Soviet Russia.

1. The Family in the U.S.S.R. *Documents and Readings, with an Introduction by the editor. 434 pp. 1949. 30s.*

2. The Nationalities Problem and Soviet Administration. Selected Readings on the Development of Soviet Nationalities Policies. *Introduced by the editor. Translated by W. W. Gottlieb. 324 pp. 1956. 30s.*

13

Reports of the Institute
of Community Studies

(*Demy 8vo.*)

Cartwright, Ann. Human Relations and Hospital Care. *272 pp. 1964. 30s.*
Patients and their Doctors. A Study of General Practice. *304 pp. 1967.40s.*

Jackson, Brian. Streaming: an Education System in Miniature. *168 pp. 1964.* (*2nd Impression 1966.*) *21s. Paper 10s.*
Working Class Community. Some General Notions raised by a Series of Studies in Northern England. *192 pp. 1968. 25s.*

Jackson, Brian and **Marsden, Dennis.** Education and the Working Class: Some General Themes raised by a Study of 88 Working-class Children in a Northern Industrial City. *268 pp. 2 folders. 1962.* (*4th Impression 1968.*) *32s.*

Marris, Peter. Widows and their Families. *Foreword by Dr. John Bowlby. 184 pp. 18 tables. Statistical Summary. 1958. 18s.*
Family and Social Change in an African City. A Study of Rehousing in Lagos. *196 pp. 1 map. 4 plates. 53 tables. 1961.* (*2nd Impression 1966.*) *30s.*
The Experience of Higher Education. *232 pp. 27 tables. 1964. 25s.*

Marris, Peter and **Rein, Martin.** Dilemmas of Social Reform. Poverty and Community Action in the United States. *256 pp. 1967. 35s.*

Mills, Enid. Living with Mental Illness: a Study in East London. *Foreword by Morris Carstairs. 196 pp. 1962. 28s.*

Runciman, W. G. Relative Deprivation and Social Justice. A Study of Attitudes to Social Inequality in Twentieth Century England. *352 pp. 1966.* (*2nd Impression 1967.*) *40s.*

Townsend, Peter. The Family Life of Old People: An Inquiry in East London. *Foreword by J. H. Sheldon. 300 pp. 3 figures. 63 tables. 1957.* (*3rd Impression 1967.*) *30s.*

Willmott, Peter. Adolescent Boys in East London. *230 pp. 1966. 30s.*
The Evolution of a Community: a study of Dagenham after forty years. *168 pp. 2 maps. 1963. 21s.*

Willmott, Peter and **Young, Michael.** Family and Class in a London Suburb. *202 pp. 47 tables. 1960.* (*4th Impression 1968.*) *25s.*

Young, Michael. Innovation and Research in Education. *192 pp. 1965. 25s.*

Young, Michael and **McGeeney, Patrick.** Learning Begins at Home. A Study of a Junior School and its Parents. *about 128 pp. 1968. about 18s. Paper about 8s.*

Young, Michael and **Willmott, Peter.** Family and Kinship in East London. *Foreword by Richard M. Titmuss. 252 pp. 39 tables. 1957.* (*3rd Impression 1965.*) *28s.*

14

The British Journal of Sociology. *Edited by Terence P. Morris. Vol. 1, No. 1, March 1950 and Quarterly. Roy. 8vo., £2 10s. annually, 15s. a number, post free. (Vols. 1-16, £6 each; Vol. 17, £2 10s. Individual parts 37s. 6d. and 15s. respectively.)*

All prices are net and subject to alteration without notice

1267 H.B.